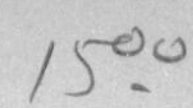

D1096208

# SPORTS CARS

# SPORTS CARS

## HISTORY AND DEVELOPMENT

GN Georgano

*Johnston & Company*

SPORTS CARS has been originated, designed, and produced by Johnston & Company.
*Design:* Nils Hermanson
*Artwork:* Lennart Molin
*Editorial staff:* Peter Coxhead, Jon van Leuven

Typeset by concept Communications, Crayford, England.
Reproduction by Offset-Kopio, Helsinki.
Printed in Italy by Grafedit SrL, Bergamo, by arrangement with Graphicom, Vicenza.

U.K. edition

ISBN: 91 87036 10 X

PHOTOGRAPHY

The Automobile: 78

B.M.W.: 87

Syb Braaksma: 196–197

Kevin Bradley: 235, 236–237

Kevin Brazendale: 214

Neill Bruce: 31, 34, 35, 37, 43, 48, 50 lower, 54, 69 upper, 81, 116, 122–123, 132, 156, 162–163, 164–165, 166, 201, 204.

Classic and Sports Car: 45, 74

CW Editorial Ltd: 210–211

Fiat: 148–149

Graham Gauld Collection: 150–151

G N Georgano: 64, 65, 67 upper, 76 upper, 82 lower, 100, 108, 117, 124 lower, 129 lower, 136, 137, 138, 144–145, 168, 170–171, 192, 195, 200, 221, 222–223, 229, 231

Peter Haventon: 169 lower, 175, 182–183, 218–219, 224–225

Honda: 189

Björn Eric Lindh: 187, 212

Ludvigsen Library: 187, 212

Jan Melin: 83

Andrew Morland: 112–113

National Motor Museum, England: 10, 11 upper, 12 upper, 12 upper, 13, 14–15, 16, 18, 19, 20, 21, 22, 24, 25, 26–27, 33, 36, 38, 39, 40, 41, 44 upper, 46, 47, 49, 50 upper, 51, 52, 53, 55, 56, 59, 66, 67 lower, 68, 69 lower, 70, 71 upper, 72, 73, 75, 79, 80, 82 upper, 84–85, 86, 88, 89 upper, 90, 91, 92, 94–95, 98, 99, 101, 103, 104, 105, 106, 109, 114, 115, 118, 119, 120, 121, 124 upper, 126, 127, 128, 129 upper, 130, 131, 133, 134, 135, 136, 140–141, 142, 143 146–147, 157, 158, 159, 160–161, 167, 178, 179, 202, 203, 206, 207 upper, 215, 216–217, 227

Panther Cars Co. Ltd.: 198–199

Cyril Posthumus Collection: 89 lower

Porsche Cars (G.B.): 207 lower

Reliant Motors plc: 194 lower

Renault: 228

Saab-Scania: 174, 176–177, 194 upper, 209

Toyota (G.B.) 213

Mick Walsh: 71 lower

Nicky Wright/NMM: 180–181

# CONTENTS

# INTRODUCTION

Any book on sports cars must attempt a definition, and this has exercised the minds of all who have written on the subject. Definitions have varied from the fanciful, 'Any car through which it is impossible to walk while wearing a top hat' (Cecil Clutton), to the logical, 'Any car in which performance takes precedence over carrying capacity'. (Cyril Posthumus). To these we must add the idea of enjoyment, which should be implicit in the word sport anyway. A 1946 M.G. TC Midget did not have the performance of a contemporary Buick Eight Roadmaster sedan, yet no one would deny the term sports car to the M.G. rather than the Buick. Because weight is inevitably an enemy of performance, most sports cars have had two seats rather than four (but what about the Bugatti Type 43?) and up to the 1950s had open bodies rather than closed.

The term sports car was unknown before World War 1, although there were many vehicles fully deserving of the title. The 'brute force and ignorance' school of thought which produced the Gordon Bennett and Grand Prix racing cars with capacities of up to 18 litres gave way around 1910 to more carefully thought-out cylinder-head design, typified by some of the cars built for the Prince Henry Trials, such as Laurence Pomeroy's Vauxhall and Ferdinand Porsche's Austro-Daimler with single overhead camshaft. By the outbreak of war sporting cars were being built in even smaller sizes, Bugatti, Mathis and others showing the way to extracting performance from limited cylinder capacity.

It was during the 1920s that the sports car really came into its own, with exciting cars being made in every price category. Some were more sporting in appearance than in anything else, but there were also notable advances brought about by the involvement of so many car makers in the aero-engine business during the war. In Britain alone, aero engines were made by Rolls-Royce, Napier, Daimler, Wolseley, Crossley, Humber, Siddeley-Deasy, Arrol-Johnston and Swift. Not all of the cars they made were sports cars, of course, but Wolseley and Napier used overhead camshafts from 1919 onwards, and the famous Hispano-Suiza 6-cylinder engine was virtually half of a projected V12 aero engine. The use of aluminium pistons, pioneered by W.O. Bentley before the war in the D.F.P. cars he ran at Brooklands, became widespread, permitting a higher piston speed and consequent increase in power per square inch of piston area. Coupled with the improved breathing offered by overhead valves, this gave a great increase in engine efficiency.

Superchargers had been tried on the American Chadwick as early as 1907, but it was in the 1920s that they became widespread. Mercedes used them from 1921 onwards, and by the end of the decade a considerable number of makers, including small sports-car builders like Amilcar and Salmson, offered superchargers. W.O. Bentley never approved of the idea, but they were used in the Bentleys developed by Sir Henry Birkin, and, although they proved unreliable, they did enable very high speeds to be achieved. In the 1930s even popularly priced small sports cars, such as the M.G. Midget and Austin Seven, were made in supercharged form.

The 1930s saw the disappearance of a number of the great sports cars of the previous decade, such as the Bentleys, the Alvis 12/50, and the Mercedes-Benz S series. However, by the end of the decade a new generation of much more modern cars had appeared, characterised by independent suspension, at least at the front (on some cars all round), tubular frames and twin overhead-camshaft engines. Cars such as the Bugatti Type 57SC and Alfa Romeo 2900B had a performance which was not equalled until more than twenty years later, although this was achieved at a very high price. At the other end of the scale, popular sports cars, such as the M.G. Midget and the Singer Le Mans, grew in numbers. Some were bought by those who wanted to look like sportsmen without the expense or driving ability demanded by the genuine sports car. In 1930s America the sports car was practically unknown, apart from the dramatic-looking supercharged Auburns and Cords. These went better in a straight line than round corners, because there were no races in which their handling could be developed.

However, all this was to change after World War II, when America discovered the sports car through the medium of such machines as the M.G. TC Midget, and later the Jaguar XK120 and the big Allards. This led the giants of Detroit to decide that it was worth entering the sports-car market themselves with Chevrolet's Corvette and Ford's Thunderbird.

During the 1950s the structure of many sports cars changed, the conventional frame with side and cross members being replaced by a built-up space frame with small-diameter tubes forming the basis of both body and chassis. One of the first examples was the A.C. Ace, which also had all-round independent suspension. Fibreglass was popular for a while, even being used by General Motors on their Corvette. The Lotus Elite was the first car to use a combined body/chassis unit in fibreglass. The advantage of fibreglass is that small firms can produce varied designs in limited quantities. However, the material is not flexible, and any lack of torsional stiffness in the chassis can result in the appearance of cracking in the bodywork.

In engine design the twin overhead-camshaft layout became almost universal for high-performance engines, and some expensive Italian units, such as those of Lamborghini, adopted a total of four camshafts, two for each bank of cylinders. The tuning of engines of popular cars became widespread, and there was a direct feed-back from the world of racing. Cars such as the Lotus-Cortina, Brabham-Viva, Dauphine Gordini and Fiat Abarth are examples of a trend which had no prewar equivalent. This has led the mass-producers to build high-performance versions of their family cars. Today there is virtually no mass producer, whether it be Renault, Peugeot, Volkswagen or Mazda, which does not have a 'hot hatchback' in its range. The success of these cars has undoubtedly damaged the sales of the traditional open sports car, and it is unlikely that successors to the M.G. Midget or the Triumph Spitfire will ever be built in such large quantities again. High motorway speeds and the increasing amount of diesel fumes from heavy trucks have made the open car less attractive, certainly for long-distance journeys. Thus most of the high-performance cars, such as the Ferrari Testarossa, Lamborghini Countach and Porsche 959, have closed coupé bodies. This trend is likely to continue, although there will always be those who enjoy 'wind in the hair' motoring. The industry has not forgotten them, particularly in Britain where traditional open two-seaters, such as the Morgans and the very stark Caterham Super Seven, still carry on prewar tradition.

The demise of the sports car has been predicted several times over the past sixty years, but the breed continues to flourish in changed form as dictated by changing circumstances. It is likely that so long as there is any motoring at all, there will always be those who demand something above basic transportation, and for them sporting vehicles will be made.

# CHAPTER ONE

# SPORTS CARS PRE-1914

The term sports car was unknown before World War I, yet there were many cars of that era which deserved the title every bit as much as those that came later. If we take the definition of a sports car as being one with above-average performance, and which is built for enjoyment rather than utility, the first such cars were seen in the earliest years of the century, being derived from racing cars.

**Mercedes 60, 1903**
This version of the famous 60-hp Mercedes is shown stripped for competition, the rear part of the chassis and the mudguards having been removed. It would take about half-an-hour to turn the car into a fast, five-seater tourer.

## Europe

Before 1898, the term racing car had no meaning, as the machines used in the great town-to-town races, Paris–Bordeaux–Paris, Paris–Trouville, Paris–Marseilles–Paris, and so on, were simply the most up-to-date cars that the makers could build. Competition was a valuable means of bringing them to the public's attention, but there was no distinction between the racing and the touring car. However, among the twenty-two starters in the 1898 Paris–Amsterdam–Paris Race were four cars, built by Amédée Bollée, which were conceived with racing in mind. In particular their bodies were sharply pointed at front and rear, being the first attempts at streamlining ever made. They had a top speed of 37 mph (59.5 km/h), and Étienne Giraud's car was the first arrival at Amsterdam. A series of mechanical problems and an accident dogged them on the return to Paris, and their final positions were third and fifth, with the other two cars failing to finish. However, the public was sufficiently impressed to place orders for replicas said to be worth more than a million gold francs. Among these was a car built for the Comte de Paiva, which had a streamlined body similar to those of the racing cars, though with the radiator mounted on the offside rather than at the front. It also had road equipment in the form of lamps and sketchy wings, so it could be considered as the first sports car.

In 1901 came the first car to bear the name Mercedes, a product of the Daimler Motoren-

Gesellschaft of Stuttgart. With its low-slung lines and a host of new features, such as pressed-steel frame, gate-type gearchange, and honeycomb radiator, the Mercedes soon set the fashion throughout the world as far as high-quality, luxury cars were concerned. The best known model in the early years was the 60 hp, with a 9,235-cc 4-cylinder engine which gave it a top speed of 75 mph (120 km/h) with the right gearing and a lightweight two-seater body.

The remarkable thing about the Mercedes 60, and indeed other powerful cars of the day, was that the same chassis could double as a racing car or as a limousine, combining in one car attributes as different as those of today's Formula 1 Grand Prix car and Rolls-Royce Phantom VI! The heaviest Mercedes 60 was probably the nine-passenger touring limousine with twin rear wheels, built for the company's French representative, Emile Jellinek, who had given his daughter's name to the marque. At the other end of the scale were the three stripped tourers which competed in the 1903 Gordon Bennett Race. The company had planned to enter specially prepared 90-hp racers for this, the leading event in the motor-sporting calendar, but they were destroyed in a factory fire shortly before the race. Rather than withdraw, the company instructed their Paris agent to borrow three cars from owners in the city, removed their touring bodies and entered them in the race. The car driven by Camille Jenatzy won at an average speed of 49.2 mph (79 km/h) over a 327-mile (526 km) course of poorly surfaced Irish roads. His team mates finished fifth and eighth.

This, then, was the type of machine which has a good claim to be considered as a pioneer sports car. Improvements were made to racing cars every year, so the makers were glad to see the previous season's models off to anyone who dared to use their performance on the road.

For a number of years the path to greater power was simply via greater engine capacity, the philosophy of 'There's no substitute for litres.' The first events which encouraged other attributes were the Herkomer Tours and Prince Henry Trials, held in Germany and Austria between 1905 and 1911. The Herkomer Tour, or to give its full title, the International Touring Car Competition for the Herkomer Trophy, consisted of a road section of about 500 miles (805 km), from Frankfurt-am-Main to Innsbruck, followed by a hill climb and a speed trial on the level. The tour was sponsored by the well-known portrait painter, Professor Hubert von Herkomer, and one of the prizes gained by the winning driver was a free portrait of himself.

The 1905 Herkomer Tour did not reveal anything unusual among the entries, all of which were standard touring cars, some with closed bodies. In 1906, however, no marks were awarded for coachwork, so in order to reduce weight the competitors built very sketchy bodies with canvas flaps in place of doors and no weather protection. The gentlemanly tour of 1905 had, to the dismay of some observers, given way to a serious competition. *The Autocar's* correspondent, H. Massac Buist, complained that some of the drivers 'adopted scorching tactics, proceeding from the very starting line with open exhausts, and emitting clouds of blue, black and yellow smoke.' It was regrettable, he said, that a reliability trial, under whose regulations British amateurs had been induced to enter, had turned into ungentlemanly racing.

These sentiments were the embodiment of the British feeling that taking part is more important than winning, but the sports car would never have developed at all had these ideas prevailed everywhere. As it was, the first nine places in the 1906 Tour were taken by German cars, the winner being Dr Rudolf Stöss driving an 18/20 PS 4-cylinder Horch. The remarkable point about this car was that, while its 2.7-litre engine was one of the smallest in the race, it was more efficient with overhead inlet valves and ball bearings throughout. With a substantial five-seater body it hardly looked like anybody's idea of a sports car, yet it was the forerunner of many.

One of the competitors in the Herkomer Tours was Prince Henry of Prussia, younger brother of the Kaiser, Wilhelm II. He was a keen driver and an amateur mechanic who is credited with the invention of the windscreen wiper. A few months after the 1907 Herkomer Tour, the prince announced that he would present a trophy for a touring-car event to be held the following year. There would be a restriction of the cylinder bore, 146 mm for 4-cylinder engines and 120 mm for sixes, and it was stipulated that no passing would be allowed, although this rule was not kept to in the event. The cars had to be four-seaters, and all repairs had to be carried out by the driver or his crew.

A total of 160 cars assembled at the start in Berlin on June 7, 1908, and it was evident that some of the constructors had interpreted the rules very liberally. In particular the Horches had bodies of what became known as the torpedo type, with a cowl between the front and rear passengers. The cars had neither doors nor running boards, and the wings over the wheels were straight, flat affairs that resembled surf boards. The winning Benz 50 hp had similar wings, while the Mercedes, which was second, had no wings at all, and resembled a Grand Prix racing car with a four-seater body. British journalists were as uncomplimentary about these cars as they had been about the 1906 Herkomer entries, but the German and Austrian papers called them *die ideale Tourenwagen*.

The 1909 and 1911 Prince Henry Trials really were touring-car events for largely standard cars, and consequently of no interest in the history of the sports car. By contrast, the 1910 event produced two designs which have a better claim to be the first sports cars than any others. These were the 27/80-hp Austro-Daimler and the C-type Vauxhall.

Up to 1910 the products of the Osterreichische Daimler Motoren AG had been more or less copies of the Mercedes made by the German Daimler company. However, the arrival in 1905 of the inventive Ferdinand Porsche led to new designs but they were not built straightaway, and up to 1910 Austro-Daimler continued with conventional side-valve engines.

In the 1909 Prince Henry Trial a team of these 32-hp Austro-Daimlers came through without penalty marks, and the team was awarded a silver plaque. Porsche was absent from the prizegiving ceremony, and was eventually found in a small writing room at the hotel. When asked what he was doing, he replied 'Designing a *proper* car for next year.'

This 1910 Prince Henry model had a single overhead camshaft which, although not a completely new idea, was the first time it had been seen on a competition car. There were four inclined valves per cylinder: two inlet and two exhaust. The engine had light steel pistons and twin magnetos. From 5.7 litres it developed a remarkable 95 bhp, giving a top speed of 87 mph (140 km/h). The four-seater body was of unusual shape, being wider at the top than the bottom. This was because the 1910 regulations laid down a minimum width at the top of the doors, but said nothing about the lower part of the body. Other makers besides Austro-Daimler also produced these 'tulip-form' bodies, which gave a lower weight and a smaller frontal area. Indeed, the style lasted on German cars until the mid-1920s. The only old-fashioned feature of the Prince Henry Austro-Daimler was its chain drive, but this was replaced by shaft in 1912.

The Austrian company entered no fewer than ten cars in the 1910 Prince Henry Trial. Those driven by Porsche himself, a fellow director, E. Fischer, and Count Schönfeld, finished first, second and third, with another two Austro-Daimlers among the first ten.

**Austro-Daimler 27/80, 1910**
Ferdinand Porsche designed this special model for the 1910 Prince Henry Trial. The narrow bonnet with streamlined fairing, the V-shaped radiator, and the wire wheels were all signs of advanced engineering thinking in 1910.

**Prince Henry Vauxhall, 1912**
A rare photograph showing a Prince Henry Vauxhall taking part in speed trials on ice in Sweden in the late 1910s or early 1920s.

**Hispano-Suiza Alfonso XIII, 1912 (*over*)**
This is a two-seater version of the Hispano-Suiza Model 15T sports car, which became known as the Alfonso XIII when Queen Victoria Eugenia of Spain gave such a car to her husband, King Alfonso XIII.

**Vauxhall 30/98, 1914**
One of the twelve Vauxhall 30/98s made before the outbreak of war. The light four-seater body is very similar to that of the Prince Henry, but note the flatter radiator, less distinctive but giving better cooling. At the wheel is the owner, Mr. Waterhouse, who used the car for European trials in 1914.

The Prince Henry Austro-Daimler pointed the way forward because it was a special sporting model built for competitions and more powerful than any of its side-valve touring sisters, although it was not the largest in the range. It developed 95 bhp from its 5.7-litre engine, while the largest contemporary Austro-Daimler produced only 60 bhp from one of nearly 7 litres. The Prince Henry was also the most expensive model in the range. Nevertheless, about 200 were made between 1911 and 1914, mostly with open four-seater touring bodies, though some two-seaters were made, not supplied by the factory, but by various coachbuilders.

Vauxhall's entry for the 1910 Prince Henry Trial was less dramatic than Austro-Daimler's, yet it was an equally significant car. It was developed from the 3-litre monobloc 4-cylinder engine which Laurence Pomeroy had designed in 1908. By dint of careful tuning, and with efficient pressure lubrication (which the Austro-Daimler lacked), Pomeroy was able to raise output from 38 bhp at 1,600 rpm to 60 bhp at 2,800 rpm. The cars had light open four-seater bodies without doors, and distinctive pointed radiators.

Three Vauxhalls were entered in the Trial, and two made non-stop runs, the third being only slightly delayed. A few of these models, known officially as the C-type, came into private hands by the end of 1910, and a four-seater tourer was exhibited at the London Motor Show in 1911. Early models had no doors, so they clearly aimed at the customer who put performance before comfort, but soon Vauxhall provided small doors which extended about halfway down the body sides. The beautiful car owned for many years by the designer's son, Laurence Pomeroy Jr, has a body of this kind, though it also has the later 75-bhp engine of nearly 4 litres capacity. These cars often had heavier coachwork with conventional doors, such as the 1915 tourer now owned by the National Motor Museum at Beaulieu in Hampshire, England.

The Prince Henry Vauxhall soon won a good reputation for its high-geared steering, smooth running and a flexible top gear, important in the days when gearchanging was the greatest problem facing drivers. Maximum speed was around 75 mph (120 km/h), but the car could cruise happily at 55–60 mph (88–96 km/h), and surviving examples still can. Like the Austro-Daimler, it was the fastest car in the maker's range, but not the largest. About fifty 3-litre and 140 4-litre models were made, production continuing for several months after the start of World War I.

Good road car that it was, the Prince Henry Vauxhall was becoming outclassed in competition by 1913, so a keen private owner, John Higginson, suggested that a larger

engine be provided. This 4½-litre unit went into a basically unchanged Prince Henry chassis, the result being christened the 30/98. The figures probably referred to 30 bhp, which was developed at 1,000 rpm, and the maximum power developed at 3,000 rpm. For better cooling, the Prince Henry's distinctive V-radiator was replaced by a flat radiator. Only twelve 30/98s were made before war broke out, but in the 1920s they became one of the most famous British sports cars.

A contemporary of the Vauxhall which became popular as a sporting car was the 3.6-litre Hispano-Suiza, known as the Alfonso XIII, after the Spanish king who was a keen motorist and supporter of his country's industry. It was developed from a successful racing car which won the 1910 Coupe de l'Auto. Because the race regulations imposed restrictions on the cylinder bore only, several of the competitors had very long strokes, the Hispano's dimensions being 65 × 200 mm. On the production cars this was revised to 80 × 180 mm, but it was still a very high stroke/bore ratio. To obtain adequate valve area the designer, Marc Birkigt, used the old-fashioned T-head layout, whereby valves on each side of the combustion chamber were operated via twin side-camshafts. Output was quoted as 64 bhp at 2,300 rpm.

With the higher of two alternative rear-axle ratios (3 to 1 or 3.25 to 1) a top speed of 80 mph (128 km/h) was possible, and the cars sold in Britain were guaranteed to reach 72 mph (116 km/h). Several Alfonsos were raced at Brooklands, their lap speeds varying between 73 and 81.51 mph (117.5 and 131.17 km/h). The car's effortless top-gear cruising was appreciated by owners, not least the Spanish king, who drove one such model on many long-distance journeys, including the 250 miles (402 km) from San Sebastian to Madrid at an average speed of nearly 50 mph (80 km/h).

The Alfonso was made in Hispano-Suiza's French factory at Levallois Perret from 1911, but was not revived in either country after the war. However, there was a brisk market for

**Hispano-Suiza Alfonso XIII, *c.* 1914**
These cars were often fitted with long, low chassis, and were preferred by younger, sportier drivers. This version has a four-seater body.

second-hand models in the early 1920s, and one was entered in the RAC (Royal Automobile Club) Rally as late as 1934. One of the founder members of the British Vintage Sports Car Club, Kent Karslake, used a 1912 Alfonso for daily transport and in Inter Varsity competitions when he was at Oxford in the later 1920s.

By 1913 there were numerous cars of medium size and sporting performance on the market. Some, like the Sunbeam 12/16, were derived from Coupe de l'Auto competition cars, while others such as the Crossley 15.9-hp Shelsley were tuned and lightened versions of staid touring cars. They generally had well-spaced gear ratios and catered for a new generation of keen drivers who were not afraid to use the gearbox, and were able to use it intelligently. For the great majority of drivers, gearchanging was to be avoided whenever possible, hence the appeal of the large slow-turning engine which could cope with most road conditions without recourse to the gearbox. Makers vied with each other to show how flexible their engines were: typical was the RAC-observed run of 1911 when a Rolls-Royce Silver Ghost was driven from London to Edinburgh entirely in top gear. Even driving manuals recommended hanging on in top as long as possible on a hill, and if necessary slipping the clutch rather than dropping down a gear. The wear on clutch linings resulting from such a technique was not mentioned.

Cars such as the Vauxhall, Hispano-Suiza and Sunbeam represented the new philosophy of high-speed engines and sensible gear ratios, but there were still a number of the older generation of monsters around in the immediate prewar years, and they provided very sporting, if unsophisticated, motoring. The great German rivals, Daimler and Benz, both produced large and powerful cars. Daimler's best known offering was the Mercedes 37/90 PS, known in Britain as the 90. It was designed by Paul Daimler and had a 9½-litre 4-cylinder pushrod overhead-valve (ohv) engine. Each cylinder had one inlet and two exhaust valves. The latter gave an adequate opening area, but kept the size of each valve relatively small to avoid a build-up of heat on the surface. Made from 1911 to 1913, it was the last Mercedes to have chain drive. Earlier Mercedes carried their gearboxes just behind the engine, but the 90's four-speed box was mounted further back, in unit with the differential from which the power was taken by cross shafts to the chain final drive.

The earlier 90s had the flat radiator which characterized all Mercedes cars from the beginning, but for 1913 a sharply V-shaped prow was adopted. This typical German design was used on the 90's successor, the 28/95 of 1914, and subsequently on every Mercedes made up to the merger with Benz in 1926. The chassis could carry heavy limousine bodywork, usually with artillery wheels, but the sporting models often had disc wheels. The engine gave its maximum power of about 90 bhp at a modest 1,350 rpm, at which the car's speed would be between 75 and 80 mph (121 and 129 km/h) with a reasonably light body. The 90 was replaced by the 7.3-litre 28/95, which was a more modern design, with 6-cylinder single overhead-camshaft (ohc) engine and shaft drive. Although some were built before the outbreak of war, it achieved most of its fame in the 1920s.

In England some sporty-looking Mercedes were built on touring-car chassis. These were mainly the work of Gordon Watney, whose premises were within earshot of Brooklands. He acquired large touring cars, often only two or three years old, removed the bodies and replaced them with light aluminium shells of his own design. Mostly doorless, these were made for Watney by the Ewart Geyser Company, famous for many years for their gas-fired hot-water generators. Some were raced at Brooklands, but they were not sports cars in the accepted sense; their appeal was to the young enthusiast who was happy with bright colours, an amusing name on the bonnet, and the appearance of a racer. One owner of a Gordon Watney Mercedes was Count Louis Zborowski, who was to achieve fame after the war with his specially-built Chitty-Chitty-Bang-Bang aero-engined cars.

Benz produced several powerful contenders in the field of monster cars, one of which had the largest engine ever seen in a catalogued road-going car. This was the 200-hp model which had originally been built for the 'Blitzen Benz' racing cars, one of which took the World Land Speed Record in 1910 at 131.72 mph (211.97 km/h). This massive 4-cylinder ohv engine had dimensions of 185 × 200 mm, giving a capacity of 21,495 cc. In 1912 the 200 hp was offered to the public, at a chassis price of 36,000 marks, compared with 25,500 marks for a complete Mercedes 90. One of those made was said to have been used as a staff car by Field Marshal von Hindenburg during the war. This car later came to Britain, and was raced at Brooklands intermittently up to 1930. Even as late as this, it lapped the circuit at 115.55 mph (185.95 km/h) at which speed the engine was turning at

no more than 1,600 rpm. Designers like Pomeroy and Porsche might have observed that there was nothing particularly clever about such performance, given the enormous size of the engine, but the 200-hp Benz is notable as being the last of the real monsters.

Italy also made several of what William Boddy has described as White Elephants. The Isotta Fraschini Tipo KM was the most interesting, for it was not only large, at 10,618 cc, but of advanced design. Its designer, Giustino Cattaneo, used a single overhead camshaft driven by a vertical shaft, with four valves per cylinder. The cylinders were cast in one block, and in place of the exposed valve gear seen on most ohv engines, the Isotta had a very neat cover. In fact, the KM engine looked not unlike that of a 4½-litre Bentley made

**Mercedes 37/90, 1913**
A contemporary photograph of the 9.5-litre Mercedes owned by the Marquess of Cholmondeley. This was one of the last Mercedes to be chain-driven (the very last was the 38/100, which left the factory in 1915).

**Mercedes, c. 1909**
This photograph of a Mercedes with a body by Gordon Watney, the British coachbuilder, was taken in France in the summer of 1921.

**Isotta Fraschini, 1914**
Chassis of a 1914 Isotta Fraschini KM. The neat appearance of the 10.6-litre 4-cylinder engine can be seen. Also visible are the front wheel brakes and gearbox, which is separate from the engine and mounted halfway down the chassis.

fifteen years later. More unusual than any of the foregoing were the four-wheel brakes, which Isotta had introduced in 1910, and standardized on their larger models by 1914. The pedal operated the rear-wheel and transmission brakes, while the front-wheel brakes, actuated by a large outside lever, were described as emergency brakes. No braking system could be called satisfactory unless all brakes were coupled and pedal-operated, but Isotta Fraschini had more commercial success with their system than their British contemporaries Argyll and Crossley.

The Isotta Fraschini KM had a four-speed gearbox and chain final drive, with a top speed around 90 mph (145 km/h). Most of the fifty cars made had V-radiators similar to those of the Mercedes, with the IF badge on both sides of the V. Isotta also made twenty of a smaller sporting chassis, the 6.2-litre TM, which could be had with either chain or shaft drive.

Other Italian companies to produce large sporting cars were Bianchi and Fiat. The former made a chain-driven 8-litre chassis up to 1916, which must have been the last passenger car in the world to use double chain drive, while Fiat's 10.1-litre Tipo S61 had shaft drive on its later models. One of the first S61s, rejected by its Parisian customer because of late delivery, was stripped of its touring body and entered by Victor Hémery in the 1911 Grand Prix de France, which it won. About fifty S61s were made, later examples having rounded V-radiators. Dimensions were 130 × 190 mm, and output 115 bhp.

## THE SPORTING LIGHT CAR

Just as the Prince Henry Trials and Coupe de l'Auto races produced sporting cars for the road, so the Coupe des Voiturettes events of 1906 to 1909 bred some attractive small cars with exciting performances. Strictly speaking, these races were also for the Coupe de l'Auto, the cups offered by the well-known French magazine, *l'Auto,* but to distinguish them from the 1910 to 1913 races for 3-litre cars, we will use the alternative title of Coupe des Voiturettes.

The first of these was organized in 1905, with the express purpose of encouraging the sporting light car. Engine capacity was limited to 1 litre, and chassis weight to 227 lb (500 kg). The lateness of the season (end of November) made a race inappropriate, so the event was organized as a six-day trial. For various reasons, including the strewing of nails

**Sizaire et Naudin, 1908**
Queuing up for the start of a hill climb. The independent front suspension by sliding pillars and transverse leaf springs can be clearly seen.

over part of the course by someone described by the magazine as a 'malicious imbecile', the event was a fiasco.

1906, however, was another matter, and saw the appearance of interesting small cars made by Sizaire et Naudin and Delage. These finished first and second respectively. Both had single-cylinder engines, and while the Delage did not become really famous as a production car until it used a 4-cylinder engine, Sizaire et Naudin made quite a number of singles derived from their 1906 racers. Engine size varied from the original 918 cc to more than 1.5 litres, but the basic design remained unchanged for six years. Its most unusual features were the transmission, which provided three direct speeds by means of a propeller shaft that shifted to engage corresponding rings of teeth on the crown wheel, and the independent front suspension by sliding pillars and transverse leaf springs. It was one of the first cheap cars with a reasonable performance. Whereas the average single-cylinder light car of 1906 was hard put to reach 30 mph (48 km/h), the Sizaire et Naudin could do 50 mph (80 km/h), although it took some time to reach this speed. According to Kent Karslake, who owned one in the early 1930s '. . . in its early stages the opening of the throttle seldom seemed to effect much change in the situation. Suddenly, however . . . the Sizaire would take a full gulp of mixture which it really appreciated, and with a series of resounding *plop-plop-plops* it would go bounding off down the road.'

The Sizaire et Naudin and Delage had De Dion Bouton engines, and this general provider of power units made a number of sporting light cars themselves, derived from successful racing cars. In 1908 4-cylinder engines began to appear among the Coupe des Voiturettes entrants, and while the cars powered by such units did not figure among the leaders in the race, they gave rise to some very pleasant and fast light cars. They included the French-built Rolland-Pilain, the Swiss Martini and the Italian Isotta-Fraschini. The latter was particularly attractive, with a 1,208-cc single ohc engine which turned at the very high speed of 3,500 rpm. It was in limited production from 1908 to 1911, and sold in England for £285 complete. This was not excessive for a well-made 4-cylinder car, but the market was not ready for a quality small car, and few were sold. One competed successfully in Dorset Automobile Club events, driven by a Mrs Bradburne, but the small Isotta's most lasting mark on history is that the chassis of one was used by Lionel Martin for his first Aston Martin.

One of the best known of all sporting marques appeared in 1910, when Italian-born Ettore Bugatti began production of a light car in a disused dye works in the Alsatian town of Molsheim. It had a 1,327-cc 4-cylinder engine with single ohc, the valves being operated

**Bugatti Type 13**
An early Bugattt Type 13, seen at the start of the 1913 Coupe de la Meuse.

by curved, sliding tappets. Three metric wheelbases were offered: 2 m (6ft 6½in) – Type 13, 2.4 m (7ft 10in) – Type 15, and 2.55 m (8ft 4½in) – Type 17. The Type 13 was the most suited to sports, and became the best known, although at first the new make attracted little attention. Indeed, when *The Autocar's* correspondent reported on the 1910 Paris Salon for his British readers, he said that 'a little Bugatti and a little Bédélia seemed most delightful looking runabouts.' He evidently did not look very closely, for he went on, 'In these, two people can sit one in front of the other,' which was true enough of the Bédélia cyclecar, but never of the Bugatti.

The celebrated journalist W.F. Bradley, writing in *The Motor,* was more fulsome and accurate, though he did comment that 'Those who estimate motorcar value on seating capacity and superficial area are not likely to become purchasers of the Bugatti.' However, he went on to say that 'M. Bugatti has sought to produce what may be termed the motorcar pony, but a pony that is fit to stand comparison with the most costly product of the best factories, and able, not withstanding its small size and low power, to hold its own in the matter of speed with any touring car built.'

When he tried it out in the suburbs of Paris, Bradley found that he could keep up with a big Benz Prince Henry tourer 'driven by a hot-blooded sportsman in his teens,' and over abominable road surfaces. He said that the makers claimed 60 mph (96.5 km/h) for the Bugatti, although he was not able to prove it. By 1914 a Bugatti had lapped Brooklands at 72.7 mph (117 km/h).

They soon gained an excellent reputation for ease of control; the well-known vintage-car collector, Cecil Clutton, wrote of a survivor after World War II, 'It is essentially to be controlled with fingers and toes rather than with hands and feet. The gear lever is flicked rather than pushed or pulled.' By the outbreak of war in August 1914 a total of 345 small Bugattis had been made, and the marque was well launched on its illustrious career.

## THE SPORTING CYCLECAR

Around 1910 a new breed of ultra-light car began to appear, aimed at the motorcyclist who wanted a little more comfort and carrying capacity, but who could not afford a conventional car. The manufacturers used many motorcycle components, including engines and gearboxes, while frames were often made of ash (wood had been totally superseded by steel for the chassis of larger cars) and bodies of plywood.

The first cyclecars appeared almost simultaneously in Britain and France. The best known British make was the G.N., built by H.R. Godfrey and Archie Frazer-Nash. Starting as a home-built effort, the G.N. went into production in 1911, using a 90° V-twin J.A.P. engine mounted in line with the chassis. Later models used engines of the company's own make, which, from 1913 onwards, were mounted transversely. The pioneer French cyclecar was the Bédélia, made by two 18-year-old Parisians, Henri Bourbeau and Robert Devaux. Like the G.N., it had a V-twin engine, belt drive and wooden frame, but driver and passenger sat in tandem, with the driver at the rear.

**Morgan Grand Prix No. 3**
The Morgan 3-wheeler which won the 1913 Cyclecar Grand Prix at Amiens. At the wheel is W.G. McMinnies, editor of *Motor Cycling* magazine, who was so impressed by the popularity of cyclecars in France that he persuaded his magazine's proprietor to start a journal devoted to these new small cars. This was *The Cyclecar,* which sold 100,000 copies of its first issue.

If cyclecars did not all have a sporting performance, and many were very slow indeed, the owner needed a sporting attitude to life, mixed with ingenuity, patience and a sense of humour. It was inevitable that before long cyclecar competitions would be organized – these mostly took the form of road trials, but in France there were two Cyclecar Grands Prix, both held in 1913.

They attracted a large number of entries, and many firms produced special competition models. These resulted in sports models of cyclecars being offered to the public. The G.N. Vitesse had staggered seating and a tuned engine, being good for 62 mph (100 km/h), while the Morgan 3-wheeler was made in three forms, the Grand Prix No. 1 with side-valve J.A.P. engine and narrow body, the No. 2 with the same engine and a wider body, and the No. 3 with ohv engine, virtually identical to the car which had won the Amiens Cyclecar Grand Prix. These were in addition to the ordinary touring Morgans.

**G.N. Cyclecar**
This is actually a postwar model. The photograph was taken at the Sutton Bank hill climb in 1930. Hill climbs were very popular throughout Britain in the 1920s and 1930s.

# The United States of America

At first sight the United States in the 1900s would seem to be very unpromising territory for sports cars. Outside the cities the roads were extremely bad; of nearly 2,500,000 miles (4,000,000 km) of road throughout the country, only 204,000 miles (328,000 km) were paved with a hard surface. The rest ranged from corduroy (logs laid transversely across the road as closely as possible) to dirt, which in winter often became impassable sloughs of mud. A traveller reported in 1905 that the average rural road in America was worse than its equivalent in Eastern Poland.

Thus, although America's first motor race, held in 1895, was a town-to-town event, it covered only 54 miles (87 km), from Chicago to Evanston and back, and there was nothing in the nature of the great European town-to-town races such as Paris–Bordeaux–Paris, or Paris–Vienna. American races were held on closed circuits, sometimes those used for horse events, and there were few long-distance trials. The exceptions were the Glidden Tours for touring cars, and the famous New York-to-Paris Race of 1908, which followed a route from New York City to San Francisco, whence the cars were shipped to Alaska and then Russia to continue their journey. In places, competitors drove along the railroad tracks, which provided a better surface than the roads, despite bumping over the sleepers.

The cars which ran in these events were in no way sports cars – the Thomas Flyer which won the New York-to-Paris marathon was a stock 6-cylinder tourer, albeit with a lighter body than one might have found in the showroom. By 1910 a number of American manufacturers were offering a sketchy-bodied two-seater in their ranges. Variously known as roadsters, speedsters or raceabouts, they had large, relatively slow-turning engines that also powered the makers' touring or town cars. Performance was provided by high gearing rather than engine output, and with a 2.5:1 top gear a 60-bhp speedster was good for 75 mph (120 km/h). Many of these speedsters started life as dealers' specials. A dealer would enter a stripped chassis in local hill climbs and demonstrations at a State Fair in order to boost sales of the regular touring cars. If successful, this might lead to orders for replicas, which the dealer would pass on to the manufacturers, and so a sporting model would enter the catalogue for the following season. The low-priced mass producers like Ford and Chevrolet did not go in for this, but manufacturers of comparatively cheap cars, such as Maxwell, who had their Sportsman roadster, did while at least twenty-five makes in the higher-price ranges also offered roadsters.

Among the makes whose reputation was won by their sporting cars were Mercer, Stutz, Lozier and Chadwick. Of these, the first two have tremendous charisma today, probably more than when they were new, although they always had keen partisans. 'There's no car worse than a Mercer', chorused Stutz enthusiasts, to which Mercer owners reposted 'You have to be nuts to drive a Stuts.' The Mercer Automobile Company was founded in 1909 in Trenton, New Jersey, offshoot of the Walter Automobile Company whose descendants still make airport fire engines today. The first Mercers used L-head Beaver engines, but in 1911 the company began to make its own T-head units, designed by Finlay Robertson Porter. These were used in a variety of models, including touring car, closed town car and taxicab, but the only one to achieve fame was the Raceabout.

The 1911 Mercer Model 35R had a 4.9-litre T-head engine which developed 60 bhp, and gave the light car a top speed in the region of 70 to 75 mph (112.5 to 120.5 km). It had a multiplate clutch, which was smoother than most of its time, three-speed gearbox and shaft drive. The body consisted of little more than two bucket seats ahead of a large bolster-type fuel tank and a small tool box. There was no windscreen, but a monocle fitted to the steering column was an optional extra. This was more of an affectation than a useful accessory, for it must have given very little wind protection. Drivers of such cars wore goggles anyway.

The Model 35 Raceabout was made for four seasons, designated 35R in 1911, 35C in 1912 and 35J in 1913 and 1914. Prices rose from $2,250 to $2,600 over the years – rather higher than the rival Stutz Bearcat, which may explain why Stutz registrations outnumbered Mercers by about three to one. Production of the Mercer Raceabout was roughly two per week, and all were sold before they left the factory. Few changes were made to the design, apart from a four-speed gearbox, with overdrive top, on 1913 and 1914 models.

The Mercer earned a reputation for a delicacy and sensitivity of handling that the Stutz lacked, but unfortunately the light frame tended to crack after hard use, and the brakes left much to be desired – it was said that by the time the car had stopped, the emergency was sixty feet (eighteen metres) behind. However, a 1914 advertisement claimed that it was

**Mercer 22-70, 1916**
Designed by Eric H. Delling, the 22-70 was faster than the Type 35, but it was raced much less, because races had largely become the preserve of specialised machines by 1916.

possible to thread a needle when travelling at 60 mph (96.5 km/h) – presumably on one of the rare stretches of well-paved road.

Mercer Runabouts were seen in a variety of competitions, from local sprints and hillclimbs to the Indianapolis 500-Mile Race, where they finished 12th and 14th in 1911. Both cars were then driven home by their owners. Among professional Mercer drivers was the flamboyant Barney Oldfield, who earned much publicity for the New Jersey car.

In 1914 Finlay Porter left the company, to be succeeded as chief designer by Eric H. Delling. He replaced the Model 35 by the L-head Model 22-70, a more civilized car with full height bodywork and a 72-bhp L-head engine, wire wheels and an electric starter. The ride was improved by the use of Houdaille shock absorbers. However, the 22-70 disappointed the older generation of Mercer enthusiasts, who rather liked the starkness and discomfort of the 35. Delling left in 1916, though his designs continued until 1923, when an ohv Rochester-six engine was adopted.

The Mercer's great rival, the Stutz Bearcat, was developed directly from the first car that Harry C. Stutz built under his own name. Stutz had worked for a number of Indianapolis car makers, and set up a company to manufacture parts in 1910. The following year his Ideal Auto Parts Company built a racing car powered by a 4-cylinder T-head Wisconsin engine of 6.3 litres. They entered it in the Indianapolis 500-Mile Race, finishing 11th on its first outing. As a result Stutz called it 'The Car that Made Good in a Day', which became the company slogan. Within two months the new company was listing three models, a two-passenger roadster and four- or five-passenger tourings, all with the same 6.3-litre T-head 4-cylinder Wisconsin engine that had powered the first racing car.

In 1912 the roadster was given the name Bearcat, possibly by association with the Marion Bobcat on which Harry Stutz had worked for the Marion Motor Car Company, also of Indianapolis. A 6-cylinder engine was offered on all Stutz models as an alternative to the Wisconsin four, though the Bearcat was usually sold with the 4-cylinder unit. An unusual

**Stutz Bearcat roadster, 1918 or 1919**
The bodywork on this model is more enclosed than that of the 1914 model on page 27, but there are still no doors, although a proper windscreen has replaced the virtually useless monocle.

feature of the design was the placing of the three-speed gearbox in unit with the rear axle.

The lively and powerful Bearcat with its skimpy body and large bolster fuel tank soon attracted the attention of sportsmen, and became a natural rival to the Mercer Raceabout. The Bearcat looked, and indeed was, the heavier car, turning the scales at 3,000 lb (1,451 kg), compared with the Mercer's 2,500 lb (1,134 kg). It lacked the Mercer's delicacy of handling, but had a less fragile chassis, and the heavier fuel consumption was hardly likely to worry the rich enthusiasts who bought Bearcats. As a rule, none of these American roadsters was driven for long distances, although Erwin 'Cannonball' Baker crossed the North American continent in a Bearcat, from San Diego, California, to New York, in 11 days, 7 hours and 15 minutes. On one day he covered 592 miles (953 km).

Bearcats were raced privately, but did not achieve the nationwide fame of the Mercers because for Indianapolis and other major events Stutz used specially-built racing cars with overhead-camshaft engines.

The Bearcat was continued until 1925, like its rival becoming more civilized in appearance from 1918 onwards. Stutz began to make their own engines in 1917, and the rear-axle gearbox was dropped in favour of a conventional placing in 1921. Left-hand steering did not come in until the 1922 models, and initially only on closed cars.

The Lozier was in a different class from the Mercer or Stutz, being one of the most expensive cars made in America – the company was more famous for its touring cars than for its sporting models. Made in Plattburg, New York from 1905 to 1910, and then in Detroit up to 1918, Loziers were at their peak between 1908 and 1912. This was the era of the 6.2-litre 4-cylinder Model H and the 9.3-litre 6-cylinder Model I which carried bodies named after fashionable resorts and country clubs, such as the Meadowbrook two-seater roadster, Briarcliff four-seater toy tonneau and Lakewood four/five-seater torpedo tourer. They featured water-cooled brakes in which the hollow drums were pressure-fed with water from a supply tank, an idea used by Briggs Cunningham on his Le Mans cars of the 1950s.

Prices ran as high as $5,000 for a 4-cylinder Briarcliff and $6,000 for the 6-cylinder version, and not more than 600 Loziers of all types were made per year.

The Meadowbrook and Briarcliff models could be stripped for racing and fitted with large-capacity fuel tanks supplied by the Lozier works. Thus equipped, they were well suited for the 24-hour races which were becoming popular. Successes included the 1907 24-hour race at Point Breeze, Pennsylvania, the 1908 and 1909 Brighton Beach 24-hours, 1910 Elgin, Atlanta Speedway and Santa Monica races, and the 1911 Vanderbilt Cup, the most prestigious race in America before the Indianapolis 500 became established. Most of these victories were achieved by works driver Ralph Mulford, but many amateurs also raced their Loziers. They would drive them to the event and remove the bodies, wings and headlamps before competing in the race. Afterwards the process would be reversed, often with the help of the family chauffeur, and the cars would be driven home.

Lozier gave up their works-racing entries after 1911, saying that now that the car's desirability had been proved beyond doubt, there was no further need for racing. However, shortage of capital was probably the real reason. The company went downhill after 1912, with many of the best personnel leaving. Smaller and cheaper cars were made, which nobody wanted, and the name faded out during 1918.

The Chadwick was made in even smaller numbers, what the French would call *une production très confidentielle.* Between 1904 and 1916 only 235 cars left the little factory in Pottstown, Pennsylvania, and the make's biggest claim to fame rests on a feature that was used on only a few production cars. This was the supercharger, devised by driver Willy Haupt in order to improve breathing without enlarging the valves. This was not possible because of the copper water jackets which surrounded each pair of cylinders. Driven by a leather belt, the blower (the word supercharger was not used at that time) ran at six times the engine speed, and gave a useful short burst of speed. It was more effective in hill climbs than in racing, and was an optional extra at $375 on production roadsters around 1907/08.

The rest of the Great Chadwick Six, as it was called, was fairly conventional, although its engine was very large, at 11.2 litres. All Chadwicks up to the last, made in 1916, used chain drive which, by 1910, was pretty archaic, but Lee Chadwick claimed that when European manufacturers entered the world's great racing contests they invariably used chain drive, and the company stayed faithful to chains even after Lee left in 1911 to follow other pursuits.

Before leaving the American roadster scene, it is worth mentioning that steam had a short-lived vogue between about 1905 and 1910. The heyday of the American steam car was around the turn of the century, when about forty makers competed for a share of the market, and steamers outsold petrol cars for three seasons. However, these were all two-seater buggies on a short wheelbase, with a top speed of 25 to 30 mph (40 to 48 km/h).

By 1903 most of the steam-car makers had given up or gone over to internal combustion, but Stanley of Newton, Massachusetts and White of Cleveland, Ohio, carried on. In 1906 Stanley brought out a series of roadsters, the 10-hp Model EX, the 20-hp Model H, known as the 'Gentleman's Speedy Roadster', and the 30-hp Model K. The Model H seems to have been the most popular, and with a weight of under 15 cwt (81.5 kg) could easily exceed 75 mph (120.5 km/h). R.W. Stanley's Model K was good for 87 mph (140 km/h), a speed to which his father pleaded guilty to reaching on a country road near Boston (he was fined $5.00). Such speeds were all right so long as one did not think too much about the Stanley's flimsy wooden frame and tiny brakes.

The White was a more expensive steam car than the Stanley, and the company did not make a roadster model. However, stripped touring cars did well in hill climbs – in 1908 a 30-hp White beat all other cars in the under $3,500 class at a hill climb held in connection with the San Francisco Auto Show. White abandoned steam cars in 1910, and Stanleys became more staid as the years passed. By the time America entered World War I in the spring of 1917 the stark roadster had almost vanished from the scene. The next generation was the Jazz-Age Speedster, exciting to look at but hardly ever raced. As America became more motor-minded, there were, paradoxically, no races held for the road-going sports car.

It will be clear from this chapter that, in an age when all motoring could be considered more sporting than it is today, there was a great variety of cars in all price ranges which deserved the title of sports car. However, it was the decade after World War I which saw the type become thoroughly established, and instantly recognizable even to the layman with no interest in cars.

**Stutz Bearcat, 1914**
This was a fairly spartan design. Note the strange way in which the monocle windscreen is fitted and also the positioning of the luggage trunk, between the fuel tank and the spare tyres.

# CHAPTER TWO

# THE 1920S

At the 11th hour of the 11th day of the 11th month of 1918, the Armistice was signed between the warring powers. What was optimistically called 'The War to End All Wars' was over, and the world's motor manufacturers, like all the other survivors, turned to building the peace. In the United States car manufacture had continued, albeit on a reduced scale, right through the war, but most European firms had been compelled to contribute to the war effort, in the shape of guns, shells, torpedoes, military vehicles and trailers, aero engines or complete aircraft. A few, such as Vauxhall, Crossley, Renault and Fiat, made staff cars which were derived from their civilian models, and so were in a position to resume production easily, but for most it was more than six months into 1919 before they had any cars to sell. Steel and other materials were in short supply, and in Germany rubber was so scarce that many manufacturers sold their cars without tyres.

## Europe

In February 1919 *The Autocar* carried an article entitled 'The Appeal of the Sporting Car' by B.H. Davies who was a Canon of the Church of England and a regular writer on motorcycling under the pen-name Ixion. It was illustrated entirely with prewar cars, from a baby Peugeot to a 100-hp Isotta Fraschini, and the author admitted that, Vauxhall and Crossley apart, the field had been dominated by foreign machines. But he was more of a prophet than perhaps he realized, when he went on: 'Every country has its own particular cliché for some commodity or other – Paris for frocks, Germany for spas and music, the Riviera and Cairo for winter holidays, Switzerland for winter sports, Scotland for grouse, Italy for architecture and pictures. Why not England for sports cars?' The Canon ended his article, which included a sound denunciation of the theory that speed and danger go hand in hand, by calling for sporting cars in every class from 10 hp upwards, and at every step in price from £200 upwards.

The first British company to announce a sporting model was Hillman, at that time a small and relatively little-known Coventry manufacturer of light touring cars. They took what was to be the most popular path to building a sports car, that of modifying an existing tourer rather than designing a new model from scratch.

The touring Hillman Ten had a 1,593-cc 4-cylinder side-valve (L-head) engine which developed 18 bhp. By using lighter pistons and connecting rods together with larger valves, even though capacity was lowered to 1,496 cc, power was increased to 28 bhp. A very high top gear of 3½ to 1 was provided, but it proved too high for the available power, so although the sports Hillman could achieve 60 mph (96.5 km/h) in second gear, changing up to top effected no improvement at all – indeed, timed speed in top gear was only 56 mph (90 km/h). This was put right on later models, and a special version took the hour record for its class at Brooklands at 78.9 mph (126.9 km/h). However, high gearing was always a drawback, and the 9:1 bottom gear made hill starts awkward.

The Hillman Speed Model looked completely different from the tourer – the flat radiator was replaced by a handsome V design, the artillery wheels were given disc covers that matched the rakish body of polished aluminium, and the ensemble was completed by a burnished copper exhaust pipe and a large Klaxon horn. For a small car it was by no means cheap, costing £620, but even the touring Hillman was £600, more than similar light cars such as Calcott, Calthorpe or Wolseley. Not more than 120 Hillman Speed Models were made in four seasons. The makers ran a works car in a number of races and hill climbs, driver George Bedford finishing seventh in the 1921 200-Mile Race for light cars at Brooklands.

The Hillman was announced in May 1919, and deliveries began during the summer, an early customer being Raymond Mays who was to achieve fame with his work on ERA and BRM racing cars. Before long other British manufacturers began to cater for what was obviously a growing market. Calthorpe brought out their Sporting Four, with aluminium pistons and drilled connecting rods, and handsome bodies in polished aluminium, made in the Mulliner factory which was next door to Calthorpe's own works at Bordesley Green, Birmingham. Wolseley had a promising engine in their 1,264-cc single-ohc Ten and offered a sports model with aluminium body, pointed tail and disc wheels.

Many other makes of light cars followed the same path, from the flat-twin ABC and Douglas to up-market machines like the 4- and 6-cylinder A.C., with three-speed gearboxes mounted on the rear axle. Between 1920 and 1925 practically every British light-car builder offered a sporting model – even William Morris, devoted as he was to cost-cutting and mass production, built 107 Sports Cowleys, with skimpy wings, the mandatory disc wheels, and polished aluminium bonnet. Sometimes the engines would be tuned, but in many cases what improvement there was in performance was provided only by a lighter body. Their buyers were mainly impressionable young men who liked a car to look fast, and were not sufficiently discriminating to demand good handling or speeds in excess of 55 mph (88.5 km/h). If they were, and could afford the price, they bought an Alvis, Aston Martin or Bugatti.

In France the tuning of light cars was practised to a greater extent, and some of the country's best-known sports cars originated in this way. Most began, at any rate, in the under 1,100-cc group as this marked an important distinction in France. Not only was it a sporting category, as in England, but cars below this engine capacity were taxed at only 100 francs a year, compared with 400 francs for larger cars. The best-known makes were Amilcar and Salmson, both of which progressed to making full-blown racing cars, and

**Amilcar-Italiana CGS, 1926**
The Amilcar-Italiana CGS was assembled in Verona from imported parts and fitted with a locally made body.

there was a 'second division' represented by Sénéchal, B.N.C., Derby and Rally. As well as these, countless other manufacturers built light cars with sporting derivations. They were helped by the ready availability of engines from makers such as Ruby, Chapuis-Dornier, CIME and SCAP. The basic version of these engines had side valves, but the makers soon began to offer overhead-valve units which the car builder could put into his *type sport*. These gave perhaps twenty per cent more power than the side valves of the same size, though often the ohv engine was somewhat larger, say 1,095 cc compared with 950 cc.

With the extra power, higher gearing and a lightweight pointed-tail body, the *type sport* could do 60 mph (96.5 km/h) compared with 45 to 50 (72.5 to 80.5) from its touring equivalent. It produced a lot of noise, from engine and exhaust, but to the average young owner this was not necessarily a drawback, nor was the cramped seating. Some of the bodies were so narrow that the seats were staggered to give the driver reasonable elbow room. Doors were seldom seen, and weather protection was rudimentary, if it was provided at all.

Such was the *type sport*, which gave a lot of fun to mostly young owners on both sides of the English Channel, though the lesser known makes such as Benjamin, EHP, Majola and Marguerite were barely exported at all. Those that achieved more than passing fame, such as Amilcar and Salmson, did so because of better financing and sporting successes which were all-important to sales in this market. 'The Car that Wins on Sunday sells on Monday' was coined in the American stock-car scene of the 1950s, but it was every bit as true of France thirty years earlier. Increased sales brought greater profits which could be ploughed back into development of both the racing and road-going cars.

The Amilcar was launched in late 1920 by two engineers, André Morel and Edmond Moyet. They had worked for the makers of the Le Zèbre light car, whence came one of their backers, Joseph Lamy, as well. They also made use of the Le Zèbre dealer network, so it could be said that the Amilcar grew, phoenix-like, from the ashes of Le Zèbre, though the latter did stagger on, under different ownership, for a few years. The first Amilcar had a 903-cc side-valve engine developing 18 bhp. Unlike most of its contemporaries, it was made in the Amilcar factory which was, from the start, larger and better equipped than its rivals.

The basic Type CC was made in touring form only, but it was joined in 1922 by the 23-bhp 985-cc CS which could be had with a staggered two-seater body with pointed tail. Known as the Petit Sport, it was replaced two years later by the CGS or Grand Sport. This had a similar body but engine capacity was up to 1,074 cc and output to 30 bhp. Front-wheel brakes of Moyet's own design were fitted, and this was an effective little sports car, with a top speed of 75 mph (120.5 km/h).

By 1926 the CGS was beginning to look rather high and narrow, so a new model called the CGSs or Surbaissé (lowered) made its appearance. This had a much more modern appearance, thanks to its lowered chassis and radiator, three inches shorter wheelbase and cycle-type wings which replaced the spidery full-length wings of the CGS. In fact both models were made side by side until Amilcar ended production of sports cars in 1929. Later models of the Surbaissé (1928 onwards) had four-speed gearboxes, and could do 75 to 80 mph (120.5 to 129 km/h). The engine was the same 1,074-cc, now giving 35 bhp, and unlike many of the Amilcar's contemporaries, still had side valves. Some of the last CGSs models had Cozette superchargers which raised output to 54 bhp and gave a top speed not far short of 100 mph (161 km/h).

Amilcar production was quite high, running at between thirty and thirty-five cars a day in the years 1926 to 1928, and total production of the CGS and CGSs models was around 4,700. The cars were also made under licence abroad, as the Pluto in Germany and Grofri in Austria. In Italy they were assembled with locally built bodies, by S.I.L.V.A. of Verona. They were exported widely, including to the USA and to Australia. In New York Amilcars shared a showroom with the massive Maybach luxury car from Germany.

The Salmson, Amilcar's great rival, had much more advanced engine designs, though its chassis was similar to the Amilcar's, and generally inferior in roadholding. It began life as a French-built G.N. cyclecar, but in 1921 a 4-cylinder engine was mounted, far back in the frame. The valves were overhead, operated by four pushrods – the cams were recessed to allow a second spring to push the tappet into this recess at the appropriate time so that the pushrod became a pullrod, hauling the rocker down with it and so opening the inlet valve against a weaker spring, the other end of the rocker actuating the exhaust valve in the usual manner. This valve gear was noisy but the Salmson was a spritely performer, having a very light chassis and body.

In 1923 a twin-ohc layout replaced the unconventional push/pullrods, and Salmson became the first company to make twin-cam engines in serious numbers. They were used in their touring as well as sports cars, and in fact no Salmson engine had any other layout up to the end of production in 1956. Twin-cam engines were made in 1.1- and 1.2-litre sizes in the 1920s, and the 1,100-cc models had many successes in racing. The cars which finished first and second in the 1923 Bol d'Or (Europe's first twenty-four-hour race) had specially light bodies made of papier maché.

**Salmson Grand Prix 100, *c.* 1928**
This period photograph of the 1,100-cc sports two-seater clearly shows the outside silencer and the pronounced scuttle hump in front of the driver. The passenger sat further back, so did not have a hump ahead of him.

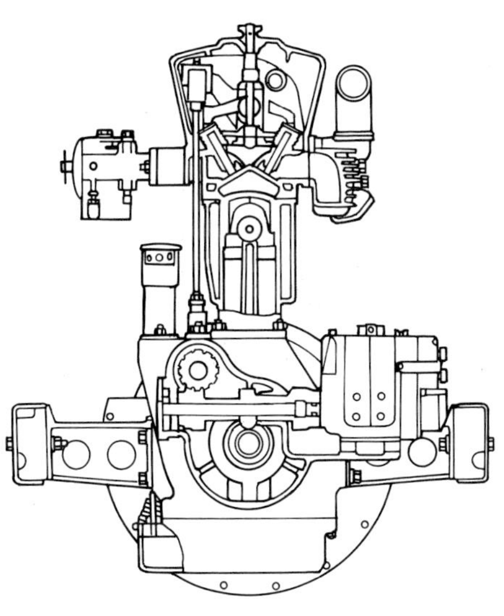

End elevation of the Salmson pushrod engine.

The best-known sporting Salmsons of the mid-1920s were the Grand Prix and the San Sebastian. Both had 1,087-cc 4-cylinder engines, but while the Grand Prix had one plug per cylinder, the higher-performance San Sebastian had two, and could be fitted with a supercharger. They were outwardly similar, both with lowered chassis in the manner of the Amilcar CGSs, and cowled radiators.

Although many other French firms produced light sports cars in the Amilcar/Salmson class, few were particularly distinctive. B.N.C. (Bollack, Netter et Cie) claimed to be the first to offer a supercharger, which they did in their 1925 Montlhéry model. From 1927 B.N.C. had sloping radiators which gave them a very attractive appearance. The S.A.R.A. (Société des Automobiles à Refroidissement par Air) was unusual in having an air-cooled engine, while the Soriano-Pedroso, made by two Spanish marquises at Neuilly, near Paris, had the outdated double-chain drive.

The light sports cars of France were entirely products of the 1920s, and none survived into the next decade. The smaller firms either faded away like B.N.C. or were absorbed by larger concerns as Sénéchal was by Chenard-Walcker. Amilcar and Salmson both decided to aim at the market for more comfortable touring cars, Amilcar with a not too successful straight-8 and Salmson with 4-cylinder twin-cam models which saw them through to the postwar years.

In Britain the position was almost exactly reversed. In the early 1920s there were few good small sports cars, and the importers flourished. By the end of the decade two outstanding vehicles brought sporting motoring within the reach of a wider public than the French cars had ever done. These were the Austin Seven and the M.G. Midget. Introduced in 1922, Herbert Austin's tiny Seven, with 10.5-bhp 747-cc engine, did not seem to offer the basis of any kind of sports car, but within two years a two-seater with raked steering column and pointed tail appeared, followed by the Brooklands model based on the racing cars developed by E.C. Gordon England. This had a staggered-seat aluminium body with an undershield of the same material, while engine modifications included a high-compression head, high-lift cams and double-valve springs. Top speed was raised from around 50 to 75 mph (80.5 to 120.5 km/h), and the Brooklands Super Sports won many races, including first three places in the 750-cc class of the 1925 200-Mile Race.

Such performance was available only at a price, which was £265 compared with £175 for the factory sports model. Gordon England then introduced the less highly tuned Cup model which featured a domed tail containing the spare wheel, and which cost £150. Soon numerous coachbuilders were offering sports bodies on the Seven chassis, some very striking such as the Burghley by Wilsons of Victoria (London) which had highly flared wings reminiscent of a 1908 Prince Henry Trial car. One of the best looking was the Swallow, offered in saloon and open two-seater form by William Lyons' Swallow Coach Building Company of Blackpool. Demand for the Seven Swallow was so great that the

**Salmson Grand Sport, 1929**
Unlike the Grand Prix this does not have a cowled radiator, though both cars wear the St. Andrew's Cross on the radiator.

company moved to Coventry and later built SS cars, ancestors of today's Jaguars.

The Austin works did not offer a tuned engine for several years, and the owner of a sporting Seven who wanted performance to match its appearance (not all did) either tuned it himself or went to a specialist who would do a reasonable job for as little as £7.50. However, in July 1928 Austin brought out the Super Sports with Cozette supercharger, a lowered frame and a neat pointed-tail body. Third and fourth places in the 1928 Ulster Tourist Trophy earned it the name Ulster, and in 1930 a production version was offered to the public in blown and unblown forms. The works cars developed 46 bhp at 6,000 rpm, but the production models were less powerful, at 33 bhp with supercharger and 24 bhp without. They cost £225 and £185 respectively, and only 168 were sold in three seasons.

The M.G. Midget proved much more popular, and has been described by the well-known M.G. enthusiast A.F. Rivers Fletcher as a car whose importance is almost impossible to overestimate. M.G. (Morris Garages Ltd) had been founded in 1924 by Cecil Kimber to make sporting cars derived from regular Morris models. In 1928 Morris brought out his smallest car yet, and a direct competitor to the Austin Seven, the Minor. It

**Austin Seven Ulster, 1930**
The Austin Seven Ulster, with characteristic pointed tail and fish-tail exhaust.

was unusual among light modestly priced cars in having an overhead-camshaft engine, derived from a design by the Wolseley company which Morris had just bought. Kimber was quick to bring out an M.G. version, which he named the Midget, a title which was to remain in the M.G. range until 1979.

The M-type Midget used mostly Morris Minor components, slightly modified. The suspension was lowered, steering column raked, and a light fabric two-seater body with a short pointed tail was fitted. These bodies were said to have cost Kimber only £6.50 each, and the price of the car complete was a modest £175. Although the engine developed little over 20 bhp, overall weight was only 10 cwt (1,120 lb or 504 kg), and the car had a top speed of over 60 mph (96.5 km/h) with very light handling. Orders poured in, and in its first year the Midget sold more than all previous M.G.s put together. It was demand for the Midget that led Kimber to move from his small premises at Edmund Road, Oxford to a new factory at Abington, where M.G. remained until the end in 1980.

The M-type Midget was raced successfully, taking the team prize in the 1930 Double Twelve-Hour Race at Brooklands, but its importance lies in the impact it made on ordinary

**Austin Seven Ulster**
Partaking in the 1930 Irish Grand Prix. At the wheel is Captain Arthur Waite, Sir Herbert Austin's son-in-law. In the race he was flagged in a lap early, when in second place, and was consequently demoted to fifth, a decision which made Herbert Austin threaten to withdraw from racing, but he subsequently changed his mind.

motorists. Countless people who thought that sports cars were somehow beyond them, in price or in the driving ability needed, found enjoyment in the Midget, and became eager customers for its successors the J-types, P-types and T-types, or for more powerful machinery. The M-type performed well enough to attract the racing drivers John Cobb and Earl Howe. A total of 3,235 M-types were made between 1929 and 1932; most were fabric

**M.G. M-type Midget, 1930**
An M-type Midget driven by the Clerk of the Course in an M.G. Car Club Trial in the early thirties.

**M.G. Mark III Tigress 18/100, 1930**
One of the few production models of the 18/100, this car was exhibited at the Olympia Motor Show in 1930, on the stand of the bodybuilders, Carbodies Ltd. It is one of two almost identical cars owned by Christopher Barker.

two-seaters, though later models had metal-panelled bodies, and there was also an attractive little closed coupé which sold for £245, compared with £185 for the later open cars.

A larger M.G. which had its sports versions was the 18/80, derived from the 2½-litre Morris Light Six. Kimber designed a completely new cylinder block and head to take twin carburettors, fitted Rudge Whitworth centre-lock wheels and a series of handsome open and closed bodies. The 18/80 was launched at the same time as the Midget, the 1928 Olympia Show, and soon acquired a good reputation as a fast tourer. The really high-performance version was the 18/100 or Tigress, built for the 1930 Double Twelve. This had dry-sump lubrication, two plugs per cylinder and many other non-standard features that gave it an output of 90 bhp, compared with 60 bhp for the Marks I and II 18/ 80s. Top speed was around 110 mph (177 km/h), and the Tigress was priced at £895. A batch of twenty-five was planned, but only five were completed before Kimber decided that the Midget was a more promising subject for racing development. The one Tigress entered in the Double Twelve retired, and it was clear that a lot more expensive work would be needed if it were to be competitive.

**Bentley 3-litre, 1926**
Most 3-litre Bentleys had four-seater bodies, but this is a two-seater by Vanden Plas on the short chassis (9 ft 9½ in) dating from 1926.

## The Specialists

The cars described so far in this chapter were all derived from touring machines which earned most of the manufacturer's money. The alternative was to design from scratch a sports car, or tourer with performance well above average. While many of the most glorious vehicles ever made come into this category, it has to be said that few of them made much profit for their builders, and several were built at a loss.

The best-known British sports car in the 1920s was the Bentley, in particular the 3-litre Speed Model open four-seater. This car was announced in *The Autocar* in May 1919, the article illustrated by a drawing because no car had yet been built. The drawing was by the famous artist F. Gordon Crosby who carried out W.O. Bentley's ideas of what his car should look like. When the car eventually appeared it was very similar to Crosby's design, including the tall, pointed radiator and the winged-B badge. A chassis was ready for the Olympia Show in the autumn of 1919, but it was not a runner, for among other essentials it lacked a crankshaft. However, a complete running car was ready by the end of the year, although development work was slow, hampered by shortage of money, and the first car was not delivered to a customer until September 1921.

Despite lack of adequate finance, W.O. Bentley was fortunate in being able to start with a clean sheet, not needing to use any existing parts. He and his designer F.T. Burgess used a 4-cylinder engine with very long stroke (80 × 149 mm) but this had the advantage of a low horsepower rating (15.9) combined with a large capacity of 2,996 cc. In the days when cars were taxed by horsepower, which was calculated by the cylinder bore only, a small bore was a considerable asset, though as this particular taxation system was not introduced until 1921, one cannot say that Bentley chose his engine dimensions with this in mind. Four valves per cylinder were operated by a single shaft-driven camshaft.

Because all parts had to be specially made, initially by outside contractors, the Bentley was inevitably expensive, and though the announced price was £750 for the chassis, by the time the first customer took delivery, this had risen to £1,050, or £1,350 for a complete four-seater. This made it the most expensive car of its size, but the news soon spread around that here was a remarkable machine, lively and challenging to drive, with close upper ratios of the four-speed gearbox. This encouraged use of the gears for overtaking as well as for climbing hills, a new concept for many drivers who had previously tried to get into top as soon as possible and to stay there whatever the conditions.

**Bentley 3-litre, 1920**
A very early 3-litre Bentley, this is car number 3, nicknamed 'The Cab' as it was the first to have a closed body. Made in 1920, it is seen here in front of King Alfred's statue at Winchester.

BM-9771

**Bentley 3-litre, 1924**
A classic four-seater body on a 3-litre Bentley chassis, made in 1924.

Customers for a £1,350 car were a small, close-knit crowd, many of whom knew each other, so the Bentley's reputation quickly brought orders. In 1922 141 cars were made, rising to 204 in 1923, and 402 in 1924, which was very near the record for the old Bentley company. This was the year in which John Duff and Frank Clement won the 24-Hour Race at Le Mans, the first of five victories which were to link the name Bentley as firmly with Le Mans as Jaguar was to be in the 1950s. For the first time in Britain, motor racing was taken up by the popular press, and the exploits of the 'Bentley boys', the group of wealthy young men led by Woolf Barnato, made front-page headlines.

The performance of the 3-litre Bentley was increased with the Speed Model of 1924, which had a higher compression ratio (5.3:1 compared with 4.3:1), front-wheel brakes and a top speed of 90 mph (145 km/h). Also known as the Red Label from the colour of the badge, this was the characteristic vintage Bentley, typically carrying an open four-seater body by Vanden Plas, metal-panelled on early models, later fabric, though often the bonnet remained unpainted polished aluminium. Today many of these cars are painted green, this being Britain's racing colour, but when new they were more often black, with blue or scarlet mudguards which matched the upholstery. Relatively few 3-litres carried two-seater bodywork, but there were quite a number of saloons for which a longer wheelbase (10 ft 10 in/3.3 m compared with 9 ft 9½ in/3 m) was provided.

In 1925 Bentley brought out their 6-cylinder car with 6½-litre single-ohc engine, and this had its sporting version in the Speed Six of 1928 to 1930. This in fact differed little from the standard 6½ apart from a higher compression ratio and twin SU carburettors. Externally it could be distinguished by its parallel-sided radiator, compared with the tapering towards

**Vauxhall 30/98, 1920**
An early postwar Vauxhall, this is a side valve E-type with Velox four-seater body.

**Bentley 4½-litre, 1928**
Winner of the 1929 500-Mile Race at Brooklands, the car is now owned by Ann Shoosmith, seen here in the passenger seat next to Peter Hull, then Secretary of the Vintage Sports Car Club. It is still used in competitions, hence the wide tyres.

the bottom radiator of the standard 6½. The Speed Six was the most successful Bentley in terms of major competitions, winning Le Mans in 1929 and 1930, the 1929 Six-Hour Race, 1930 Double Twelve and 1931 500-Mile Race, all at Brooklands. Out of a total of 544 6½-litre chassis built, 177 were Speed Sixes.

More openly sporting than the 6½-litre was the 4-cylinder 4½-litre developed from the 3-litre when the latter had reached the safe limit of its development. This was the extra-short-chassis Green Label, of which fourteen were made in 1925/6, which could achieve over 100 mph (161 km/h) with a 3.53:1 rear axle. The 4½ had a similar design of engine, but the bore/stroke ratio was increased, at 100 × 140 mm; these were the same as those of the 6½. Capacity was 4,398 cc and output 88 bhp. A 4½ took part in the 1927 Le Mans Race, where Frank Clement broke the lap record repeatedly until it and the 3-litre car of Davis/Benjafield/Duller were involved in the famous crash at White House Corner. Two of the Bentleys were too badly damaged to continue, but Sammy Davis managed to extricate his 3-litre and carry on to victory. In 1928 Woolf Barnato and Bernard Rubin won the Le Mans event in a 4½ giving 110 bhp, but after that victory went to the Speed Sixes.

The most controversial Bentley was the supercharged 4½-litre, familiarly known as the 'Blower 4½'. This came about because Sir Henry Birkin realized that the normal 4½ could not deliver much more than 110 bhp, yet this was likely to prove inadequate against competition from Alfa Romeo and the big American cars such as Stutz and Chrysler at Le Mans and elsewhere. W.O. Bentley distrusted the idea, saying that to supercharge one of his cars would be 'to pervert its design and corrupt its performance'. He preferred to obtain greater power from a larger engine, that of the Speed Six. He was proved right as far as long-distance races were concerned, as Birkin's blown cars never won a major event, though one did take the Brooklands Outer Circuit Record twice, the final speed being 137 mph (220.5 km/h).

The first of the Blower 4½s was the 1928 Le Mans winner which was fitted with an Amherst Villiers supercharger between the dumbirons, ahead of the radiator. Development work on this and another competition car took place at the Welwyn premises of the Hon. Dorothy Paget, as Bentley was not happy with such activities at his own factory. However, if the cars were to race at Le Mans, a batch of fifty had to be built, and these were made at Cricklewood, London. Vanden Plas open bodies were fitted to twenty-six of them, while the others carried a variety of coachwork, including six saloons. These were said to be almost uninhabitable because of noise, although on the open cars the blower was relatively unobtrusive.

On the competition cars the blower more than doubled the available power, to 240 bhp, but at a cost of heavy fuel consumption, 10 mpg (3.5 km/l) compared with 16 mpg (5.6 km/l) for the unblown 4½, and a healthy appetite for sparking plugs. 'The blower eats plugs like a donkey eats hay,' commented leading Bentley mechanic Nobby Clarke. Although the blower 4½ was not a sporting success, and was blamed by W.O. for the collapse of his company in 1931, it has acquired a great charisma among vintage-car collectors, and a good example will command a higher price than any other model of Bentley. It also has a very high survival rate – of the fifty-five cars made at least forty-eight are known to exist today.

For the man with more than £1,000 to spend there were several alternatives to the Bentley. The obvious choices were the Vauxhall 30/98 and the twin-cam 3-litre Sunbeam. The Vauxhall was descended from the prewar 30/98, itself derived from the Prince Henry, and was really a fast tourer rather than a sports car. That is not to say that its performance was inferior to the contemporary Bentley, but it was never raced like its rival from Cricklewood, and there were no glamorous personalities like Barnato and Birkin to earn the headlines. However, the Vauxhall had the advantage of going into production about six months after the Armistice, more than two years ahead of the Bentley, and during that time it was the leading British high-performance car. Raymond Mays, in his autobiography *Split Seconds,* describes how he and his father went to collect their glistening aluminium car from the Vauxhall showrooms in Great Portland Street, London in the autumn of 1919, and how the salesman begged them to leave the car for another day because so many enthusiasts were flocking to the showroom to see what was still a rare machine.

The 30/98 chassis was a shortened version of the 25-hp staff car that had been made in considerable numbers during the war. The engine was basically the same 90-bhp 4½-litre unit of the prewar car, and with the standard Velox four-seater body gave a top speed of 80 to 85 mph (129 to 136.5 km/h). At this speed the engine was turning at no more than 2,800 rpm, so the car had a delightful 'long-legged feel' about it, ideal for fast drivers over the generally uncrowded roads of the period. The brakes, on the rear wheels only, were not the 30/98's strong point, but emergency stops were mercifully rare.

Between 1919 and 1922 a total of 274 E-type 30/98s were sold, and for the 1923 season C.E. King, who had replaced the famous Laurence Pomeroy as chief engineer, evolved a straightforward overhead-valve conversion, the resulting car being called the OE 30/98. The stroke was reduced from 150 to 140 mm, giving a slightly smaller capacity of 4,224 cc, but power was increased to 112 bhp at 3,300 rpm. Because a lower rear-axle ratio was

**Vauxhall 30/98, 1923**
OE-type Vauxhall 30/98, with ohv engine and front-wheel brakes.

K 205

used, top speed remained about the same. Cable-operated front-wheel brakes were an optional extra from late 1923, at a cost of £25. The last 30/98s from 1926 to 1928 had hydraulic brakes, though front and rear were still uncoupled.

Most 30/98s had the factory-built open four-seater body called the Velox, though from 1924 there was also the Wensum, still a four-seater but with pointed tail, V windscreen and flared wings. Other coachbuilders, notably Grosvenor of Kilburn, London, made two-seaters and saloons, but there was never the variety of coachwork on the Vauxhall that was seen on the Bentleys. The 30/98 was a limited-production prestige car for Vauxhall, which also made several other cheaper touring cars. Only 584 were made from 1919 to 1928, compared with 2,985 Bentleys between 1921 and 1930. Since about fifty per cent of 30/98s were exported to Australia, they were never common on British roads, yet they have a keen following today. There is a 30/98 section of the Vintage Sports Car Club, and their owners rate them higher than a Bentley for sheer pleasure of driving.

Like Vauxhall, Sunbeam had made staff cars during the war, and were well placed to return to passenger-car production in 1919. Some sporting models with single-ohc engines were announced in 1921, but very few were made, and the first sports Sunbeam of the vintage era did not appear until 1924. It was very advanced, with a 3-litre twin-ohc engine (Britain's first in a road car) which was in effect a larger version of the engine that powered the 2-litre Sunbeam racing car, victor of the 1923 French and Spanish Grands Prix. The camshafts were driven by a train of gears from the front of the seven-bearing crankshaft, pistons were of aluminium and lubrication was by the dry-sump system. The four-speed gearbox was in unit with the engine.

The Sunbeam's chassis was not so advanced, being basically a touring-car frame with cantilever rear springs, and very long at 10 ft 10 in (3.3 m) wheelbase, the same as the longest 3-litre Bentley chassis, and 15 in (0.4 m) longer than the 30/98. Cycle-type wings gave a sporty appearance, and the 3-litre was a genuine 90-mph (144 km/h) car. The classic, factory-built body was an open four-seater, but some two-seaters and saloons were also made. Curiously, considering he was not only a Bentley team driver but also managing director, Woolf Barnato owned two twin-cam Sunbeams, a tourer and a saloon.

Although announced in 1924, and entered for that year's Le Mans Race, they did not appear, and the cars were not available to the public until the end of 1925. Before that, two

**Sunbeam 3-litre, 1926**
The Sunbeam twin-cam 3-litre four-seater owned by the Marquess of Cholmondeley. Note the long cantilever rear springs.

**Bentley and Sunbeam**
1927 Sunbeam twin-cam with its closest rival when new, a 1928 4½-litre Bentley.

**Lorraine-Dietrich 3.5-litre, 1926**
A French competitor for Sunbeam and Bentley, both on and off the track, was the 3½-litre Lorraine-Dietrich. This is Bloch's car on its way to victory in the 1926 Le Mans 24-Hour Race.

cars had run at the 1925 Le Mans race, that of Sammy Davis and Jean Chassagne finished second, behind a Lorraine-Dietrich but ahead of the Bentleys. This auspicious debut was not followed up by further victories, largely because the Sunbeam company did not provide the necessary funds to develop the 3-litre as a competition car. They were part of the international Sunbeam-Talbot-Darracq group, and in 1926 it was decided that the sporting side of the group should be represented only by the French Talbot-Darracq racing cars. Total production of the twin-cam 3-litre between 1925 and 1930 was about 250, including some Cozette-supercharged cars in 1928/29. Of these, forty-two survive today.

There were numerous French-built rivals for the large sporting car market, although in their own country they tended to be regarded as fast tourers rather than sports cars. They were admirably suited to the fast straight roads, free of any speed limits, which were the envy of British motorists. Not many were imported, though the 2-litre Ballot with single-ohc 4-cylinder engine had quite a following in Britain, especially in its 2LTS form, with hemispherical combustion chambers and larger valves. Panhard and Peugeot made sporting tourers with sleeve-valve engines, as did Gabriel Voisin whose 4-litre cars tuned to give 150 bhp took the first three places in the 1922 Touring Car Grand Prix. Other cars in this category included Lorraine-Dietrich which defeated the Bentleys at Le Mans in 1925 and 1926, Cottin-Desgouttes, Georges Irat and Delage.

France's leading luxury car in the 1920s was the Hispano-Suiza, and unlike its rival the Rolls-Royce it had several sporting derivatives. The H6B, announced in 1919, was a brand-new design with practically nothing in common with the Alfonso. For one thing, it was developed in the company's French factory at Bois-Colombes, near Paris, and soon became so famous that many people forgot the company's Spanish origins, though it was also made at Barcelona, together with cheaper models. The heart of the car was a 6-cylinder engine with single ohc which displaced 6,597 cc and developed 135 bhp. It was very flexible, so that the car could remain in top gear for most of the time – hence the wide-ratio gearbox with only three speeds, a direct contrast to the closer-ratio four-speed boxes of the Bentleys. An advanced feature for 1919 was four-wheel braking assisted by mechanical servo.

The H6B was intended as a luxury touring car, and most were sold as such, but it clearly had sporting potential, as André Dubonnet, of aperitif fame, showed when he won the 1921 Georges Boillot Cup with a standard four-seater. This led the company to consider making a more competitive car; the result was the H6C with engine enlarged to 7,982 cc and 200 bhp, and a shorter wheelbase. Six works cars were built, winning many events in 1922 and

1923. Their success in the Boillot Cup at Boulogne earned them the title Boulogne, which came to be applied to all the 8-litre cars but really belongs only to the short-chassis sports models. The H6C, with two wheelbases, was put on the market in 1924 alongside the smaller car. They were made up to 1934 in France, and a year or two later in Spain. The H6C was much rarer, only 264 being made compared with about 2,200 H6Bs. Unfortunately the H6C became less sporting as the years passed. Hispanos were always somewhat noisier than rivals such as Rolls-Royce or Panhard, and the H6C more so than its slower sisters. Therefore, in 1928 a lower cam profile was used which did achieve the desired effect, but reduced power to 144 bhp, not much more than the smaller engine. The most desirable Hispano to the sportsman would be a short-chassis H6C of the years 1924/27, preferably with a boat-decked body by one of the great *carrossiers* such as Labourdette.

Another class of sports car was the small specialist-built machine, generally less than 1½ litres capacity. Before the war firms such as Isotta Fraschini and Bugatti catered to this limited market, and the latter quickly revived their ohc 4-cylinder Type 13, now with engine enlarged to 1,368 cc and with four valves per cylinder. The short-chassis racing version was still called the Type 13, larger cars being designated Type 22 (7 ft 10½ in/2.4 m wheelbase) or Type 23 (8 ft 4½ in/2.5 m). After their success in the Italian Voiturette Grand Prix at Brescia in 1921, when they took the first four places, they became generally known as Brescias, the name still used today. Even a touring model would do 75 mph (120.5 km/h), and a short-chassis car with high axle ratio could exceed 85 mph (136.5 km/h). Sometimes the ratio was too high, and the Brescia would suffer from the sports Hillman's defect of being faster in third than in top.

The sporting Brescia was far from civilized, being incredibly noisy, with poor brakes and minimal passenger comforts, yet it had more performance than any other small car in the early 1920s, and indeed could see off a 3-litre Bentley. Two of the fastest were those owned by Raymond Mays and tuned by his friend Amherst Villiers; christened *Cordon Bleu* and *Cordon Rouge*, they earned 250 awards in sprints and hill climbs between 1922 and 1924. By using special camshafts, lightened components and alcohol fuel, Villiers was extracting 6,900 rpm from *Cordon Bleu* by 1924, compared with 3,000 for the standard product.

Only the short-wheelbase cars were officially called Brescias, touring models being known as Brescia Modifié. They could be had with a variety of coachwork, and there was at least one four-door saloon. Four-wheel brakes came in 1925, and the cars were made until 1926. Total production was about 2,000, more than any other Bugatti model.

The Brescia was by no means cheap, but it was reasonable compared with the 8-cylinder cars. The first of these was the Type 30 which had a 2-litre single-ohc straight-8 engine with three valves per cylinder, mounted in a modified Type 23 chassis. Introduced

**Bugatti Type 22/23**
A four-seater model of the Brescia Bugatti, at the Scottish hill climb, Rest-and-be-Thankful, in the early twenties.

**Bugatti Type 43, 1927**
A wolf in sheep's clothing. The Bugatti Type 43 was in principle the same as the supercharged racing model, Type 35B, equipped with a four-seater chassis.

in 1922 it was the first Bugatti with four-wheel brakes, hydraulic at first, but later cable-operated as at the rear. It was not Bugatti's most successful design, but it paved the way for later straight-8s, particularly the Types 35 and 43. The 35 was the most successful racing car of the inter-war period, being made with engines of 1½, 2 and 2.3 litres. Available to private owners as well as being the works Grand Prix car from 1924 to 1930, the 35 won twelve major Grands Prix in 1926 alone, and the following year Ettore claimed to have won 2,000 sporting events to date – this presumably included the successes of the Brescia. Together with the 4-cylinder Type 37 racing car, the 35 could be used on the road, and was frequently driven to and from races. As French law did not demand mudguards as in Britain, all that was needed to make the Bugatti racers strictly legal were headlamps and a horn. The Type 35 was priced in Britain at £1,100 complete in 1927, with the cheaper Type 35A with touring engine costing £675.

The Type 35 engine in its 2.3-litre version combined with the touring Type 38 chassis made up the Type 43, a four-seater sports car of remarkable performance made from 1927 to 1931. It was the only road-going Bugatti to have a full roller-bearing crankshaft and had a top speed of 105 mph (169 km/h). With acceleration of 0 to 60 mph (96.5 km/h) in twelve seconds, its performance was quite up to that of a 1960s sports car such as MGA or Triumph TR3A, though achieved with very much more noise! The standard body was a factory-built open four-seater with pointed tail, but some two-seaters and coupés were also made. Williams drove a dual-cowl four-door four-seater in the 1928 Monte Carlo Rally, but the factory body had only one door, the nearside front. In this form it cost £1,200 – expensive, but not unduly so for what was probably the fastest four-seater car made at the time. A total of 160 Type 43s were made.

Reverting to the small specialist sports car, three British makes stand out from their contemporaries, Alvis, Aston Martin and Frazer-Nash. Of these the Alvis company was the least of a specialist, in that they made touring versions of their 12/50 and 12/60 sports cars, and the most successful in terms of numbers built. Like Bentley, the Alvis was a brand-new postwar design, which appeared in 1920 as a conventional 4-cylinder light car whose 1400-cc side-valve engine developed just over 30 bhp at 3,500 rpm. It had aluminium

**Bugatti Type 43 and 40**
A Bugatti Type 43 (left) competing with a Type 40 in a Bugatti Owners' Club gymkhana. Though the body styles are similar, these were very different cars, the 43 having a 2.3-litre straight-8 engine, while the 40 had a 1½-litre 4-cylinder engine.

pistons which hinted that the designer, G.P.H. de Freville, had some sporting ambitions. Despite being expensive for a 1½-litre car (£750 to £870) the 10/30 Alvis sold quite well, with 120 cars finding customers in 1920, and 344 in 1921. In the latter year there was a more sporting version, the 11/40 with shorter wheelbase, 1,598 cc and 40 bhp. One of the body styles was a polished-aluminium two-seater with pointed tail, nicknamed the 'duck's back', and this became the most famous body on the 12/50 which appeared in 1923.

The 12/50 came in two sizes, 1,496 cc for the sports cars and 1,598 cc for the touring version. Designed by the new chief engineer, Captain G.T. Smith-Clarke, they both had overhead-valve engines, and the short-wheelbase SA 12/50 was good for 75 mph (120.5 km/h). It was soon recognized as a quality car in which a useful performance was combined with reliability, and sales jumped from 710 in 1923, to 933 in 1924, and over 1,000 in 1927. The 12/50, and its companion twin-carburettor 12/60 with close-ratio gearbox, were made until 1932 with little change, although front-wheel brakes were fitted for 1924, and in the later twenties the duck's back with its straight-through outside copper exhaust pipe was replaced by the beetle back which carried its exhaust more discreetly under the car. The 12/50's popularity is revealed by the sales figures of about 7,000 (including the 12/60), and in the 1930s it became one of the makes championed by the newly formed Vintage Sports Car Club (VSCC). It has remained a favourite vintage car up to the present day, and about 650 are known to survive.

Much more of a specialist car was the front-wheel-drive Alvis, which used a modified 12/50 engine turned back to front, with independent front suspension by eight transverse quarter-elliptic springs, two upper and two lower on each side. The engine had a gear-driven overhead camshaft, and a Cozette blower boosted power from 50 to 75 bhp. Performance was good, but the cars were very noisy, temperamental and difficult to drive – everything that the 12/50 was not, and Alvis withdrew them in 1930 after about 150 had been made. Even more complex was the straight-8 front-drive car, but only ten were made, and nearly all were works racing cars. The 4-cylinder cars were quite successful in racing, winning their class in the 1928 Le Mans race, and coming second in that year's Tourist Trophy. In 1930 a straight-8 won its class in the T.T.

**Alvis 12/50**
A later beetle-back on a 12/50, taking part in a Junior Car Club Inter Club Trial in 1929.

Aston Martin and Frazer-Nash were magical names to the sports car enthusiast between the wars, and the former is still one of the most highly regarded performance cars, but they were made in minuscule numbers, with a very uncertain financial background. The first Aston Martin was a home-assembled special which consisted of a 1.4-litre Coventry Simplex engine in the chassis of an Isotta-Fraschini voiturette. Completed in 1914, its builder, Lionel Martin, added the name Aston to his own because he had achieved a number of successes in his Singer at the Buckinghamshire hill climb at Aston Clinton. In 1921 came a production sports car, also using a Coventry Simplex engine, which was finished off in Martin's little works in the residential London district of Kensington. The chassis was built by Rubury Owen, and was unusual for having front-wheel brakes from

**Alvis 12/50, 1923**
The sportiest of the Alvis models, this has the classic duck's back body and a wheel-base of 9 ft (275 cm).

the earliest models. The bodies were all made by outside firms, for the Abingdon Road 'factory' was little more than a garage. The price was a hefty £850, and sales were very few, not more than fifty cars in three seasons, 1923 to 1925. However, Martin managed to attract some well-known drivers to race his cars, including Sammy Davis, Clive Gallop, B.S. Marshall and Count Louis Zborowski who also provided some welcome financial aid. Probably most of the cars sold went to friends of these drivers who achieved quite a lot of success with twin-cam racing Aston Martins. More capital came from the Hon. John Benson, later Lord Charnwood, but by 1925 the little company had lost £50,000. They would have been no worse off if they had given each customer £1,000 to go and buy a car from someone else!

The company was bought in 1926 by a Birmingham firm of consulting engineers, Renwick & Bertelli, and a completely new single-ohc engine, still of 1½ litres, was used in a new car made at a new factory at Feltham, Middlesex. It was lower and more modern-looking than the previous Astons but even more expensive, at £925 for a tourer and £1,025 for a saloon. Sales were even lower than before, only seventeen cars between 1927 and 1930, but two competition two-seaters were also built, which were entered at Le Mans in 1928. They were unusual in having dry-sump lubrication, in which the oil was kept in a reservoir between the dumbirons, the crankcase being scavenged by a pump mounted in tandem with the oil-delivery unit. This system went into production on all Aston Martins from 1930 onwards. Although unsuccessful in 1928, Astons were entered in every Le Mans race from 1931 to 1964, achieving many class successes and, in 1959, outright victory.

The Frazer-Nash grew out of the G.N. cyclecar (see page 22) as Archie Frazer-Nash and his friend Ron Godfrey left the G.N. company in 1922 in protest at the decision to abandon chain drive. While G.N. made a few unsuccessful shaft-driven light cars and then folded up, Frazer-Nash bought the chaindrive components that G.N. no longer needed and set up his own company at Kingston-upon-Thames, Surrey. A few modified G.N. chassis were sold under the name Frazer-Nash-G.N., but in 1924 he brought out a sports car powered by a 4-cylinder 1½-litre ohv Plus Power engine. The three-speed chain and dog-clutch transmission was retained, and was used on all Frazer-Nash cars until 1939. It was unconventional but in skilled hands very rapid changes could be made, it weighed less

**Frazer-Nash**
Chassis view of a Frazer-Nash, showing the unique transmission by four separate chains, engaged by dog clutches. The reverse gear chain is on the right.

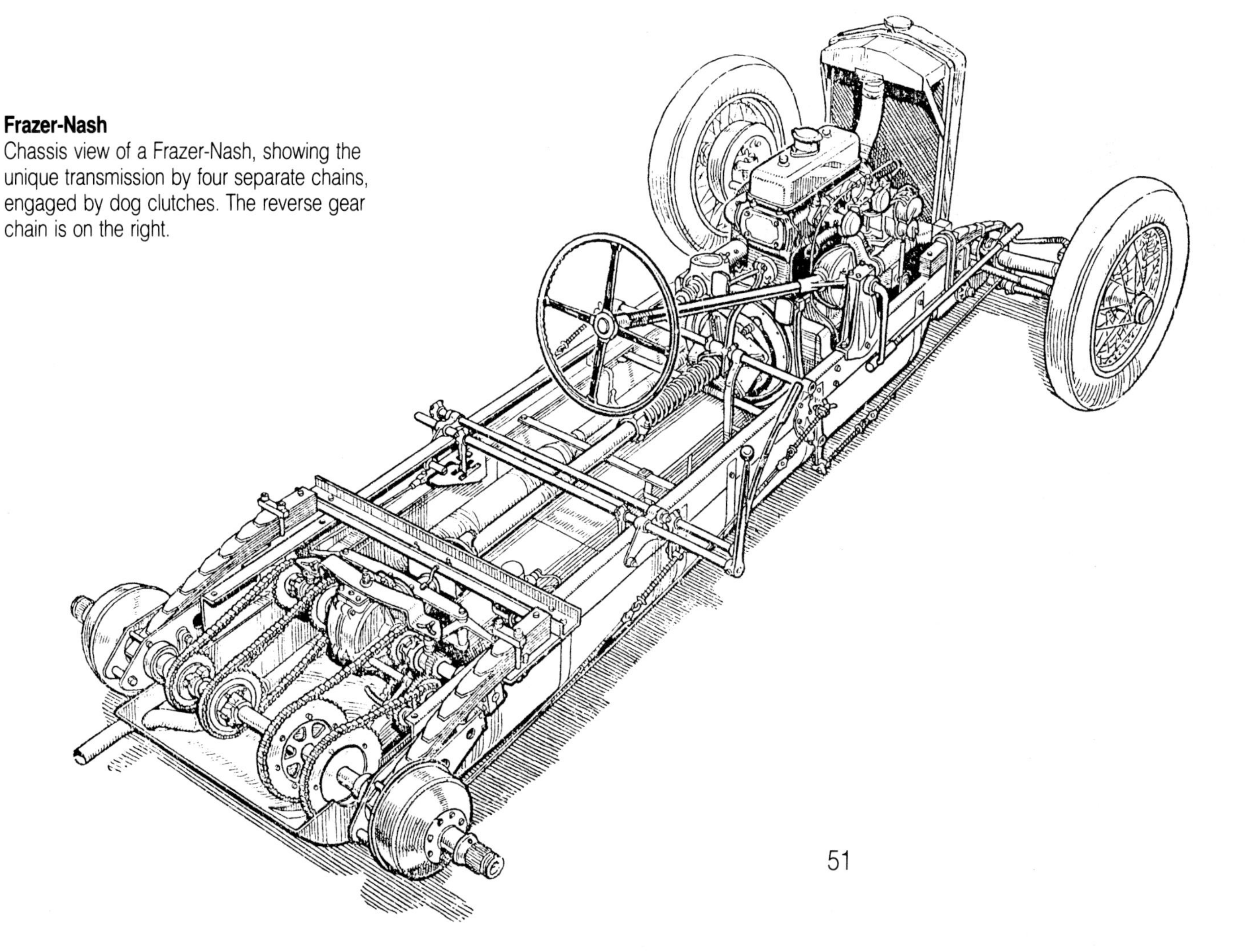

than an ordinary gearbox and gear ratios could be quickly altered for, say, hill climbing one day and racing or road work the next. Unlike the Aston Martin, the Frazer-Nash was not over-priced, at £285 to £300 complete.

Little change was made to the basic design over the years, apart from power units. The 1½-litre Anzani engine was adopted in 1925, and used on most models until 1932, after which Meadows, Blackburne and Gough engines were employed. Four speeds were available from 1929. Few concessions were made to creature comforts (only two closed saloon Frazer-Nashes were ever made) and a 'Nash owner was, and is, expected if not to welcome at least not to grumble about a bumpy ride, cramped accommodation, an inadequate hood and a tendency for oil to find its way into trouser legs. This, combined with the unconventional transmission, made Frazer-Nash owners a clannish brigade, fiercely loyal to their marque. Nearly all of them collected their cars from the factory, and often inspected them during construction. The makers, Frazer-Nash at first and from 1929 the Aldington brothers, were happy to incorporate customers' requests so long as they did not compromise the basic Frazer-Nash philosophy.

The best known sports-car maker from Italy was Alfa Romeo, who made two distinctive series of 6-cylinder cars in the 1920s. The 3-litre pushrod ohv cars were designed by Giuseppe Merosi, while their successors, the 1,500- and 1,750-cc ohc designs, were the work of Vittorio Jano. The Merosi cars began as tourers, but in 1923 a sports model appeared, with dry-sump lubrication and a handsome V radiator in place of the flat one of the tourer. The new model was known as the RLS in Italy and in Britain, where horsepower ratings were so often used, as the 22/90. It was joined in 1925 by the more powerful RLSS which had a top speed of 80 to 85 mph (128.5 to 136.5 km/h), and could be considered as the Italian equivalent of the 3-litre Bentley. Most RLSS cars had open two- or four-seater bodies, although there were a few lightweight saloons as well. One British owner, who raced his 22/90 in early postwar VSCC events, said of it 'The steering and look are just "Alfa" in their perfection. The brakes are surprisingly effective considering the year and have no need of adjustment for 2,000 miles (3,218 km). The radiator is about the most handsome ever designed. Compared to it, that of the Mercedes is a monument of Teutonic crudeness and the 4½ Bentley almost Imperialistic in its aggressiveness.' The only complaint he had was that third gear was too low for English roads: all the ratios seemed to have been chosen with the mountainous roads of Italy and Sicily in mind. Total production of the RLSS 22/90 was 392 cars.

In 1923 Vittorio Jano joined Alfa Romeo, and designed for them the highly successful P2 racing car which dominated the Grand Prix scene in 1924 and 1925. The new series of 1½-litre ohc cars which he produced in 1927 owed much to the racing models, and was notable for having a relatively short-stroke engine (62 × 82 mm). The first series, known as

**Alfa Romeo RLSS**
An Alfa Romeo RLSS with striking pointed-tail four-seater body. The discs were not standard wear for Alfas, but were doubtless recommended by the coachbuilder.

**Alfa Romeo 6C-1500, 1929**
Vittorio Jano's little masterpiece – a 1929 Alfa Romeo 6C-1500 in twin-cam Gran Sport form.

the 1500 Turismo, was available with two wheelbases: 10 ft 2 in (3.1 m) for touring and saloon bodies, and 9 ft 6 in (2.9 m) for sports cars. As yet the engine was not highly tuned, and top speed was not more than 65 mph (104.5 km/h) for the tourers and 70 mph (112.5 km/h) for the sports models. In 1928 a twin-cam model joined the range which was available only with the shorter wheelbase. This was known as the Gran Turismo with a top speed of 75 mph (120.5 km/h), and there was soon an even faster car available, with Roots supercharger and a wheelbase of only 9 ft (2.75 m). This was called the Gran Sport, and won numerous events in 1928, including the Mille Miglia, Belgian 24-Hour Race, Georges Boillot Cup and Circuit de Routes Pavées.

In 1929 came the ultimate development of Jano's 6-cylinder cars, when the engine was enlarged to 1,752 cc. Known as the 1750, this car, too, was made with three wheelbases: the 3.1-m Turismo (with single-ohc engine), the 2.9-m or 2.75-m Gran Turismo (twin ohc, unsupercharged) and the 2.75-m Super Sport (twin ohc supercharged). The latter was capable of 95 mph (153 km/h): works-backed cars won every race in which they were entered in 1929, including the Mille Miglia, Belgian 24 Hours, Eireann Cup and Irish Grand Prix. In 1930 they again won the Mille Miglia and Belgian 24 Hours, and also the Tourist Trophy. The classic body on the 1750 Super Sport was an open two-seater by Zagato, which many consider to be one of the most beautiful sports cars ever made. It was, inevitably, far from cheap; while the Turismo cost £875 complete, a Zagato Super Sport was £1,275, or more than a 4½-litre Bentley.

After 1930 the 1750 was overshadowed by the straight-8 2300, but it continued in production until 1933, by which time 2,579 had been made, of which 369 were the short-chassis Super Sport models.

**O.M. Tipo Superba, 1928**
This 2-litre tourer, known in Britain as a 15/60, and by its makers as a Tipo 665 Superba.

No other Italian make came within striking distance of Alfa Romeo, though there were a number of fast tourers which had their sporting versions. Best known of these was the O.M. (Officine Meccaniche) which was unusual in extracting a very satisfactory performance from a side-valve engine. The Tipo 665 Superba, made from 1923 to 1931, had a 45-bhp 1,991-cc 6-cylinder engine, from which 70 mph (112.5 km/h) could be obtained. In 1928 came a short-wheelbase low-chassis model whose sloping radiator gave it some resemblance to a 1750 Alfa. This was given a larger engine of 2,200 cc and a Roots supercharger in 1930, but it was still no match for the Alfas, or a Type 43 Bugatti. Because there was less competition, it was the earlier touring models which had the greatest competition success, taking the first three places in the 1927 Mille Miglia and coming second in 1928 and 1929. Always popular in England, where L.C. Rawlence, the concessionaire, fitted some with overhead-valve conversions, the O.M. still has a keen following in the VSCC.

The unconventional Lancia Lambda was thought of as a sports car in Britain, but in its homeland it was considered a well-made fast tourer, and many of the saloons were used as taxicabs. It was really too long to be a satisfactory sports car, and in the 1930s and later there was quite a vogue in England to 'cut and shut' the Lambda, taking out a foot (third of a metre) or more of the wheelbase.

With the exception of Mercedes-Benz the 1920s German car, sporting or otherwise, was relatively unknown in Western Europe and America, though quite a number were exported to Scandinavia and Eastern Europe. No cars from east of the Rhine were exhibited either at the Paris Salon or London's Olympia until 1927. Mercedes and Benz were the first to re-

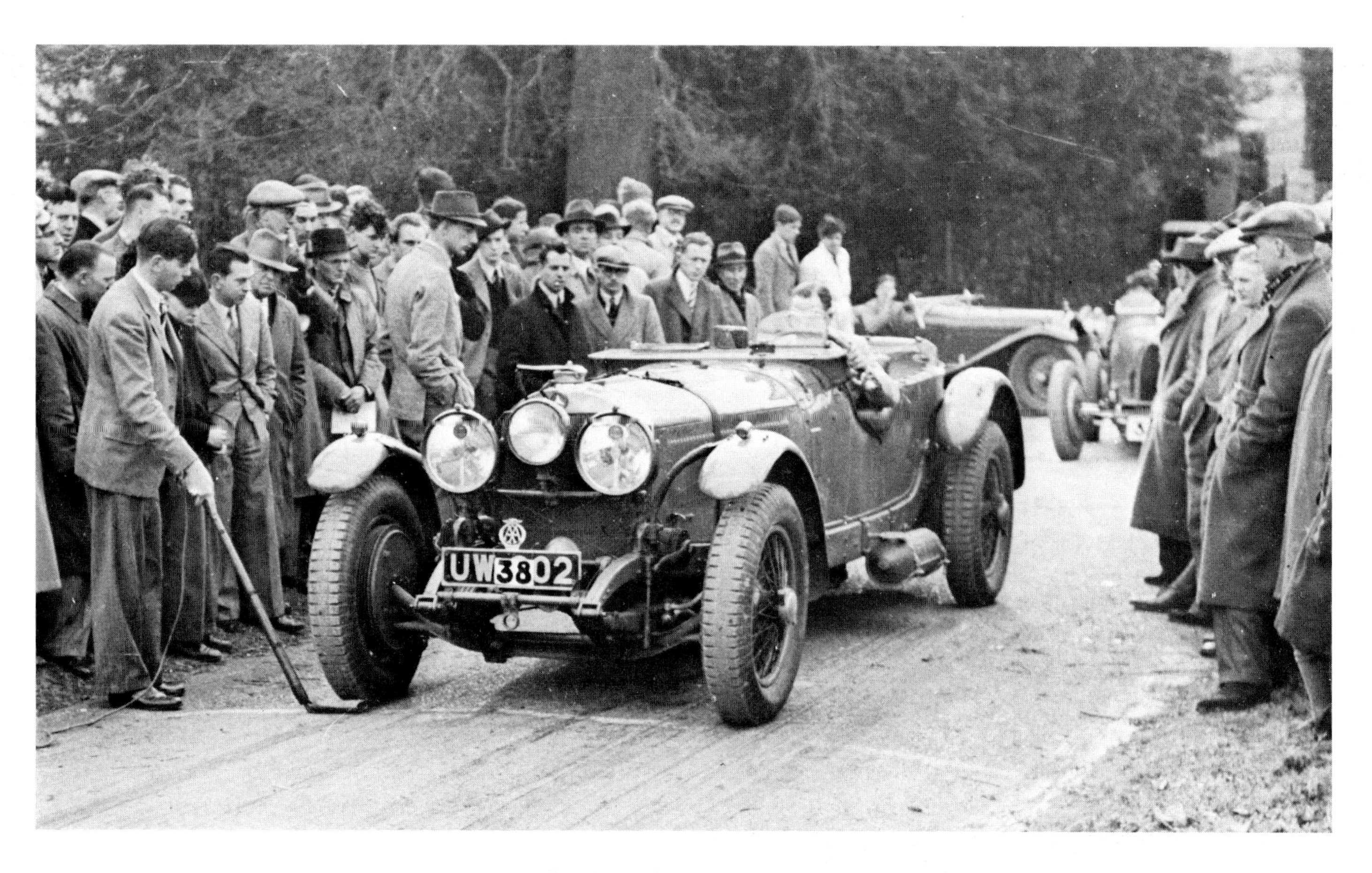


**Mercedes-Benz S, 1929**
A Mercedes-Benz S 36/220 on the starting line at a sprint in Syston Park, Nottinghamshire. Behind it are a Bugatti Type 35 and an Alfa Romeo 2300, so the photograph cannot have been taken earlier than 1931.

establish themselves, even before their merger in 1926, because they had good contacts inherited from prewar days. The British Mercedes Co. had remained in business selling and servicing used cars, and they took up new ones again when they began to arrive in the country around 1925.

The most interesting innovation on the Mercedes was the supercharger which had been first tried on a 28/95 PS which won the 1921 Coppa Florio. Unlike the blower used a year or two later on Fiat and Alfa Romeo racing cars, the Mercedes system blew air into the carburettor instead of being located between carburettor and engine. Also the blower was engaged by the clutch and did not operate continuously, but only for short bursts. Certainly on the later cars, using it for more than twenty seconds at a time was likely to result in a blown gasket.

Although blown Mercedes were advertised as early as the 1921 Berlin Motor Show they did not appear in any numbers until 1923, when three were listed, the 1.6-litre 6/25/38 PS, 3.9-litre 15/70/100 PS and 6.2-litre 24/100/140 PS. In these German designations, the first figure was the rated, taxable horsepower, the second the brake horsepower without the blower and the third the maximum power with blower in operation. In Britain, where rated horsepower was calculated differently, the small car was called the 12/40 hp, and the big six the 33/140 (touring) or 33/180 (sports). It is simpler to use the German letter designation, in which the basic model with the 6.3-litre engine was the 24/100/140 PS from 1924–1926 and the Type 630 from 1926–1929, while the sports variant, which had a shorter chassis, was known as the Model K from 1926–1929.

The Mercedes 15/70/100 PS (later called the Typ 400) and the 24/100/140 PS were the first car designs which Ferdinand Porsche produced for Mercedes after he joined the company in 1923. The engine had a light-alloy crankcase-cum-block, with a detachable cast-iron head. There was a single overhead camshaft driven by a vertical shaft and silent gears. Model K in its original form was not an ideal sports car because of its high centre of gravity and poor brakes. However, in 1927 Porsche produced a lower model with servo-assisted brakes and engine capacity increased to 6.8 litres. This Typ S 26/120/180 was a genuine 110-mph (177-km/h) car, and with its long, low bonnet headed by the handsome V radiator it was the best-looking of all the big Porsche-designed Mercedes-Benz cars. It had a number of sporting successes to its credit, including the first three places in the 1927 German Grand Prix and the first two in 1928.

In 1928 came the SS 27/170/225 PS, or 38/250 as it was known in Britain. The engine was enlarged further, to 7 litres and 225 bhp with supercharger, and the bonnet was higher than on the S. The typical SS body was an open four-seater, though drophead coupés were also made. Coachwork was built by a variety of German firms such as Neuss, Gläser and Erdmann & Rossi, and also by foreign companies such as Castagna in Italy, James Young in England and D'Ieteren in Belgium. However, the standard tourer by Mercedes-Benz' own coachworks at Sindelfingen took a lot of beating for looks.

**Mercedes-Benz SS**
The higher bonnet line shows this car to be an SS 38/250. It is, in fact, the car which Malcolm Campbell drove in the 1929 Tourist Trophy.

**Mercedes-Benz SS**
Dashboard and gearbox view of a Mercedes-Benz SS chassis. The large central dial is the rev counter, to its right are speedometer (calibrated in km/h) and a clock. Note the drilled cross member of the chassis. The SSKL was much more liberally drilled.

Soon after the SS came the SSK 27/170/225 PS with wheelbase shortened from 11 ft 2 in (3.4 m) to 8 ft 8 in (2.6 m) and partially drilled chassis frame for lightness. Top speed was around 120 mph (193 km/h), and output 250 bhp with the larger supercharger. Three sizes of blower were used on these big Mercedes-Benz, the standard compressing at 8½ lb/in$^2$ (0.6 kg/cm$^2$) which was fitted to all SS and SSK models, the large (10 lb/in$^2$/0.7 kg/cm$^2$) and the competition, nicknamed 'the Elephant' (12 lb/in$^2$/0.85 kg/cm$^2$). The latter was only used on works-sponsored cars driven by nominated drivers; private owners, even one as well known as Malcolm Campbell, were refused the Elephant. Caracciola's SSK, equipped with the Elephant blower, was barred from the 1930 Tourist Trophy because it was not standard production equipment.

The ultimate development of this series was the SSKL 27/240/300 PS (Super Sports, Kurz, Leicht), of which only seven were made, all retained by Mercedes-Benz for competition work. The Elephant blower gave over 300 bhp and the frame was copiously drilled to get weight down to 2,700 lbs (1,215 kg). These formidable cars were said to have a top speed of 147 mph (236.5 km/h), while one with a special streamlined body was timed at 156 mph (251 km/h) on the Avus banked circuit in 1931.

Many successes came to these cars, including Caracciola's win at the 1929 Tourist Trophy on an SS, in the 1930 Irish Grand Prix and 1931 German Grand Prix on an SSK, and in the 1931 Mille Miglia on an SSKL. In the latter event he drove single-handed for the whole 1,000-mile (1,609-km) race. The SSK was also very successful in hill climbs, winning the European Championship in 1930 and 1931. The SS and SSK remained in production until 1934, though very few were made after 1932 – Mercedes-Benz was concentrating on smaller machines which earned the company's bread and butter. Various production figures have been claimed, and it is possible that truly accurate numbers will never be obtainable. However, according to recent research, the figures are these:

| | |
|---|---|
| S | 174 |
| SS | 151 |
| SSK | 42 |
| SSKL | 7 |

No other German sports car had the international impact of the Mercedes-Benz, but some advanced designs were made for domestic consumption. Among these were the Simpson Supra Typ S which featured a twin-ohc 4-cylinder engine, with four inclined valves per cylinder. Made from 1924 to 1926 by a small firm in Suhl, Thuringia, the Typ S developed 60 bhp from two litres and had a top speed of 85 mph (136.5 km/h). Wheelbase of the sports model was only 8 ft 5 in (2.5 m). It was expensive, and only thirty were made, compared with about 700 of the company's single-ohc Typ SO and 750 of the pushrod-ohv Typ R. The Simson Supra was designed by Paul Henze who had previously been responsible for another sports car, the single-ohc 50-bhp 2.6-litre 4-cylinder Steiger. The engine was notable for having a very long stroke for the period (72 × 160 mm), but the design was spoilt by the absence of four-wheel brakes. These only arrived on the last models, made in 1925, but they were too late to save the firm, which closed down the following year.

Other German sports cars included the NAG C4b, a Bentley-like fast tourer which, like the O.M., managed very well with a side-valve engine, the Dürkopp which could be had with a supercharger, boosting power from its 2-litre engine from 32 to 60 bhp, one of which gave Hans Stuck his entry into motor sport, and the attractive, low-slung 1½-litre single-ohc Stolle. With its smooth two-seater body and Rudge-Whitworth wire wheels, the Stolle would not have looked old-fashioned in the early 1930s, yet it was made in 1924. However, its price was against it, and only fifteen ever reached the public. There were also numerous small sports cars mostly derived from tourers, also the Pluto which was a licence-built Amilcar, and the Bugatti-based Rabag.

# The United States of America

During the 1920s car production reached record levels in America, which would not be equalled until the 1950s. Paradoxically this was not reflected in any growth in motor sport, and in fact there was less than in prewar days. The Indianapolis 500-Mile Race was the leading event, and the board tracks flourished in the earlier part of the decade, though the last closed down in 1931. These were all for racing cars, and there were no competitive events for cars like Mercer and Stutz. Thus the sports car as it developed in Europe was nonexistent in America, yet a number of sporty looking cars, generally known as speedsters, were made.

The most striking feature of the speedster was its body, generally a two-seater with cycle-type wings and step plates in place of running boards. Wheels were generally wire-spoked, whereas the touring equivalent would still have used artillery wheels. These changes were all cosmetic, and usually the speedster was quite unaltered in engine, suspension, brakes and wheelbase, all areas where European sports cars differed markedly. They handled no better than their touring equivalents, and if they were a little faster, this was thanks to a lighter body. Most speedsters were driven relatively short distances, to the golf club or yacht marina. They were more popular in temperate climates, and in the northern states were almost always laid up in the winter.

A typical vintage speedster was the Paige 6-66 Daytona. In 1921 a stripped Paige touring car established a stock-car record of 102.8 mph (165.5 km/h) for the flying mile at Daytona Beach, Florida, and the following year the Paige-Detroit Motor Car Co. put into production a speedster named Daytona in honour of the record. The engine was the standard Continental 5.4-litre six which developed 66 bhp (hence the name 6-66), and the body was a striking two-seater. An unusual feature was a third seat which, with its accompanying footrest, could be pulled out like a drawer from the side of the body. This was very much in keeping with the carefree attitudes of the time, but the thought of riding on this seat at any speed above 20 mph (32 km/h) is pretty daunting.

The Daytona was priced at $3,400, compared with $2,875 for a five-passenger tourer, but did not sell well. The 1923 model was better equipped, with automatic windscreen wiper, cigar lighter and eight-day clock, and cheaper, at $2,400 (tourers were down to $2,195) but still it did not attract the customers, and it was dropped at the end of its second season. Only fifty-six were made in all.

The Kissel Motor Co. of Hertford, Wisconsin, offered a speedster throughout the twenties. This originated as a special, designed by the New York agent for the make, Conover T. Silver, who thought he had a market for a distinctive car. The first Kissel Silver Special was built in 1917, on lines which were to become familiar, with cycle-type wings, no doors, and two of the folding seats later offered by Paige. Silver ceased to handle the make in 1919, but the trend he started continued. The 1919 show car was painted chrome yellow all over, and was christened the Gold Bug, a name used for Kissel speedsters for several years afterwards. By the mid-twenties the folding seats had been dropped, replaced by a two-passenger dickey seat. A Lycoming straight-8 engine was adopted in 1925, and speedsters used this as well as the smaller six. They were made up to 1931 when Kissel went out of business.

There were at least ten other American speedsters, including the Argonne, Revere, and Richelieu, all powered by the large 4-cylinder Rochester-Duesenberg engine, the 6-cylinder Marmon, Jordan, and Noma, and the Daniels with its own make of 6.4-litre V8.

By 1925 all the foregoing cars except for Kissel had vanished, as had the leftovers from the previous decade, the Mercer and Stutz Bearcat. Towards the end of the twenties, though, some new speedsters appeared, coinciding with the first stirrings of American interest in European sports-car races. In fact a Chrysler had competed at Le Mans in 1925, and the make was there again in 1928 and 1929, but with stock roadsters rather than sports cars. Stutz introduced a new line of cars in 1926 with their Safety Stutz Vertical Eight, powered by a 4.7-litre single-ohc straight-8. The wide range of coachwork included two- and four-seater speedsters, and a four-seater ran at Le Mans in 1928, entered by the French pioneer of fabric bodywork, C.T. Weymann. The Stutz finished second, behind the Barnato/Rubin 4½-litre Bentley, but ahead of two other Bentleys. Indeed, for much of the race it had led the field. This seriously alarmed the Bentley camp, resulting in two different solutions – supercharging by Birkin and the larger-engined Speed Six by W.O. himself.

In fact, 1928 was Stutz' best year at Le Mans; in 1929 they were fifth, and in 1930 and 1932 they did not finish. However, their speedsters were continued, culminating in the

Super Bearcat of 1932, which had a 5.2-litre twin-ohc engine with four valves per cylinder. The Bearcat name was revived for the 11-ft 2½-in (3.4-m) wheelbase model, while the Super Bearcat had a 9-ft 8-in (2.9-m) wheelbase and a top speed in excess of 100 mph (161 km/h).

Another make which came to the fore in the late 1920s was Auburn. This Midwestern car, from the Indiana town of the same name, had been a conventional touring car with nothing to distinguish it from countless others until the company acquired as its general manager Errett Lobban Cord, in 1925. He proceeded to revamp the styling of the staid sedans and in 1928 brought a speedster into the range. This had a pointed-tail two-seater body and a 115-bhp engine. That year an 8-115 speedster recorded 108.46 mph (174.51 km/h) over a mile (about 1.6 km) at Daytona Beach. Later models were more powerful, the 8-120 coming in 1929 and 8-125 in 1930. They were all remarkably good value, selling for around $2,000 when a Stutz cost up to $5,895 for a Super Bearcat.

**Mercer Series 5 Raceabout, 1922**
A far cry from the classic Mercer 35 of prewar days, the Series 5 had a 70-bhp 4-cylinder engine. The huge spotlight mounted on the running board can hardly have helped the aerodynamics.

# CHAPTER THREE

# THE 1930S

Seldom does the end of a decade neatly round off a period in history, and one cannot say that the world of the motorcar changed dramatically in 1930. However, if one looks at the decade as a whole, the 1930s scene was very different from its predecessor. Among sports cars, familiar names such as Bentley, Vauxhall, Sunbeam and Mercedes-Benz were making cars of very different character, while most of the little French cars of the Amilcar/Salmson persuasion had disappeared altogether.

## Great Britain

National characteristics emerged more clearly in the thirties; generally speaking, the continental countries of Europe led in design, particularly in chassis and suspension, while the British manufacturers built cars whose charm lay, and still lies, in their traditional design and appearance. It is significant that, in a race held at Brooklands in 1939 to ascertain the fastest road car in Britain, of the seven cars entered only one was of British manufacture.

However, if the British motor industry did not make the most up-to-date cars, it built sports cars in a greater variety than any other country. They ranged from inexpensive machines like the M.G.s, Austin Sevens and Wolseley Hornets to the V12 Lagonda and the very rare Squire, which cost almost as much as the Lagonda although it was only a 1½-litre car.

M.G.s were made in great variety throughout the period, and can be seen as the archetypal British sports car of the thirties, as the Bentley was of the twenties. They entered the decade with the M-type Midget already described, adding in 1931 the C-type, whose engine was reduced to 746 cc to enable it to compete with Austin Seven Ulsters in the 750-cc class. With a Powerplus supercharger it could reach 90 mph (145 km/h), but performance had to be paid for, and a C-type cost £295 unblown and £345 blown, compared with £185 for the M-type. It is doubtful if many people bought a C-type unless they wanted to race it, and only forty-four were made, in 1931/32. In 1931 came the D-type four-seater with a lengthened C-type frame, and this led to the J series which used a D-type frame with an engine derived from the C-type, but with the same dimensions as the

**M.G. TA Midget**
The first M.G. Midget with pushrod ohv engine, the TA was criticised by dyed-in-the-wool enthusiasts, but it was more comfortable and better braked than its predecessors, and led directly to the famous TC of the postwar years.

**Singer Nine Sports, 1933**
The Singer cars did not have the same reputation as the M.G.s, but their road-holding was just as good as that of their rivals. With passengers in the minimal rear seat, however, the Singer underwent a change of character, and less experienced drivers could be caught out.

old M-type. It was, however, a much better power unit, with strengthened crankshaft and opposed-port head. Power was now up to 36 bhp, and the two-seater J2 offered 70 mph (112.5 km/h) for less than £200. The first J2s had cycle-type wings, but in 1933 flowing wings and running boards were adopted, and the classic M.G. look had arrived. This persisted without great change through the P series and up to the TC of postwar years.

The PA Midget had a three-bearing crankshaft which made it more suitable for tuning, and capacity was unchanged at 847 cc. It was increased to 939 cc on the PB of 1935/36 which now gave 43 bhp, with a top speed of 76 mph (122 km/h). Most PAs and PBs were open two-seaters, but there was a pretty, if rather claustrophobic, Airline coupé also available. Prices were up a bit, at £222 for the open car and £290 for the coupé, but they sold well, 2,526 Ps finding buyers between 1934 and 1936.

The PB was the last of the ohc Midgets, being replaced by the TA which had a 1,292-cc pushrod engine based on that used in the Wolseley Ten. This was part of the rationalization process brought in by Leonard Lord, which also saw the M.G. competition department disappear almost overnight. 'That bloody lot can go for a start,' Lord is reputed to have said when he made his first visit to the Abingdon works. Enthusiasts deplore the TA, but it did have a similar top speed to the PB, was wider and more comfortable, with hydraulic brakes and (within a month of its introduction) synchromesh on the upper two ratios. The price remained at £222, and in place of the Airline coupé there was a drophead coupé with full-height doors, made by Tickford. In 1939 the TA gave way to the TB, generally similar but with a shorter-stroke Morris Ten-derived engine of 1,250 cc. Few of these were made (379 in about five months) but it was the ancestor of the postwar TC which became such a success on the export market and sparked off the sports-car boom in America.

Before looking at larger M.G.s, we should consider the rivals to the Midgets: the Austin Sevens, Singer Nine, and Morgan 4/4. The Austins were less sporting than the Ulster which was dropped in 1933. Its replacement was the '65', renamed Nippy for 1935, which had a nearly standard 23-bhp engine and underslung rear springs. Its price of £152 undercut the M-type M.G. by £33, but it was less of a sports car and was not so popular. In 1935 it was joined by the Speedy, which had a pointed tail compared with the Nippy's rounded back, higher gearing and a pressure-fed crankshaft. This engine was used in later Nippies, but Austin gave up their sports Sevens in 1937.

Singer had introduced an 848-cc ohc 4-cylinder engine on their Junior in 1927, and this had its sporting version in the Porlock two-seater of 1928. This had barely any performance advantage over the saloon, and it was not until 1933 that the Birmingham firm brought out a sports car, the 972-cc Nine. This had a lowered chassis and remote-control gearbox, and was made in two models, the 35-bhp Nine Sports and the 42-bhp Nine Le Mans, the latter with high-lift cams and counterbalanced crankshaft. Body styles included two- and four-seater sports, a coupé and a saloon. The fastest model, the Le Mans two-seater, was good for 75 mph (120.5 km/h), and at £215 it provided keen competition for the P-series M.G. They raced with some success at Le Mans, but blotted their copybook badly in the 1935 Tourist Trophy, when three works cars crashed because of broken steering drop-arms. Two actually crashed at the same spot, piling one on top of the other, while the third ended its run in a bank only a few yards away. This episode did a lot of harm to the Singer reputation, and though they redeemed themselves in the 1937 T.T. (fourth and sixth overall, the best performance by British cars) the factory never raced them again. The Le Mans was discontinued in 1937, and the Nine Sports Tourer of the immediate pre- and postwar years was in no way a sports car, in either handling or performance. The Le Mans body was also seen on a 1½-litre 6-cylinder Singer made from 1934 to 1937.

For years Morgan had been the most famous name among British 3-wheeled cars, and they were the only ones to be consistently campaigned in races and trials. In 1935 H.F.S. Morgan decided to enter the 4-wheeled market with a light sports car very much in the M.G. Midget idiom. Although he used a Ford 8-hp engine in the prototype, the production cars of 1936 had a 34-bhp Coventry Climax 1,122-cc engine, and a Moss four-speed gearbox which was mounted amidships, directly next to the gear lever, so avoiding the slightly woolly remote controls of the M.G. and the Singer. The frame was underslung and front suspension was independent by sliding pillars, as it had been on all the 3-wheelers made since 1910. Top speed was 78 mph (125.5 km/h), and the 4/4 as it was called (four wheels, four cylinders) cost £192, undercutting the M.G. TA by £30. It took a little time to get established, for the 3-wheeler enthusiasts considered it a heresy and too soft, while others found difficulty in getting into and out of it, with an awkward hood. However, the fact that H.F.S. and his son Peter regularly entered their cars in rallies and trials pleased sporting customers. By the time World War II interrupted production, 824 had been made. Models for 1939 included a drophead coupé, and the engine was now a 1,267-cc Standard Ten.

Many rude things have been said about the Wolseley Hornet ('. . . typifies the small six both at its worst and at the pinnacle of its commercial success' – Michael Sedgwick. 'More than any other model it typifies the decay of British motorcar design in the early '30s' – D.B. Tubbs) yet these strictures were aimed more at the saloons than the Hornet Special sports models. The Hornet began life in 1930 as a stretched Morris Minor with a 1,271-cc 6-cylinder engine and the same tiny four-seater saloon body as the Morris. In 1932 came the Hornet Special which was offered as a chassis only, with engine tuned to give 45 bhp with the aid of twin carburettors, high-compression pistons and duplex valve springs. The

**Morgan 4/4, 1937**
A Morgan 4/4 two-seater. A four-seater was also offered from the start, and a drophead coupé was added to the range in 1939.

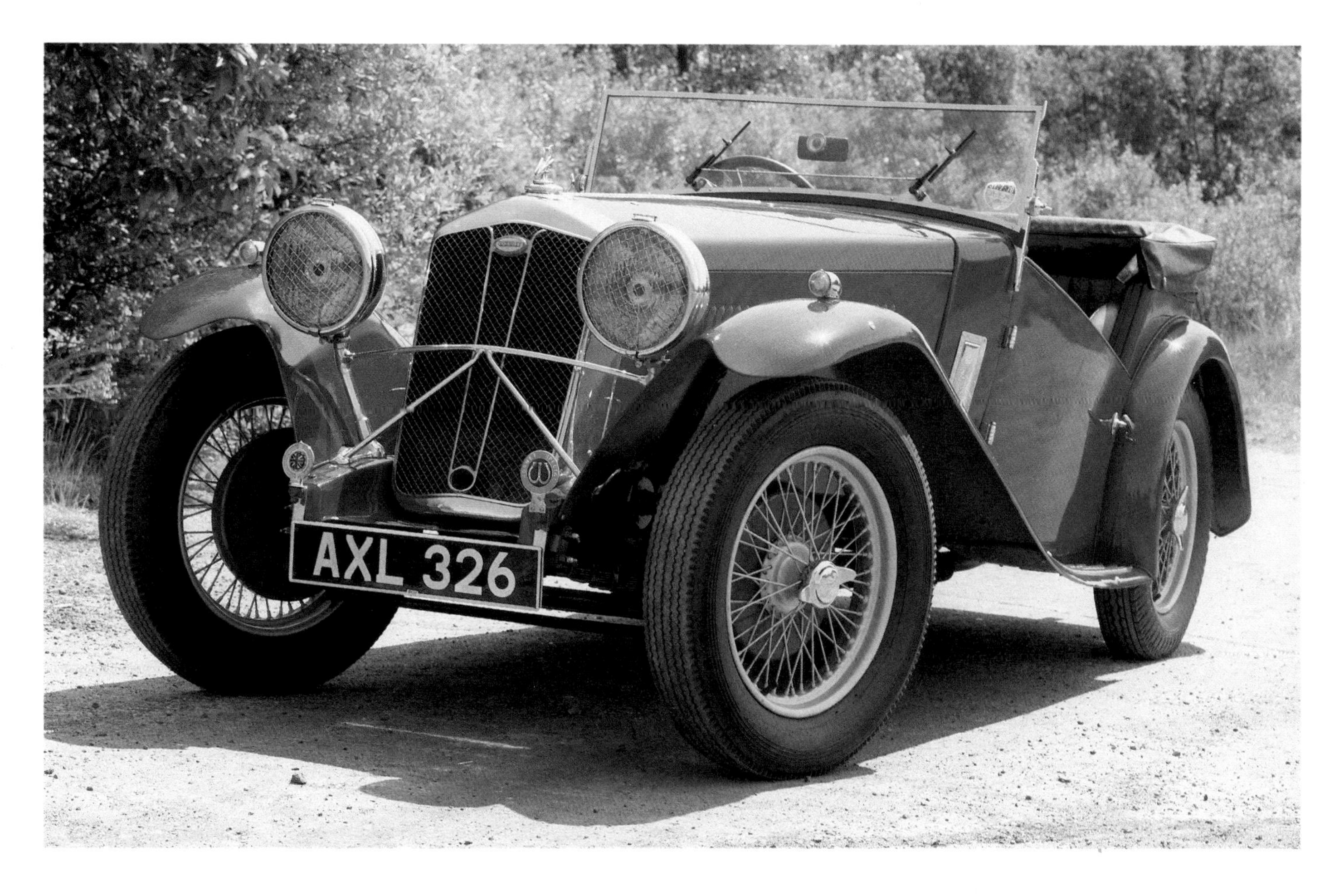


**Wolseley Hornet Special**
One of the later Wolseley Hornet Specials, with 1.6-litre engine. Note the stoneguards on headlamps and radiator.

coachbuilders soon realized that the Hornet Special's long bonnet could make for a very handsome sporting car, and a considerable number of firms produced offerings on this chassis, including Abbey, Swallow and Salmons. The Abbey-bodied cars were called E.W. Daytonas, after the London distributors who sold them, Eustace Watkins, and sold for £275. A top speed of 75 mph (120.5 km/h) was by no means discreditable, but they did not handle very well, and were never used for serious racing. However, they were much in evidence at gymkhanas and *concours d'elegance* where many extras would be flaunted, such as an aero screen for the driver's use when the windscreen was folded flat, wire-mesh stoneguards over the headlamps, and special horns. The 1935 Hornet Specials had 1,604-cc engines, but ohc engines were discontinued in 1936, when Lord moved the Nuffield Organization so firmly away from motor sport, and that was the end of the Hornet Special.

The 'promenader' or 'boy racer' such as the Hornet Special was a phenomenon of the 1930s, although not so different in spirit from such 1920s cars as the Morris Cowley Special Sports. Both hinted by their appearance at sporting performance that was not there. Among other promenaders of the 1930s were the Hillman Aero Minx whose dropped frame and sporty body styles made it look completely different from the staid Minx saloon on which it was based, the Morris Ten Six Special with humped scuttle, fold-flat screens and bonnet straps on a car that was hard pressed to reach 65 mph (104.5 km/h), and the Avon Standards which carried handsome bodies on unmodified Standard Nine Sixteen or Twenty chassis. The Avon bodies were designed by the Jensen brothers, who became car makers in their own right in 1936.

For the more serious driver with up to £500 to spend, there was a wide variety. M.G. offered the Magnette, a small six with 1,087-cc ohc engine derived from the Wolseley Hornet – the K1 saloon had a four-speed pre-selector gearbox but the shorter K2 sports had a crash box. Saloons sold for £445 and the K2 for £390. The most potent Magnette was the K3, a true road-racing car which frequently competed without road equipment. The engine was still a 1,087-cc unit, but greatly developed, with triple valve springs, straight-cut bevel gears for the cam drive, machined and balanced crankshaft and a No. 9 Powerplus supercharger. Output was a formidable 120 bhp at 6,500 rpm, compared with 45 bhp at 5,500 rpm from the K2. It was, of course, not cheap, at £750, but it could beat all the opposition in its class, including specialized racing cars such as the 1,100-cc Maseratis. Its greatest success was Nuvolari's outright win in the 1933 T.T., and K3s also took the team award in the Mille Miglia and won the Coppa Acerbo, both in 1933. Although they were sold with full road equipment, including twin horns, a K3 would never have been bought by someone uninterested in racing. Thirty-one were made for sale, together with two prototypes. Before the advent of the E.R.A., which was strictly a racing car, the K3 was Britain's most successful competition car.

Later Magnettes were the KN saloon and the N series made in open two- and four-seater form, or as an Airline coupé. All these had larger engines of 1,271 cc, the most powerful giving 74 bhp and over 80 mph (129 km/h). The most highly developed was the NE which gave Charles Dodson victory in the 1934 T.T.

Riley was one of the best-known names in the 1930s, for attractive saloons of above-average performance, as well as sports cars. The latter were derived from the Brooklands Nine which had been introduced in 1928. This used Percy Riley's ingenious 1,087-cc 4-cylinder engine with hemispherical combustion chambers and twin camshafts set high in the block in a very low chassis designed with the help of Parry Thomas and Reid Railton, and built at the Brooklands track. So low was the Brooklands Nine that the driver could touch the ground with his hand when seated at the wheel. It was made until 1932, selling at £420, and was succeeded by the Imp which used the same engine in a shorter chassis, upswept over the front axle and underslung at the rear. Rather stubby in appearance, it was a delightful little car to drive, provided one could get behind the wheel. This was a very close fit, and virtually impossible for a six-footer. With a 6-cylinder engine it became the MPH Six, capable of 90 mph (145 km/h) compared with 75 mph (120.5 km/h) for the Imp. However, the £550 price tag for the MPH discouraged most would-be customers, and only twelve were made, compared with about seventy-five Imps. Three sizes of engine were offered in the MPH, 1,458 cc, 1,633 cc and 1,726 cc.

**M.G. K3 Magnette, 1933**
The second prototype K3 Magnette competing in the 1933 Mannin Beg ('Little Man' in the Manx language) race through the streets of Douglas, Isle of Man. Magnettes finished 2nd and 3rd in this race. The car is stripped of its road equipment, as K3s frequently were for racing purposes.

**Riley Imp, 1935**
English sports cars were built with performance in mind, and their driving qualities satisfied drivers who did not put comfort first. The clean lines of the Riley Imp, especially of the beautifully defined rear section, are typical of this school.

In 1935 Riley brought out a 1,496-cc 4-cylinder engine designed for them by Hugh Rose. It was on the same lines as the Nine, and went into a range of touring cars such as the Falcon, Kestrel and Merlin saloons, and the Lynx tourer. In 1936 came a sports version with a chassis similar to the Imp and MPH. Known as the Sprite, most of them had a curious fencer's-mask grille unlike the traditional Riley front end. The engine was considerably modified, with different cams, larger sump and magneto ignition, giving the Sprite a top speed of 85 mph (137 km/h). This engine was also available in the Lynx and Kestrel. Between forty and fifty were made.

**Riley Imp, 1934**
Mike Hawthorn's first competition car was a 16-year-old Riley Imp which he ran in speed trials and races in 1950 and 1951. He is seen here at Goodwood, where he was awarded the *Motor Sport* Brooklands Memorial Trophy in 1951 for consistent success at club meetings.

**Frazer-Nash TT Replica, 1935**
One of fourteen made that year, this car is driven by A.F.P. Fane at a hill climb organised by the Bugatti Owners' Club at Amersham, Bucks.

Frazer-Nash and Aston Martin continued to make very traditional sports cars during the decade. The Frazer-Nash recipe was much as it had been in the 1920s, apart from changes in engines as the 50-bhp Meadows unit became increasingly uncompetitive. Alternatives were the 1,660-cc 6-cylinder twin-ohc Blackburne which gave 75 bhp, the 60-bhp 1½-litre 4-cylinder unit designed by Albert Gough and built by Frazer-Nash themselves, and the 6-cylinder 2-litre BMW. The most powerful model was the Shelsley with twin-supercharged Gough engine, capable of 100 mph (161 km/h). However, the chain-gang appeal dwindled rapidly: in 1934 Frazer-Nash sold thirty-nine cars, in 1935 fourteen, and in 1936 eleven. Figures for 1937, 1938 and 1939 were two, one and one respectively.

Aston Martin made a greater variety of models, although there were only two basic engines, the 1½-litre single-ohc Bertelli-designed unit, employed up to 1936, and a 2-litre unit, still with single ohc, which was made from 1936 to 1939. Designed by Claude Hill, a long-time assistant of A.C. Bertelli, it originally had the dry-sump lubrication of the earlier unit, together with such traditional features as magneto ignition and crash gearbox. After thirteen of the very expensive Speed Model had been made, Hill turned to a 'softer' design using conventional lubrication, coil ignition and a synchromesh gearbox. This was made in two wheelbase lengths, with two- and four-seater bodies including a saloon. Prices were £475 to £525, compared with £775 asked for the 1956 Speed Model. Of the earlier

**Frazer-Nash TT Replica, 1935**
The chain-driven Frazer-Nashes were considered eccentric even in England, a country that has had its share of odd sports cars. They also had most of the characteristics one attributes to the English sports car of the period: big wire wheels, cut-down doors, large instrument dials, fold-down windows, and spartan interiors.

**Aston Martin Ulster, 1934**
In addition to the spare wheel, the pointed tail can hold a small amount of luggage.

1½-litre cars, the International did well at Le Mans in 1931 and 1932, winning the Biennial Cup, but the fastest model was the Ulster two-seater. This had twin carburettors, special valves and springs, a Laystall crankshaft and a higher compression ratio, giving 80 bhp at 5,500 rpm. Its appearance was quite in keeping with its performance – a long pointed tail which concealed the spare wheel, outside exhaust pipe and cycle-type wings. The price was a hefty £750, but each car came with a 100-mph (161-km/h) guarantee. Only twenty-four were made, between 1934 and 1936.

Several new makes appeared in the 1930s, including Alta, H.R.G., Squire and S.S. Of these the last was the most important, being the ancestor of today's Jaguar and providing looks and performance way beyond what one would expect from the price. The S.S. was the first complete car made by William Lyons' Swallow Coach Building Co. and first appeared in 1931 as a long, low coupé powered by a 2-litre Standard Sixteen engine. These and smaller cars derived from the Standard Nine, Ten, and Twelve made up the S.S. range until 1935 when they brought out the 90. This used the 2.7-litre Standard Twenty engine in a short (8 ft 8 in/2.6 m) wheelbase, with a handsome and functional two-seater sports body. The next step was an increase in power when the engine received overhead valves designed by Harry Weslake and W.M. Heynes. This engine, now giving 104 bhp, was also used in the S.S. Jaguar saloons, and the sports model was called the S.S. Jaguar

**Aston Martin Ulster**
An Aston Martin Ulster competing at a club race at Silverstone in 1956. Note the headlamps turned sideways to avoid damage from flying stones.

**S.S. Jaguar 100, 1937**
The team of 2½-litre S.S.100s that took part in the 1937 Welsh Rally.

100. The final development was to equip this car with the 125-bhp 3½-litre engine, so that the car could justify the 100 mph (161 km/h) claim of its title.

With their long flowing wings and large headlamps, the Jaguar 100s looked as good as any sports car on the market, yet cost only £445. It was this price tag, combined with the humble origins of the engine, that led some people to sneer at them: 'The Bentley of Wardour Street' (centre of London's film business) was one epithet, and the infant Vintage Sports Car Club refused to accept them as post-vintage thoroughbreds, though they gladly welcomed Alvis, Aston Martins, Bentleys and Lagondas. Not that Bill Lyons cared, for he sold as many of the 100s as he wanted to (314 between 1936 and 1939), although saloons always claimed around ninety per cent of the factory's output.

At the opposite end of the scale were Alta and Squire, both built by perfectionists with little eye to profits. The Alta was the work of Geoffrey Taylor, operating from tiny premises at Surbiton, Surrey. Aided by not more than a dozen employees, all skilled mechanics, he built his own engines and superchargers, buying his chassis from Rubery Owen. The engines were advanced twin-ohc units with aluminium-alloy block and head. A 1,074-cc unit was listed throughout the 1930s, joined by a 2-litre in 1935, but production was very small, only seventeen road cars being made. Taylor was one of the few people to offer single-seater racing cars for sale, and more of these were made (eighteen) than of the sports cars. These were not overpriced, at £350 for the smaller car, and £575 for a supercharged 2-litre, but they made little impact on the scene because so few were made. It is doubtful if Taylor would have wanted to become a large-scale manufacturer – his main business was supplying aluminium cylinder heads to improve the performance of other cars, and he was content to make a few cars a year for himself and like-minded friends to drive. The only British-built car to take part in the Fastest Road-Car Race, mentioned at the beginning of this chapter, was a 2-litre Alta. Driven by Robert Cowell, it finished fifth.

The Squire was an even rarer bird, with only seven cars made, yet it has always attracted a lot of attention. It was designed and built by Adrian Squire who had worked out the basic idea while still at school. He was only twenty-four when he announced his car, to be made at a small garage just outside Henley-on-Thames. Unlike Geoffrey Taylor he did not make his own engine, but chose a very powerful unit, the supercharged 1½-litre twin-ohc Anzani

**S.S. Jaguar 100, 1937**
The 1937 3½-litre S.S.100 was the first S.S. model which was a genuine 100-mph car.

**Squire, 1935**
Much more attractive than the 'Skimpy' was the Vanden Plas body on the earlier Squires. This is DMP 219, the prototype.

R1. This had been acquired by H.J. Aldington of Frazer-Nash when he took over the Anzani company, but he did not want to install it in his own car, so saw Adrian Squire as a useful customer. The engine developed 110 bhp, a remarkable output for 1½ litres, and was mated to an ENV pre-selector gearbox. Very powerful Lockheed brakes stopped the car from 30 mph (48 km/h) in twenty feet (six metres). The original body was a beautiful two-seater by Vanden Plas, which itself cost £200. The total price of the Squire was £1,220, more than a 4½-litre Lagonda and not far short of a 4¼-litre Bentley. It is hardly surprising that buyers did not flock to pay this kind of money for a 1½-litre car. A much cheaper body was used for two subsequent cars, known privately as the 'Skimpy,' with cycle-type wings and no hood. Even this did not enable Squire to get the price below £995. Most of the seven cars made at Henley were bought by Adrian Squire's wealthy young friends, and in 1936 the Squire Car Manufacturing Co. was wound up. Two further cars were assembled by Val Zethrin, who had been a customer for one of the original models. David Scott-Moncrieff sums up the Squire story as 'a grisly example of the inescapable fact that it is much easier to make money by building a bad car down to a price than by building a good car up to an ideal'.

CORONATION
178
JB 8776

**Squire 1½-litre, 1936**
A Squire 1½-litre with the 'Skimpy' body by Markham, in the 1937 Scottish Rally. This was the penultimate Squire made.

The H.R.G.s were also built to an ideal, but a more modest one, with the result that the company lasted for twenty years, with a total output of 240 cars. They were built by H.R. Godfrey who had been Archie Frazer-Nash's partner in the G.N. cyclecar way back in 1910. In conjunction with E.A. Halford and G.H. Robins, he built a prototype in 1935 and, after it had been successfully received by the press, formed a private company in February 1936. The design was 'conventional-traditional,' with a 1½-litre Meadows 4ED engine, four-speed Moss gearbox, leaf-spring suspension at front and rear, and Rudge-Whitworth wire wheels. The body was a simple open two-seater, priced, not excessively, at £395. Top speed was 85 mph (136.5 km/h) and 0 to 60 mph (96.5 km/h) took 11 seconds. Only thirty-six H.R.G.s were made up to the outbreak of war, but they had a loyal and keen following, and did well in racing and rallies. At Le Mans they took second place in their class in 1937 and 1938, winning it in 1939. The last cars made before the war had ohc Singer engines of 1,074 and 1,496 cc.

Before leaving the under 3-litre cars, it is worth pointing out that there were several others to claim the attention of the British sports-car enthusiast. A.C. used the same 1,991-cc 6-cylinder engine from 1922 to 1963, and although their postwar Ace won more fame than any prewar sports car, there were some handsome models made, starting in 1935 with a short-chassis two-seater known as the 16/80 which in supercharged form became the 16/90. Only four of these were made, out of forty-four sports A.C.s. Then there was the British Salmson; most were saloons and tourers derived from the French Salmson, but the South London company made about fifteen sports cars using a 6-cylinder twin-ohc 2½-litre engine which had no French counterpart.

There were fewer large British sporting cars in the 1930s than in the previous decade, and most were fast tourers rather than genuine sports cars. Lagonda and Talbot made some derivations of their touring models which did well in competitions, though, the

**A.C. 16/80, 1938**
The later version of the AC 16/80, with taller radiator and rounded back in place of the slab tank. Nine of these were made in 1938 – this is the last works-owned demonstrator which had an active competition life.

**A.C. 16/90 and S.S. Jaguar 100**
The AC 16/90 was similar to the 16/80, apart from its Arnott supercharger which gave it a top speed of 95 mph. It is seen here (right) next to an S.S.100.

former's 4½-litre Meadows-powered car winning the Le Mans 24-Hour Race in 1935 at 77 mph (124 km/h) average. In that year W.O. Bentley joined Lagonda, and he supervised the final stage of the Meadows engine, and also designed the 4,480-cc V12 which was introduced in 1938. The 1936 Rapide was a very striking sports car, with 150-bhp crossflow-head version of the Meadows, known as the Sanction III, shorter wheelbase and four-seater body with pointed tail and outside exhaust pipes. This body was seen on the 1936 LG45 and the 1938 LG6 with independent front suspension (ifs), though very few of this style were made on either chassis. Most Lagondas carried very elegant drophead coupé or saloon bodies. No sports bodies were sold on the V12 chassis, though two tuned versions ran at Le Mans in 1939, finishing third and fourth.

Talbot had a high reputation for a few years in the early thirties, aided by Swiss-born Georges Roesch's excellent 6-cylinder ohv engines. The best-known sporting models were the 2.3-litre '90' and 3-litre '105', the former finishing third and fourth at Le Mans in 1930, behind two Speed Six Bentleys but ahead of a 7-litre Mercedes-Benz SSK and a 5-litre twin-cam Stutz. They and the 105s also did very well in long-distance races at Brooklands, and in the Alpine Trials. Production models included some handsome open tourers with pointed tails, but after 1934 the 105 gave way to the 3.3-litre 110 which was a handsome fast tourer. They were made up to 1937 when, as a result of the Rootes Group acquisition of Talbot, all models with even a pretence of sporting attributes were dropped.

The Lagonda's 4½-litre Meadows engine was also used in the Invicta. This was the product of another small company run by enthusiasts for enthusiasts. From the start in 1925 the maker's aim was to avoid gearchanging as much as possible, so large, relatively slow engines in the American manner were the order of the day. In 1931 the Meadows engine was fitted to a new low frame which was swept up over the front axle and underslung at the rear. The result was the S-type low-chassis Invicta which was capable of 90 mph (145 km/h), or more than 100 mph (161 km/h) from 1934 when the engine output had been raised from 115 to 140 bhp. It was a very 'long-legged' car, and at 60 mph (96.5 km/h) the engine was turning at no more than 2,000 rpm. At £875 complete with a four-seater body the Invicta was good value. Although they did not do particularly well in races, where their reputation was badly dented by a serious accident to Sammy Davis at Brooklands in 1932, they had a good reputation on the rallying front. They won cups in the Austrian and Hungarian Alpine Trials of 1930, and in the International Alpine in the same year, while in 1931 Donald Healey gained Britain's second victory in the Monte Carlo Rally. About sixty were made at Invicta's Cobham, Surrey, factory, where production ended in 1933. A further dozen or so were assembled from parts on hand, at the Chelsea service depot.

**Lagonda 4½-litre, 1938**
A Lagonda 4½-litre Rapide, taking part in a FIVA (Fédération Internationale des Vehicules Anciens) Rally in Scotland.

322
PD 939

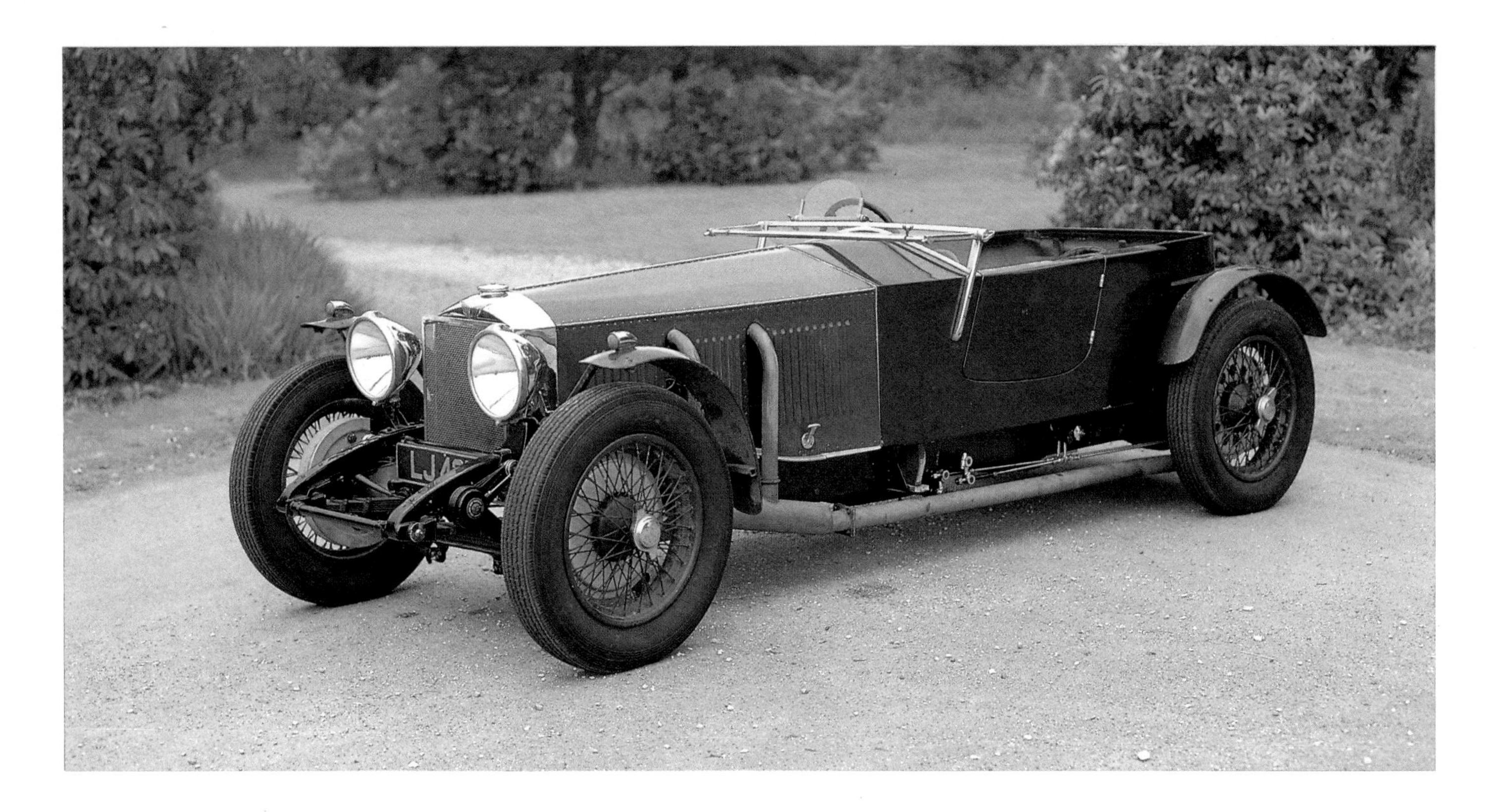

The 1930s saw a new type of motorcar in Britain which had several sporting models. This was the Anglo-American hybrid consisting of an American engine with its qualities of easy power from a slow-turning engine, combined with coachwork of traditional British lines and quality. On paper it was an ideal recipe, for American cars were very popular for untiring long-distance driving. Except for the very expensive models, however, their coachwork let them down, being uninspired in styling and with dashboards and interior trim which did not appeal to British tastes.

The first Anglo-American hybrid to appear was the Railton, which was made in the old Invicta works at Cobham. This used a 4-litre Terraplane Eight engine in an unmodified chassis (they were not lowered as many historians have claimed), clothed with a light open four-seater body by Ranalah. A simple, rather squared-off radiator headed a long bonnet which had rivets down the side in the manner of the Invicta. The Railton made a great impression on British journalists for, if its top speed of 88 mph (141.5 km/h) was unexceptional, its acceleration was remarkable: 0 to 50 mph (80 km/h) took 7 seconds, less than a Jaguar XK120, the outstanding sports car made seventeen years later. Bill Boddy

**Invicta 4½-litre S-type, 1931**
An Invicta 4½-litre low-chassis S-type. The wings on this car are rather skimpier than on the production models, but the owner prefers them for racing.

**Invicta 4½-litre S-type, 1930**
The first Swedish Winter Grand Prix competition was held on the ice of Lake Ramen in southern Dalecarlia, and many foreign drivers participated. This Invicta was borrowed from England by the Swedish driver Henrik Widengren, but it had to withdraw after the third lap.

recalls trying a Railton at Brooklands on the same occasion as a 3½-litre Bentley, and marvelling at the way the £499 Anglo-American outperformed the £1,380 Rolls-Royce-built 'Silent Sports Car'. Engine capacity went up to 4,168 cc when the Hudson engine was adopted in 1934, and an improved engine of the same size but better breathing was used for 1937 models. The ultimate sports model was the Light Sports Tourer of 1935, in which the engine was moved back in the chassis and a higher-geared rear axle used. With a very light four-seater body this car could do 0 to 50 mph (80 km/h) in 6.4 seconds, and exceeded 100 mph (161 km/h). There is a famous picture of one of these cars leaping in the air at the top of the Test Hill at Brooklands – it remained airborne for about thirty-three feet (ten metres)!

As the years passed the Railton became heavier, and bodies were mostly saloons and drophead coupés. However, one of the last chassis delivered, in 1939, was acquired by the young racing driver Richard Shuttleworth, who planned to build a two-seater sports body on it. He was killed in a flying accident in 1940 before it was ready for him, but it was completed for his mother who used it for commuting to London in connection with her Red Cross work. It is now in the motor museum at Schloss Langenburg in Germany, which is owned by the husband of Shuttleworth's niece, Princess Charlotte von Hohenlohe-Langenburg.

The Railton was the best known of the Anglo-Americans, but others included the Ford V8-powered Allard, Batten, Jensen and Leident, the Hudson-powered Brough Superior, the Graham-powered Lammas, and the Atalanta which used a V12 Lincoln Zephyr engine. Of these the Jensen and Lammas were tourers or saloons, as were most of the Brough Superiors, while the Allards and Battens were stark trials cars made in very small numbers – twelve Allards were made prewar of which three had V12 Lincoln Zephyr engines, and about the same number of Battens. The Atalanta was made in two-seater sports form as well as saloons, and was unusual among prewar British cars for having independent suspension all round.

**Railton Series 1, 1934**
Reid Railton was known for his fast sports cars, which were among the first Anglo-Americans, being based on the Hudson chassis and the Hudson straight-8 side valve engine.

## Europe

The variety of sports available in Europe was much smaller than Britain's, and much less than it had been in the 1920s. On the credit side, many of those available were more advanced than those north of the English Channel. Features such as independent suspension and tubular chassis were quite common by the end of the decade, while 'supercars' such as the Alfa Romeo 2900B had no British equivalent.

Among the traditionalists, Bugatti continued his individualistic way. Although design passed increasingly to Ettore's son Jean, the company resolutely ignored synchromesh gearboxes and independent suspension right up to 1939. In 1930 they were still making the Type 43, as well as the Types 35 and 37 racing cars and several touring models. The 43 was replaced in 1932 by the 55, one of the most desirable of all Bugatti models. Made only in two-seater form, it used the 2.3-litre twin-cam engine of the Type 51 racing car in the chassis of the Type 54 Grand Prix car, clothed in a curvaceously beautiful two-seater body designed by Jean Bugatti.

The race-bred twin-cam 2.3-litre engine developed 135 bhp and gave the 55 a top speed of over 120 mph (193 km/h) when stripped for racing, and 112 mph (180 km/h) with road equipment. The engine had roller bearings, in common with the Type 35, 43 and several racing models, whereas the more touring Bugattis such as the Types 44, 49 and 57 used plain bearings. It was, inevitably, very expensive, and in the wake of the Depression not many people were prepared to pay 70,000 lire (£1,350) for a two-seater. Only thirty-eight were made, between 1932 and 1935, mostly with Jean's classic open body, though a few neat but noisy coupés were made, and there was at least one custom drophead body by Figoni. Because of its rarity and high performance, the Type 55 has always been in great demand, and they seldom come onto the market. When one was auctioned by Sotheby's in London in December 1985, it fetched £440,000, a European record for a motorcar.

**Bugatti Type 55, 1932**
A Bugatti Type 55 with the standard body designed by Jean Bugatti. This is the car which sold for £440,000 at Sotheby's in 1985.

**Bugatti Type 55, 1934**
The distinctive lines of Jean Bugatti's Type 55 are well displayed in this shot of a 1934 model at the Prescott hill climb.

The other 1930s Bugatti was more of a *Grand Routier* or fast tourer, though some excellent sports cars were derived from it. This was the Type 57 with 3,257-cc twin-ohc engine which developed 140 bhp and gave 95 mph (153 km/h) even with a saloon body. The brakes were still mechanical, although Lockheed hydraulics had arrived by 1938. The sporting models came in 1936/37 with the 57S and 57SC. They had lowered chassis on which the rear axle-beam passed through the frame, magneto ignition and dry-sump lubrication. They were the only Bugattis to have V radiators, by which they could be distinguished at a glance from the touring Type 57. They were also thirteen inches (0.3 m) shorter in wheelbase. These engines developed 170 bhp, and when supercharged (57SC)

**Bugatti Type 57S, 1936**
A Bugatti Type 57S, showing the V-radiator which distinguished the S models from the ordinary 57. This car was raced regularly in Bugatti Owners' Club events up to the 1970s by its owner Ronnie Symondson.

**Bugatti Type 57, 1938**
One of the most beautiful bodies ever fitted to a Type 57 is this two-seater by Corsica on a 1938 57SC chassis. It was designed by Eric Giles for his brother Colonel G.M. Giles, both men being founder members of the British Bugatti Owners' Club.

over 200 bhp. Some beautiful open and coupé bodies were fitted to these Bugattis, which had a top speed of 125 mph (201 km/h). The supercharger was also available on the standard-chassis 57, in which form it was known as the 57C (Compresseur).

Various production figures for the Type 57 have been claimed, but the following, taken from the instruction manual published by the Bugatti Owners' Club, are probably the most accurate:

| Type 57 | | | Type 57C | | Type 57S* | |
|---|---|---|---|---|---|---|
| 1934 | 124 | | | | | |
| 1935 | 106 | | 1935 | 1 | | |
| 1936 | 128 | | 1936 | 4 | 1936 | 17 |
| 1937 | 71 | | 1937 | 12 | 1937 | 19 |
| 1938 | 103 | | 1938 | 41 | 1938 | 5 |
| 1939 | 14 | | 1939 | 38 | | |
| Total | 546 | | Total | 96 | Total | 41 |

*(some cars being SC, or so converted) Grand total 683

From this it will be seen that the S and SC models had been discontinued well before war broke out, further reducing the number of sports cars available to the enthusiast in the last year of peace.

There were no other French sports cars to match the Bugattis, but several excellent *Grands Routiers* which had their competition versions. The Delahaye was a phenomenon of the thirties as their earlier products had been very staid touring cars and the power unit of the Type 135 was based on that of a 3-ton truck. Hence the late Michael Sedgwick's summing up the Delahaye compared with the Bugatti: 'By contrast. . . an uprated hack rather than a downrated race horse, which made it a different car for a different clientele.' It was also a larger clientele, for the 3.2-litre Superluxe and more powerful Type 135 had easy gearchanging, by courtesy of M. Cotal's electromagnetic pre-selector transmission, while the bodies were much more spacious and the cars quieter.

In 1936 the Type 135's engine was bored out to give a capacity of 3,557 cc, and Delahaye began to figure in races as well as rallies where they had been successful since

1934. The 1936 French Grand Prix was a sports-car event, and Delahaye finished 2-3-4-5, being beaten only by a Bugatti 57S. In 1937 they were second and third at Le Mans, and won the 1938 Monte Carlo Rally. For competitions the 135 carried lightweight and stark open bodies in which form they were capable of around 115 mph (185 km/h). The Fastest Road-Car Race at Brooklands was won by Arthur Dobson's Delahaye, particularly creditable as he had to stop during the race to put out a fire.

In 1937 Delahaye made a bid for Grand Prix honours with a 4½-litre V12 engine, and a detuned version was used in a very limited production road-car called the Type 165. Its chassis was similar to that of the 135, though slightly longer and with hydraulic brakes in place of the Bendix mechanical system. The chassis was priced at 138,000 francs, compared with 65,000 francs for a 135, and only five 165s were ever made, although a few more came into existence when the Grand Prix cars were fitted with roadgoing bodywork.

In the same mould as the Delahaye was the Talbot Lago, made by Automobiles Talbot and representing a new range of cars designed by Walter Becchia and sponsored by Major Antony Lago who had taken over the company in 1935. Like the Delahayes they had 6-cylinder ohv engines, and the largest, the 3,996-cc Major, was made in short-wheelbase form as the Baby, while the competition version on the same wheelbase was called the Lago Special. The open models of these were mostly works cars which had a number of successes including winning the Montlhéry Sports Car Grand Prix and the Tourist Trophy, both in 1937, but the chassis was available to private buyers who could choose their own coachwork. The majority carried closed coupé bodies by Figoni et Falaschi with sweeping fastbacks and spatted rear wheels. Like some of the coachwork on Delahayes, they were considered hopelessly flashy by many people, but they carried off the prizes at *concours d'élegance* all over France.

**Delahaye 135, 1937**
A Delahaye 135 competition two-seater, used for many years by the racing driver and later entrant of Stirling Moss' cars, Rob Walker. It is now at the Midland Motor Museum, Bridgenorth, Shropshire.

**Delahaye 135, 1937**
Eugene Chaboud's Delahaye 135 in trouble during the 1938 Le Mans Race, though he later went on to win. Passing it is the Marcus Chambers/PCT Clark H.R.G. which finished 10th.

The small sports car in France was not quite dead, though the few makes there were made little impact on the market, and virtually none in competitions. The largest producer was Georges Irat, who made about a thousand of a little car with 950- or 1,095-cc Ruby engines driving the front wheels, followed by a much smaller number of Citroën-powered cars, also with front-wheel drive and all-round independent suspension by thick strands of rubber cord. Other companies competing in roughly the same market included Remi Danvignes who used the 950-cc Ruby or a 750-cc ohc vertical twin in an all-independently sprung chassis, Lambert who made a few front-drive Ruby-powered sports cars in Rheims from 1931 to 1936, and Sandford, who was best known for his Morgan-like 3-wheelers, but also made a few 4-wheeled models. Apart from their Ruby engines, they could be thought of as French-built Morgan 4/4s.

The sports-car scene in Germany can really be summed up in two names, Mercedes-Benz and BMW, and only the latter took an active part in racing. Mercedes, of course, was predominant on the *grands prix* circuits, but their road cars fall more into the category of high-speed tourers than sports cars.

The big SS and SSK models were continued nominally until 1934, but hardly any were made after 1932. Meanwhile, the foundations of the next generation of high-performance

**Talbot Lago, 1938**
A Talbot Lago 4-litre cabriolet.

**Mercedes-Benz 380**
The Mercedes-Benz 380 roadster driven in the 1934 Deutschland Fahrt by Prince Max zu Schaumberg-Lippe and Otto Merz. This was a special car, and differed from the regular 380 in having cycle-type wings and cut-away doors.

cars from Stuttgart were being laid with the appearance of the 380. This was intended to combine the virtues of a powerful engine with the handling and ride offered by an all-independently sprung chassis. Daimler Benz already had experience of independent suspension with their 170, a 1.7-litre family saloon introduced in 1931. The 380 had parallel wishbones and coil springs at the front, and swinging axles at the rear. The engine was a 3,822-cc pushrod ohv straight-8 which developed 90 bhp (120 with supercharger), not enough to give the car the performance its appearance deserved. The bodies were very handsome, mostly two-door four-seater cabriolets, though there were some sporty-looking two-seater roadsters. A total of 157 were made before the 320 was replaced by the more powerful 500K.

This had a larger chassis and larger engine (5,016 cc), but design was similar, and at first glance it was not easy to distinguish a 500K from a 380. The main identifying feature was that the larger car had external exhaust pipes. Power was now up to 160 bhp with the supercharger in action, and top speed 102 mph (164 km/h). The Daimler Benz company now had the comfortable high-speed *Autobahn* cruiser that they and their customers wanted. A Swiss owner reported that he could comfortably drive from Zürich to Berlin, about 560 miles (900 km), in a day, holding an average speed of 50 to 55 mph (80.5 to 88.5

**Mercedes-Benz 500K**
Mercedes-Benz 500K Autobahn Kurier at a checkpoint in the 1934 Deutschland Fahrt. Driven by Bernet and Muller, this was also a specially built car with sketchier wings than other Autobahn Kuriers.

**Mercedes-Benz 500K, 1936**
A Mercedes-Benz 500K Spezial Roadster. This was a new design for 1936, previous Spezial Roadsters having smaller doors and two external spare wheels. This car, which is almost identical to the Spezial Roadster on the 540K chassis, also has two spare wheels but the lower one is concealed inside the tail.

km/h) even on bad roads. Coachwork on the 500K chassis resembled that on the 380, but included a streamlined closed coupé, the *Autobahn Kurier,* of which fewer than ten were made.

The final development of this series was the 540K, made from 1936 to 1939. As its name implies, it had a 5,401-cc engine, giving 180 bhp and a top speed of 105 mph (169 km/h). Otherwise there was little change in design from the 500K – bodies were similar, though more curvaceous in some cases. Production of the 540K was 419 units, and for the 500K, 342. Although chassis production ended in 1939, some bodies were mounted later, and 540Ks were still being delivered to favoured customers in 1941 and 1942.

These big Mercedes were not seen much in competitions, their main appearances being in the 1,240-mile (2,000-km) Deutschland Fahrt of 1934. This was a high-speed rally for which all speed limits were lifted. More than 600 cars took part, of which 74 were Mercedes-Benz. Most were small 170s, but there were several 380s and 500K, as well as older SS and SSKs. Two gold medals were won by 500Ks, and one by a 380.

Germany's other important offering in the sports car field was very different from the big cars from Stuttgart. BMW (Bayerische Motoren-Werke) entered car manufacture in 1928 with the Austin Seven-based Dixi light car, proceeding to six cylinders and independent front suspension with the 1,173-cc Typ 303 of 1933. Later derivatives were the 1,490-cc Typ 315 and 1,911-cc Typ 319, both of which engines went into an attractive sports car, known as the 315/1 or 319/1. This had, like the saloons, a twin-tube chassis and transverse-leaf independent front suspension, with swing axles at the rear. The body was an attractive two-seater with swept tail and spatted rear wheels. With triple carburettors and higher compression ratio, the sports engine gave 40 or 55 bhp according to size.

These sporting BMWs became very popular, and laid the foundations for the marque's reputation, which was greatly enhanced by the next model, the 328. This employed the tubular frame of the 319/1, with a new engine and a two-seater body, which has become a classic of its kind. The engine was enlarged to 1,971 cc and had a new head with inclined ohv and a hemispherical combustion chamber. Only one camshaft was used; the inlet

**BMW 328, 1938**
A BMW 328 with the British rally driver, Betty Haig. The car has temporary Hungarian number plates. The rear wheel spats were usually left off for competition purposes.

Start of the 2-litre sports car race that preceded the 1938 German Grand Prix at the Nürburgring. It was dominated by the BMW 328, of which twelve can be seen in the photo. The winner was Paul Greifzu (no. 10) at 75.7 mph (122 km/h).

valves were operated in the normal way, but horizontal pushrods ran across the top of the head to operate the exhaust valves. This gave the advantages of a twin-ohc layout without the complexity and expense. The result was an easy 80 bhp, and a top speed of 95 mph (153 km/h) in standard form. With an aero screen, over 100 mph (161 km/h) was possible, and Sammy Davis put 102.23 miles (164.49 km) into an hour at Brooklands. Charges that this was achieved with a specially lightened car were refuted when a private owner with a standard car put over 101 miles (162.5 km) in the hour. There were some improved models, with higher compression ratios and improved breathing, which were capable of 120 mph (193 km/h).

The BMW 328 set new standards in road holding as well as performance, and more than any other single car made British enthusiasts realize how their native designs had fallen behind, with cars like Aston Martin and Frazer-Nash still relying on semi-elliptic springs and an appearance not far removed from that of the 1920s. BMWs were handled in Britain by A.F.N. Ltd, makers of the Frazer-Nash, and the success of the German cars led to the abandonment of the old chain-drive designs. The 328, and other models, were known as Frazer-Nash BMW in Britain, and carried special badges announcing the fact. They were among the best all-round sports cars ever made, being equally at home on the race track, in rallies, sprints and off-road 'mud-plugging' trials. Production was 464 cars, together with some streamlined prototypes built for the 1940 Mille Miglia, which finished first and third. The 328 remained competitive for several years after the war (Stirling Moss drove one in one of his first speed trials) and the engine was used in the British Bristol and Frazer-Nash cars and in the German-built Veritas.

No other German sports car of the thirties could compare with the BMW, although several firms such as Adler, Stoewer and Wanderer made roadsters, often with attractive coachwork. A team of Adler Trumpfs were successful at Spa and Le Mans between 1936 and 1938, but their highly streamlined bodies bore little relation to what the public could buy.

25 BMW

**BMW 328, 1938**
A BMW 328 roadster. Nearly all 328s made had this body style, though there were a handful of cabriolets and coupés made by Gläser, Wendler and Weinberger.

**Alfa Romeo 8C-2300, 1933**
An Alfa Romeo 8C-2300, used on the road for several years after the war by Mike Hawthorn, and now in the National Motor Museum at Beaulieu.

**Alfa Romeo 8C-2900B**
Short-wheelbase version of the remarkable Alfa Romeo 8C-2900B. This is the car which won the 1938 Mille Miglia, averaging 110 mph (177 km/h) on one 90-mile (145-km) stretch. It is seen here at Brooklands, driven by Hugh Hunter in a JCC Members Race in July 1939.

In Italy only two names come to mind among prewar sports cars, Alfa Romeo and Fiat. They were at opposite ends of the spectrum, for Alfa Romeo was a very small-volume producer at the time, with only 699 cars made in their best year (1934) and only ten in 1936. Total Alfa production in the 1930s was 5,983, of which by no means all were sports cars. By contrast Fiat made more than 50,000 in a single year.

**Alfa-Romeo 2900B**
Long-wheelbase Alfa 2900B with body by Carrozzeria Touring.

At the beginning of the decade Alfa Romeo were concentrating on the 1750 made in single- and twin-cam form, and described in the last section. It was built up to the end of 1933, being joined in 1931 by a more expensive and complex sports car, the 8C-2300. This had a 2,336-cc straight-8 engine derived from racing practice: features included camshaft drive shaft mounted between the two blocks of cylinders, the flywheel also being centrally mounted, dry-sump lubrication, a ten-bearing crankshaft and magneto ignition. A Roots-type supercharger ran at engine speed. The 8C was complex, expensive, noisy and very fast, with a top speed of 110 mph (177 km/h). It achieved 0 to 50 mph (0 to 80 km/h) in about eight seconds. Even faster were the short-chassis 2.6-litre works Mille Miglia cars, which were good for 125 mph (201 km/h), but these were never sold to the public. The model was very successful in competitions, winning Le Mans four years in a row, 1931 to 1934, and the Mille Miglia from 1932 to 1934. The 8C was very much a car for the expert, and the wealthy expert at that. A long-chassis cabriolet cost nearly 100,000 lire in Italy, or £1,985 in Britain. Only 188 8Cs were made, and it is thought that Alfa Romeo made no profit on them.

The other sporting Alfa of the thirties was also race-based, and even rarer than the 8C-2300. This was the 8C-2900A which came into being to use up the numerous 2.9-litre engines made for the Tipo B Grand Prix car. This twin-supercharged 220-bhp engine was mounted in an all-independently sprung chassis (coil springs at the front, transverse leaf and swing axles at the rear) and clothed with a variety of coachwork. The initial 2900A of 1936 was very much a competition car, finishing 1-2-3 in that year's Mille Miglia, and carried simple open two-seater bodies. Only six were made. Then in 1937 came the 2900B made in two wheelbase lengths (8 ft 10 in and 9 ft 2 in/2.7 m and 2.8 m) which carried more luxurious bodywork, mostly by Superleggera Touring of Milan. The open two-seaters were on either wheelbase, while there were also six streamlined coupés on the long chassis.

The engine of the 2900B was less highly tuned than that of the 2900A, giving 180 bhp, but the cars were still good for nearly 130 mph (209 km/h). Since between thirty and thirty-three 2900Bs were made, it seems unlikely that they all used Tipo B engines; some engines must have been specially built for the road cars. A 2900B won the 1938 Mille Miglia at an average of 84.45 mph (135.88 km/h) for the whole race. On one ninety-mile stretch from Brescia the car was averaging 110 mph (177 km/h). This came to London for the 1938 Motor Show and was bought by Hugh Hunter. Although built in numbers too small to make a serious impact on the sports-car market, the 8C-2900B was a magnificent example of how far sports-car engineering had come by the late 1930s. It would be another twenty

**Fiat Balilla 508S, 1935**
The pronounced tail fin was a characteristic of the cars sold in the UK, which were bodied there.

years before its performance would be matched. In the early postwar years ten-year-old 2900Bs had several racing successes, including the 1947 Mille Miglia and 1948 Watkins Glen Grand Prix in America.

Fiat's contribution was in the manner of the early M.G. Midgets, being a popularly priced sports car developed from a family saloon. This was the side-valve 995-cc Balilla, of which the first sports models had merely a higher rear-axle ratio and an open two-seater body, but in 1934 there came the 508S which had an ohv engine which raised power from 22 to 36 bhp. With high and close gear ratios and an all-up weight of only 1,288 lb (584 kg) the Balilla Sport 508S had a spritely performance, with a top speed of 75 mph (120.5 km/h). The body was attractively styled, with some resemblance to that of the Alfa Romeo 1750 – most cars had flowing wings (Spider Normale) but some had cycle-type wings (Spider Corsa) and there were a few closed coupés (Berlinetta Aerodinamica). They sold well in England, where they could outperform a PA Midget or Singer Nine. Tuned versions were made by SIATA in Italy and Gordini in France, while the 508S was made under licence by Walter in Czechoslovakia.

There were few native Czech sports cars, although the country had a flourishing motor industry in the thirties, with seven companies making passenger cars. The biggest was Skoda which made an advanced small family car, the 1,110-cc Popular with tubular backbone frame. Roadsters and a few streamlined coupés were built on this chassis, the

**Fiat Balilla 508S**
Fiat Balilla 508S with driver Stanley Tett in the 1935 Blackpool Rally.

latter fitted with 43-bhp 1,558-cc engines. This model was called the Monte Carlo coupé; it had come second in its class in 1937 and fourth in 1938.

Aero and Jawa both made sporty-looking cars with 2-stroke engines, the latter based on the German D.K.W., but they were not suitable for serious competition work. The only other Czech sports car worthy of note was the Wikov, made by a firm of agricultural engineers. Using the Italian Ansaldo single-ohc engine as a starting point, Wikov evolved a series of high-performance sports cars, originally of 1½ litres, progressing to 1,750 and 1,960 cc. They had wedge-shaped combustion chambers and aluminium-alloy blocks, pistons and connecting rods. Bodywork was simple and stark, the Wikovs being in the tradition of Frazer-Nash or H.R.G. Top speed was 85 mph (136.5 km/h), or 100 mph (161 km/h) in supercharged form; the make did well in the International High Tatra Rally in 1930 and 1931, as well as coming fourth in the 1931 Polish Grand Prix behind an SSKL Mercedes-Benz and two Type 35 Bugattis, and second in the 1932 Polish Mountain Race. Unfortunately these successes were not reflected in high sales – the sport Wikovs were dropped by 1934, and all car production ended three years later. The successors to the company are still in the agricultural machinery business, under the delightful name of Agrostoj.

Despite the great variety of sports cars described in this chapter, the outlook in 1939 was less encouraging than at the beginning of the decade. The genuine sports cars built with competition in mind were much fewer – Bugatti had abandoned the 57S and SC, Mercedes-Benz, Bentley and Lagonda were concentrating on fast tourers, M.G. were no longer competition-minded, the short-lived Anglo-Americans were already on the way out, and many famous names like Talbot, Invicta, Frazer-Nash, Riley and Singer had either disappeared or abandoned sports cars altogether. Perhaps people were getting softer and less susceptible to the appeal of wind-in-the-hair and oil-on-the-trousers motoring, and there was also the growing appeal of the well-handling family saloon. Cars like the BMW 315, Fiat 508 Millecento and Lancia Aprilia performed and handled as well as most sports cars in their price bracket, while providing comfortable and warm seating for four people. The Aprilia, in particular, had beautifully light and positive steering, and excellent handling, thanks to its all-round independent suspension. It could run rings round the competition from Austin, Standard and Wolseley, while the lack of synchromesh was not such a drawback as it would be in the postwar years. Saloons such as this were the 1930s equivalent of today's 'hot hatchbacks', even if there were not enough of them to erode the sports-car market in the way their successors have done.

**Auburn 851 Speedster, 1935**
An Auburn 851 supercharged speedster.

## The United States of America

There is little to say about the American sports car, for it continued the 1920s theme, even if there were fewer makes around. Although the Stutz Super Bearcat was listed up to 1932, the other sports cars were all the products of one group, the Auburn-Cord-Duesenberg Corporation. Auburn made a speedster version of their 6.4-litre V12, selling it for the remarkably low price of $1,145. The cheapest of the V12 range, a coupé, cost only $975, the cheapest 12-cylinder car ever marketed. However, American buyers in the depths of the Depression were not very interested in speedsters, bargains or otherwise, and the 95-mph (153-km/h) 12-160 was only listed for 1932 and 1933.

In 1935 Auburn brought out a range of supercharged cars, the 4.6-litre straight-8 851 series, and once again a speedster was offered. This was a very striking-looking machine with a long pointed tail and outside exhaust pipes. The body was designed by Gordon Buehrig who was also responsible for the even more striking Cord. An 851 speedster was not cheap, at $2,245, but 100 mph (161 km/h) was guaranteed. Even at this price, Auburn made no profit on the speedsters, for the bodies were all hand-built, but they attracted customers into the showrooms, who might then buy a less exotic Auburn. About 500 speedsters were made in 1935 and 1936, after which Auburn ceased production altogether.

The Cord 810 of 1935-7 has been described as 'perhaps the single most instantly recognizable car in the history of the American automobile' (Beverly Rae Kimes in *The Standard Catalog of American Cars 1805-1942*), but whether it deserves a place in a book on sports cars is more debatable. It had most striking lines, with wrap-around grille, retractable headlamps and no running boards. By the standards of contemporary American cars it was very advanced, and with a supercharger boosting power to 170 bhp, the most powerful. If it did not have European standards of handling, this is because the average American motorist, even one keen enough to buy a Cord, was not particularly interested in cornering at speed, and there were no races to improve the breed. Had events such as Le Mans or the Mille Miglia been held in America, doubtless improved models of the Cord and Auburn would have been developed to compete in them. As it was, the Cord 810 sold on its appearance and scarcity value in an era when most American cars were depressingly conventional and alike. The supercharged 812 had a top speed of over 100 mph (161 km/h), and was available as a two-seater convertible, four-seater phaeton, and a sedan. A total of 2,320 Cord 810/812s were made between February 1936 and the end of 1937.

The third member of the trio was the Duesenberg, intended by Errett Lobban Cord to be the ultimate in American luxury cars, and a challenge to the best that Europe could make. It had a 6,882-cc twin-ohc straight-8 engine developing about 245 bhp (the claim of 265 bhp, so often quoted, is unlikely to have been achieved in most production cars). Many open bodies were built on the Model J chassis, and in its supercharged version, the SJ, a few of which were speedsters in the Auburn style. They were, however, far more expensive: the SJ chassis alone cost between $8,000 and $10,000 according to year. In 1935 two extra-short chassis cars were built for the film stars Clark Gable and Gary Cooper. They were simple two-seaters with short, stubby tails, and in appearance the nearest to the European idea of a sports car the Duesenberg made. Known as the SSJ, they had a top speed of around 125 mph (201 km/h). As Don Vorderman wrote in *Automobile Quarterly,* 'Though there's no record that such a thing ever occurred, a friendly drag race between these two cars would have been something to see – and hear.'

**Cord 812 (*over*)**
'The single most instantly recognizable car in the history of the American automobile,' this is the Cord 812, distinguishable from the unsuper-charged 810 by the exhaust pipes emerging from the bonnet side.

CALIFORNIA
HISTORICAL
VEHICLE
4944

# CHAPTER FOUR

# THE UNCHALLENGED SPORTS CAR 1945-70

Looking back, this era seems like a golden age, when many of the greatest classic sports cars were made. Will any other age see the like of the Jaguar XKs and E-type, the Aston Martin DB series, the Mercedes-Benz 300SL or the Ferrari GTO? Moreover, petrol was cheap, emission controls were unheard of, and speed limits were restricted to cities. Optimism abounded, from Europe where more people could afford cars than ever before, to the USA and Canada where the joy of driving for its own sake was being rediscovered after over twenty years.

# Great Britain

In terms of quantity, if not always quality, the two and a half decades after World War II were the most important in the sports car's history. The limited-production elitist image of the breed had begun to crumble with the M-type M.G. Midget, but it was almost totally swept away by the M-type's postwar successors, the TC, TD, TF and MGA, and their rivals the Austin-Healey Sprite, Triumph TR series and Spitfire. Prosperity was more wideiy spread in Western Europe than it had been, and in America a vast new market had opened up, satisfied at first by imports such as M.G. and Ferrari, and later by the home-grown products, in particular the evergreen Chevrolet Corvette, introduced in 1953 and still going strong today.

It would have been understandable if sports cars had taken a back seat in the austerity atmosphere of the immediate postwar years, but the need to earn dollars spurred British industry into selling to the United States of America as quickly as possible. The first company to get a sports car into production was M.G., whose new TC Midget began to come off the assembly lines at Abingdon in November 1945. 'New' it was not, apart from the name, for it was very similar to the 1939 TB. The body was four inches wider and the sliding trunnions locating the springs were replaced by less expensive shackles. The general appearance was quite unchanged, as was the performance, with a top speed of 78 mph (125.5 km/h). Acceleration was hardly sparkling, 0 to 60 mph (96.5 km/h) taking 22.7 seconds. As the average American six-seater sedan could do 85 mph (136.5 km/h), it is obvious that the TC did not sell on its speed, nor its comfort which was minimal by transatlantic standards. However, it felt faster, held the road better, and was a great crowd gatherer.

Not everyone loved the M.G., though: a correspondent wrote to *The Saturday Evening Post* complaining that the postwar American car was too flashy, and begging manufacturers to look to European cars for inspiration. This drew a reply the following week from someone who said that his neighbour's M.G. Midget was much flashier than any American car going, and he, for one, would be ashamed to be seen in such an ostentatious little wagon!

American enthusiasts took the TC to their hearts, and many who were not enthusiasts were bitten by the sports-car bug. Of just 10,000 TCs made, a little over 2,000 were sold in

**M.G. TC Midget, 1947**
A 1947 M.G. TC Midget taking part in driving tests at Brighton in 1952.

**M.G. TF Midget, 1954**
A 1954 M.G. TF with the optional wire wheels which gave a better appearance than pressed steel ones, in a club race at Brands Hatch in 1961.

the United States, a lower proportion than of its successor the TD. The Sports Car Club of America sprang from one American branch of the M.G. Car Club. Among well-known American drivers who began their careers on the TC were John Fitch and Phil Hill, while several Hollywood stars bought them, including Clark Gable. In Britain, one of M.G.'s customers was a young naval lieutenant, Philip Mountbatten, who used his TC regularly when he was courting the future Queen of England. Twenty years later, when their son bought his first car, it was also a two-seater M.G. – an MGB.

In November 1949 the TC was replaced by the TD, a car which has been described as obsolete from the moment the first one rolled off the Abingdon lines. Its main improvements lay in independent front suspension (ifs) and rack-and-pinion steering, but the engine was the same as the TC's, as was styling, apart from the steel disc wheels which replaced wire ones. Although obsolete in comparison with new continental designs such as the Porsche 356 and Ferrari 166, it horrified the diehards who saw no appeal in ifs and lamented the absence of wire wheels and the presence of bumpers. However, the public as a whole liked the TD, and bought 29,644 of them during a four-year production run. Of these, 23,500 went to America so, in fact, many more Americans were introduced to sports cars by the TD than by its predecessor. In 1952, forty-two TDs were sold abroad for every one in Britain. Among the few British owners were the well-known prewar driver Sammy Davis and his son, Colin, who had a TD each.

If the TD was outdated in comparison with Ferrari and Porsche, at least it was much more reasonably priced. However, by 1953 the Austin Healey 100 and Triumph TR2 were available, both with more all-enveloping styling and capable of 100 mph (161 km/h), compared with the TD's 80 mph (128.5 km/h). Abingdon had to update their design, but until their new car which became the MGA was ready, they warmed-over the TD with a sloping radiator grille, headlamps partially faired into the wings, and gave more of a slope to the fuel tank and spare wheel. The engine was tuned to give 57 bhp, but at first its size was still 1,250 cc. This was the TF, and once more the diehards howled, though they should have been gratified that at least wire wheels were back – as an option.

Unfortunately the TF looked like the stopgap that it was, too modern for the traditionalists but outdated in terms of the competition. Yet today it is the most valued of the postwar T series, and will command at least £250 more than a TD in the same condition. This is because it has a better performance, particularly with the 1500 (1,466-cc) engine available from November 1954 onwards, and its lines have improved with age. In the author's opinion they are every bit as attractive as those of a TC or TD; it is interesting that when Alistair Naylor decided in 1980 to build an M.G. replica with modern components, it was the TF that he chose.

Before moving on to the MGA, one should look at the T series' competition. Two makes that were even more for the diehard were H.R.G. and Morgan. The former was little changed from its 1939 form, with modified Singer engines in two sizes, 1,074 cc and 1,496 cc, styling in the best 1933 tradition, leaf springs all round and cable-operated mechanical brakes. The only important changes since the original H.R.G.s were coil ignition in place of magneto, and a synchromesh gearbox, both of which were present in the 1939 cars. The ride was even harsher than that of an M.G. TC, but with the 1500 engine top speed was 85 mph (136.5 km/h), and steering superb. The H.R.G enthusiast paid £812 for an 1100 and £70 more for a 1500, compared with £528 for an M.G. This partly explains why only 187 H.R.G.s were sold between 1946 and 1955, but it was also a question of H.R.G. having a very small factory, with neither the finance nor the inclination to expand.

Although H.R.G. sold on their traditional appearance, Messrs Halford, Robins and Godfrey also offered an aerodynamic two-seater from 1946 to 1948. Unfortunately, flexing of the chassis caused the body panels to fall off, and weight distribution was not helped by having the spare wheel and the fuel tank on opposite sides of the tail. Only thirty aerodynamic cars were made, all with 1500 engines, and some were later reconverted to standard bodies. The last twelve traditional H.R.G.s had slightly larger Singer engines of 1,497 cc, hypoid axles and hydraulic brakes. In 1955 the company hoped to bring out a brand-new design with twin-ohc Singer engine, twin-tub frame dual-circuit disc brakes and full-width bodywork. Unfortunately, Rootes' take-over of Singer cut off supplies of the engine, no suitable alternative could be found, and that was the end of H.R.G.

**H.R.G. 1100, 1948**
The front axle of the H.R.G.s was so far forward that it protruded from under the radiator, giving the cars a typical appearance.

**H.R.C. 1500, 1949**
1949 H.R.G. 1500 in an MCC (Motor Cycle Club) meeting at Silverstone in 1954. Apart from badging at the rear there were no external differences between the 1100 and 1500 models.

**H.R.G. Aerodynamic, 1946**
The aerodynamic H.R.G. was very modern looking for 1946, but was not very successful. William Boddy wrote in *The Sports Car Pocketbook,* of '. . . the all enveloping bodywork which the harshly sprung HRG was all too eager to discard.' This example is racing at Goodwood in 1954.

**Austin-Healey 100, 1953**
Austin-Healey's first year at Le Mans was 1953, only a month after production began. Two cars were entered, finishing 2nd and 3rd in their class. This is the Gatsonides/Lockett car which finished 14th overall.

Morgan entered the postwar era with their 1939 4/4, in two-seater, four-seater and drophead coupé forms. With only 39 bhp from the 1,267-cc Standard Ten engine it was not a brilliant performer, but things looked up in 1951 when the 2-litre Vanguard engine was adopted. The new car was called the Plus Four, and speed was increased from the low seventies to 90 mph (145 km/h), with over 100 mph (161 km/h) obtainable when the Triumph TR2 engine was installed from 1954 onwards. Externally the Plus Four looked the same, though the wheelbase was four inches (102 mm) longer, and hydraulic brakes were seen for the first time on a Morgan. With the TR engine came a new grille with curved vertical bars – it was the first change in front-end appearance since the 4/4 was introduced, and it has altered little right up to the present. At £794 the 1951 Plus Four cost only £24 more than a TD Midget, and although the TR-engined car cost £869, it was in a different class from the M.G., and had many successes in rallies and club racing.

In 1959 Chris Lawrence of Lawrencetune Racing began to campaign specially tuned Plus Fours, and from 1962 to 1969 a limited number of these cars were sold. With twin SU or Weber carburettors you could expect 115 to 120 bhp and a top speed of over 115 mph (185 km/h). Only 102 were made, out of 3,390 Plus Four TRs produced between 1954 and 1969, but many successes were achieved, by Lawrence and others. These included the National Six Hour Relay Race in 1959, second in the 1961 Spa Grand Prix for GT cars and a class victory in the 1961 Guards Trophy at Brands Hatch. Morgan's only entry at Le Mans was in 1962, when the Lawrence/Shepherd-Barron Plus Four finished thirteenth overall, winning the 2-litre class.

The 4/4 was revived in 1956 with a Ford Ten engine, and has been made ever since, using various Ford units and, recently, a 1.6-litre Fiat engine. From 1964 to 1966 there was the curious Plus Four Plus, a two-seater closed coupé with all-enveloping fibreglass body, but this, straying from traditional Morgan appearance, pleased nobody, and only twenty-six were made. The very quick Rover-powered Plus 8 was introduced in 1968, but properly belongs to the 1970s.

If H.R.G and Morgan represented the traditional end of the British sports-car market, the Austin-Healey 100, Triumph TR2 and Jowett Jupiter made bids for those who wanted something more up-to-date. Donald Healey had been building cars under his own name since 1946. Powered by the well-tried 2.4-litre 4-cylinder Riley engine they were open or closed fast tourers which had a number of successes in rallying, and also the simple open two-seater Silverstone which was a natural for club racing, but also finished second overall in the 1949 Alpine Rally. In 1952 he produced a new sports car powered by another large four, the 2.6-litre Austin unit that had powered the unloved Austin Atlantic. Clothed in a beautiful but simple all-enveloping body, the new Healey was christened the Hundred in view of its anticipated top speed. It was exhibited at the 1952 London Motor Show and attracted the attention of Austin's Sir Leonard Lord who was looking for a car to succeed in the American market where the A40 saloon and A90 convertible had failed. Before the show ended Lord had concluded a deal with Healey whereby the car would be made in the Austin factory and named the Austin-Healey Hundred. New badges were hastily produced, and the car which had entered the show as a Healey left it two days later as an Austin-Healey.

In the event the cars were put together in the Jensen factory at West Bromwich, as Jensen were the body builders anyway, and the engines were brought from Austin's factory at Longbridge, Birmingham. Disc brakes were featured on the 100-S of 1954, and in 1957 the 100 was replaced by the 100-6, using Austin's new 2.6-litre 6-cylinder engine which gave 117 bhp. For 1960 this grew to 2,912 cc, and in this form the car became the definitive Austin-Healey 3000, now with disc brakes standard on all models. The new car was a potential rally winner, and over the next five years it fully lived up to its promise. With drivers such as the Morley twins, Pat Moss (Stirling's sister), and Ann Wisdom, they won the 1960 Marathon de la Route, the 1961 Alpine Rally in which the Morleys won the only Coupe des Alpes to be awarded, the 1962 Alpine, and the 1964 Marathon, to mention only a few of their successes.

In production from 1959 to 1968, the 3000 was made in three series, each with successively more power. The 1966 model comes into Series III, with 150 bhp, triple SU carburettor and servo-assisted brakes. It was made as a two-plus-two (2 + 2) seater, with very small seats behind the driver and passenger. The pure two-seater had been phased out during the early 1960s, and another step away from the out-and-out sports car was the use of wind-up windows in the Series III.

The 'big Healey', as it was called to distinguish it from the Sprite, was a real man's car with a top speed of 120 mph (193 km/h), but was undeniably heavy to handle, and its rather bumpy ride was no longer acceptable in the late 1960s. It had always been popular on the United States market, but could not easily have been made to conform with current safety legislation, so it was honourably retired during 1968. A total of 41,534 Austin-Healey 3000s were made.

Also at the 1952 Motor Show was a new sports car from Triumph, powered by a 1,991-cc version of the Standard Vanguard engine, with front suspension and rear axle from the Triumph Mayflower and a chassis based on that of the old Standard Eight. The body was a simple open two-seater with a curious open front to the bonnet, with the radiator grille several inches inside it. The 20TS, as it was called, had been put together very hastily, and when ex-B.R.M. engineer Ken Richardson tested it around the factory he pronounced it to be 'a bloody death trap'.

When the production model appeared in 1953 under the name TR2 the design had been greatly improved, with a new, much stiffer, chassis and a larger tail to provide some luggage accommodation. With overdrive it could do 108 mph (174 km/h), and at £555 it was the cheapest 100-mph (161-km/h) car in Britain, undercutting the Austin-Healey by £195. Both engines produced 90 bhp, but the Triumph's lighter weight and higher gearing gave it the advantage. It was also very economical, achieving 31–34 mpg (11–12 km/l) overall, compared with the Healey's 23–27 mpg (8–9.5 km/l). In 1955 it was replaced by the TR3 with egg-crate grille, overdrive on three speeds and an optional children's seat. The 1957 models had disc brakes on the front wheels – the first British production car to offer discs. During 1957 the grille was widened and power increased to 100 bhp on the TR3A, which lasted until a complete redesign in 1961 produced the TR4. This had a new full-width body styled by Michelotti, a wider track, bigger boot and all-synchromesh gearbox. The engine was a 2,138-cc unit which had been available on the last TR3As.

**Austin-Healey 100M, 1953**
This had slight engine modifications as used on the 1953 Le Mans cars, available from the factory or as a conversion kit for private owners.

**Triumph TR2, 1953**
An early production model of the Triumph TR2 at the Prescott hill climb in September 1953. The rear wheel spats were a factory option, but not widely bought, and were not available on the TR3 or later Triumph sports cars.

The TR series was steadily developed during the 1960s, independent rear suspension coming in on the TR4A (1964 to 1967), a 2½-litre fuel injection 6-cylinder engine on the TR5 (1967 to 1968) and its American-market carburetted version the TR250, and a new Karmann-styled body on the TR6 (1969 to 1976). Power was now up to 150 bhp, giving 119 mph and 0 to 60 mph (96.5 km/h) in 8.2 seconds. Fuel-consumption consideration brought the power down to 124 bhp after 1972. The TRs were among the most successful sports cars ever made in Britain, and their simple, no-frills performance endeared them to buyers all over the world. Like the M.G.s, the earlier models went largely for export; of 58,236 TR3As made, only about 2,000 were sold in Britain.

**Triumph TR2, 1955**
One of the last made before the arrival of the TR3 with egg-crate grille.

Although competing for the same share of the market, the Jowett Jupiter was a much rarer machine, only 899 being made between 1950 and 1953. It was developed from the remarkable Javelin, an 80-mph (129-km/h) 1½-litre saloon with all-round torsion-bar suspension which was the first British-built family car to rival continentals such as the Lancia Aprilia. It has been said that the chief motive for Jowett's move into sports cars was the need for steel. This was allocated by the Government according to export performance, and while family cars like the Javelin did not appeal to Americans, sports cars clearly did – hence the Jowett Jupiter.

Announced in March 1950, the Jupiter used the Javelin's 60-bhp flat-four engine in a new tubular chassis designed by Professor Eberan von Eberhorst, who had been responsible for the 1939 Auto Union racing cars. The wide body was a multi-curved affair, not fully all-enveloping like the Ferrari 166 or Cisitalia, yet much more streamlined than the M.G. or H.R.G. The bench seat could accommodate three, at the price of a steering column gearchange. This feature, so fashionable in the family cars of the 1950s on both sides of the Atlantic, yet hated by sporting motorists for its lack of precision, was the main reason why the Jupiter was never really accepted by enthusiasts. It had good roadholding and its top speed of 86 mph (138 km/h) was by no means unsatisfactory, but it was somehow never thought of as a real sports car, in the way that H.R.G., Morgan and the much cheaper M.G.s were. Nor did it find much of a welcome in America, where one might have expected a bench seat and column change to be acceptable. Jupiters won the 1½-litre class at Le Mans in 1950, 1951 and 1952, were first and second in their class in the 1951 Tourist Trophy, and won the 1951 Bremgarten Sports Car Race at Berne, Switzerland. The model disappeared from the market with the end of all Jowett production in 1954, though the company had hoped to keep going with a fibreglass Jupiter of which only three were made.

The traditional M.G. disappeared in 1955 when the MGA came out. This had a modern body derived from that of a car built four years earlier on a TD chassis for Le Mans. The engine was a 1,489-cc 4-cylinder used in the ZA Magnette saloon which developed 68 bhp in original form and 73 bhp when twin carburettors were employed. The MGA had coil ifs and rack-and-pinion steering. It was a considerable step forward from the TF, not only in

**M.G. MGA 1500, 1956**
Two MGA 1500s on the starting line at an M.G. Car Club race meeting at Silverstone in 1956. One has an aero screen, while the driver of 32D has opted for a small full-width screen.

appearance but also in performance. Top speed was almost 100 mph (161 km/h), compared with the TF's 80 mph (129 km/h), while 0 to 60 mph (96.5 km/h) took four seconds less, at 15 seconds. Later MGAs had 1,588-cc engines in pushrod and twin-ohc forms, the latter being good for 115 mph (185 km/h) at the price of heavy fuel consumption and a tendency to burn pistons. The Twin Cam had disc brakes all round while the ordinary 1600 had discs on the front wheels.

The MGA had a wide appeal, being more suitable for touring with greater comfort and luggage accommodation, and at the same time excellent performance and safe handling. Sales boomed – in 1956, its first full year of production, more MGAs were made than the total output of TC Midgets, while in 1959 MGAs outnumbered the entire prewar production for all M.G.s. Total number made between 1955 and 1962 was 101,181, of which only 2,111 were Twin Cams.

The successor to the MGA was, logically, the MGB, and this was made in even larger numbers. It had a bigger engine (1,798 cc of 95 bhp) and unitary-construction body, front disc brakes and a higher axle ratio, with overdrive as an option. In terms of comfort and performance, it was about as much of an improvement over the MGA as that was over the TF, and has been described as the world's most popular classic sports car. The open two-

**M.G. MGA roadster, 1958**
A coupé was also made, at a price of £1,087 compared with £995 for the open car illustrated.

seater was joined in 1965 by the GT, a 2 + 2 coupé that was almost an estate with its big tailgate. It weighed only 160 lb (72.5 kg) more than the open car, and with better aerodynamics performance was about the same, with a maximum 105 mph (169 km/h). An automatic transmission (what would Cecil Kimber have thought?) became available on the MGB Mark II of 1967, but the major variations on the theme both concerned the power unit.

In 1967 the Austin-Healey 3000 was nearing the end of its production run, and rather than produce a new Austin-Healey BMC management decided to drop the 6-cylinder engine into the MGB shell, calling the result the MGC. It did not receive a rapturous welcome as the additional weight of the larger engine spoilt the handling, and the gear ratios were critical. However, top speed was 118 mph (190 km/h) and the MGC soon found a niche as a high-speed motorway cruiser rather than a competitive sports car. It was available as a coupé in addition to the open two-seater. A total of 8,909 were made between 1967 and 1969, while MGB production totalled 512,880 between 1962 and 1980.

The other engine transplant involved the 3½-litre aluminium-block Rover V8 which was installed in the MGB GT shell to make the fastest road-going M.G. ever, with a top speed of 125 mph (201 km/h). Made from 1973 to 1976, it sold only 2,591 units, suffering perhaps from being overpriced and looking too much like its 4-cylinder cousins. Its performance was startling and needed careful handling. The great M.G. enthusiast, Rivers Fletcher, said of it: 'In the wet, on a low gear, it will easily turn round and bite you, but surely that is what you want with a V8!' The V8 was made only as a coupé, although a handful have been converted privately to open form.

Parallel to the big Austin-Healeys and MGBs, both companies built small sports cars in the tradition of the original M-type Midget. Austin-Healey were first in the field with their Sprite, launched in 1958. This used the 948-cc BMC A-type engine from the Austin A35 saloon in a welded platform frame with a light, two-seater body. The bonnet and wings assembly opened up in one piece for easy maintenance, and the headlamps projected from the bonnet top giving the familiar 'frog-eye' appearance. At first this was thought to be a bit of a joke, and a number of firms offered replacement bonnets in which the headlamps were less prominent, but as the years have passed, it has become an endearing feature, and today a frog-eye Sprite will fetch nearly double the price of a later example.

As modified for the Sprite, the 948-cc engine developed 45 bhp, giving the little car a top speed of 81 mph (130 km/h). Several conversion kits for improving performance soon became available, notably those offered by Speedwell Conversions. Output could be increased to between 60 and 70 bhp, and body alterations included a streamlined front end and fastback coupé top. Some of these Sprites could exceed 100 mph (161 km/h), while Graham Hill drove a specially prepared example at 110 mph (177 km/h) on a Belgian motorway. Sprites were successful in rallying, particularly in the hands of John Sprinzel who dominated British rallying in 1959 and finished third overall in the very punishing Liège-Rome-Liège Rally of 1960. In the same year he was second overall in the RAC Rally.

38,999 Mark I Sprites were made up to May 1961, when the Mark II appeared. Mechanically it was little changed, but the front was redesigned with the headlamps being mounted conventionally at the front of the wings, and the luggage boot was now accessible from the rear, instead of by folding forward the seats. Front disc brakes were standard on Sprites from the Mark II onwards, and engine capacity went up to 1,098 cc in 1962 and to 1,275 cc in 1966 when the engine was basically a detuned Mini Cooper S. The last 1,029 Sprites, made from January to July 1971, were badged simply as Austins, for British Leyland's licence to use the Healey name had run out.

In June 1961 M.G. brought out their version of the Sprite, for which they revived the name Midget. This was essentially the same car, with a slightly different grille and a chrome strip along the side of the body. The price was £38 more than the Sprite, at £669. The same changes to engines and brakes were made during the 1960s, but the Midget soldiered on through the next decade, being discontinued in the spring of 1970, about eighteen months before the last M.G. (MGB) was made at Abingdon. Total production of Sprites and Midgets was 355,888.

The only serious rival to the Spridgets, as they are familiarly called, was the Triumph Spitfire, product of what was an independent company when it was launched, though in 1968 the Leyland Group merged with the Spridget's makers, the British Motor Corporation, to form British Leyland. The Spitfire was based on the Triumph Herald, a rather superior, small family car notable for its independent rear suspension and remarkable turning circle of twenty-five feet. For the sporting model the chassis was shortened by 8½ in (216 mm), a

tuned version of the 1,147-cc Herald engine was used, and the Italian stylist Michelotti, who was responsible for the Heralds, was called in to design a simple open two-seater body. Top speed was 90 mph (145 km/h), rising to 95 mph (153 km/h) when capacity went up to 1,296 cc in 1967. The Spitfire was a very enjoyable car to drive, its only drawback being the uncertain handling of the independently sprung rear end. As the late Michael Sedgwick observed, 'It's a good thing you can't watch yourself at 10/10ths cornering'. Rear suspension was improved on the Mark IV introduced in 1970, when an all-synchromesh gearbox became a standard item. Like the M.G. Midget, the Spitfire was continued throughout the 1970s, its engine being used in its rival from Abingdon after 1974. Marginally cheaper than the Midget when it was introduced in 1962, the Spitfire became more expensive for most of the time, and by the end of the seventies when both cars were due to be phased out, it cost £4,308 to the Midget's £3,821. However, it was roomier and better equipped, and on later models, faster and quieter. Of the 314,342 Spitfires made, only 22.7 per cent were sold on the British market, the bulk of exports going to the United States.

There was never a closed Spitfire, though detachable hard tops were obtainable. However, the GT6 which used the 6-cylinder 2-litre Triumph Vitesse engine in the Spitfire chassis and front end came as a fastback coupé. Made from 1966 to 1973, it was a rival to the MGB GT with something of the styling of the E-type Jaguar.

**Austin-Healey Sprite**
The famous frog-eyed model which has become so popular among collectors.

**Austin-Healey Sprite**
Scottish agricultural students Andrew Henderson and David Philp before setting out on a round-the-world trip in a Sprite. The limited luggage accommodation has been supplemented by a well-laden rack.

Only one serious attempt was made to market a sports car smaller than the Spridgets. This was the Berkeley, designed by Laurie Bond and made by a caravan-building firm from Biggleswade, Bedfordshire. When it appeared in 1956 this little fibreglass car powered by a 322-cc Anzani 2-cylinder engine driving the front wheels was barely a sports car, having a top speed of only 65 mph (104.5 km/h), but later models received an Excelsior in-line 3-cylinder engine of 492 cc and 30 bhp, or a Royal Enfield parallel twin of 692 cc and 50 bhp. With the latter, the Berkeley could do 105 mph (169 km/h), though the noise level was shatteringly high. These B105s had some success in international competitions, defeating several Fiat-Abarths to win their class in the Monza 12-Hour Race, and they also won their class in the Mille Miglia. About 2,000 Berkeleys were made altogether, between 1956 and 1961, but once the Sprite was established at no greater price, the noisy and unrefined twin-cylinder cars from Biggleswade were no longer competitive.

One of the great success stories of the postwar motor industry began in 1951 when twenty-three-year-old Colin Chapman built a sports car powered by a tuned Austin Seven engine, with independent front suspension and a light aluminium body. Christened the Lotus, it was widely used by its builder in club events, and led to a production car seeing the light of day in 1953. This Mark VI had a multi-tube space frame, coil ifs and a light alloy body. Rather surprisingly for such a functional and no-frills car, the rear wheels were covered by spats. As the Mark VI was sold only in kit form any reasonable engine could be

**Lotus Mark VI, 1953**
At Prescott in 1954.

used. These included the 1,172-cc Ford Ten, 1,508-cc Ford Consul, 1,250-cc M.G. and 1,098-cc Coventry Climax. About 100 Mark VIs were sold between 1953 and 1955; two years later the slightly more civilized Seven arrived. This had a longer wheelbase and simple weather protection, though no doors. Indeed, its descendants right up to today's Caterham Super Seven have always been doorless. The Seven had hydraulic brakes and was again suitable for a variety of engines, of which the 948-cc BMC A-type and 1,172-cc Ford Ten were the most popular. Thus equipped, a Lotus Seven could do about 83 mph (133.5 km/h), not an outstanding speed for the late 1950s, but it was undoubtedly a fun car to drive. The later Super Seven (1961–70) with a Cosworth-tuned Ford 1500 engine could do 103 mph (165.5 km/h), with 0–50 mph (80 km/h) in 7.4 seconds.

In 1957 Colin Chapman built the first closed Lotus, the 1,216-cc Coventry-Climax-powered Elite coupé. This was intended more for fast road-work than for competitions. The completely new design featured an integral body/chassis unit made of fibreglass, the first application of this material in unit construction though it had been used for the body of the Chevrolet Corvette. The monocoque was in three parts, floor, structural centre section and one-piece outer skin, to which all mechanical parts were attached. The engine was a single 4-cylinder ohc Coventry-Climax of 1,216 cc displacement and 75 to 83 bhp, depending on

**Lotus Elan**
Overhead view of the Lotus Elan's box-section backbone-chassis branching out at the front to support the engine, and at the rear to carry the rear suspension.

whether one or two carburettors were used. Suspension was independent at front and rear, and brakes were disc all round. This advanced specification gave the Elite two other firsts: the first small British sports car with all-round independent suspension and disc brakes.

Although designed in 1956 and announced to the public at the 1957 London Motor Show, the Elite did not get into production until 1959 because of financial problems and the necessity to acquire a new factory outside London – at Cheshunt in Hertfordshire. The Elite was built from 1959 to 1963, production totalling 988 cars. Because the roof was a stress-bearing structure a convertible was out of the question, but the coupé was so attractive and functional that this did not really matter. Fuel economy was very good, at over 30 mpg (10.5 km/l) on long runs, and top speed was 117 mph (188 km/h) with the twin-carburettor engine.

The Elite had a good career in racing, including class victories in the 1959 Nürburgring 1,000-Kilometre race, and at Le Mans every year from 1959 to 1964. It was also successful in club racing. Unfortunately, the fibreglass shell proved increasingly expensive to manufacture, and in 1963 Chapman was forced to turn to a steel chassis on his next car, the Elan. The name Elite was revived in 1975 for a completely new Lotus, variants of which are still made today.

**Lotus Mark VI, 1955**
Powered by an MG 1.466-cc engine

The Elan was made in much larger numbers and was the car which established Lotus as a serious manufacturer. It was also one of the most desirable road cars of the 1960s, having a 113-mph (182-km/h) top speed combined with superb road holding. William Boddy, editor of *Motor Sport,* described it as 'one of the finest road clingers of all time'. It had a twin-ohc version of the 1,558-cc Ford Classic engine mounted in a sheet-steel box-sectioned backbone-chassis frame which branched out at the front to hold the engine. Like the Elite, the Elan had independent suspension and disc brakes all round. The body was a simple but attractive fibreglass two-seater with pop-up headlamps in the manner of the prewar Cord 810. Later developments included the S2 (1964–69) which could be had as a fixed-head coupé as well as open two-seater, the S4 (1968–71) with low-profile tyres and servo brakes, and the Sprint (1971–73) with a big-valve engine giving 126 bhp and top speed of 122 mph (196 km/h). Later models of the Sprint had five-speed gearboxes. The Elan was not cheap, prices running from £1,312 in 1964 to £2,467 for the last Elan Sprint of 1973 (MGB prices over the same period were £847 to £1,414), but it attracted many enthusiasts, total sales being 12,224 of the two-seaters and 3,300 of the longer Elan Plus 2 with four seats, equally good handling and very little loss of performance. The two-seater Elans were available in kit form as well as complete, but the Plus 2 was the first Lotus not offered as a kit.

In 1966 Colin Chapman again broke new ground with the Europa, a very low coupé with a mid-mounted engine, i.e. behind the driver but ahead of the rear axle. The power unit was a 1,470-cc Renault 16, and Chapman had an arrangement with the French company whereby the first sanction of the Europa would be sold only through Renault outlets in Europe. After two years Lotus gained permission to sell the cars all over the world. A twin-cam Cosworth-Ford engine was available for racing and from October 1971 a detuned version of this went into the road cars as well. They were the first mid-engined sports cars outside the supercar bracket. Roadholding was excellent, and the later Europa S2s had

**Lotus Elan Sprint, 1973**
The last model of the Elan was the 126-bhp Sprint, of which 1,353 were made between 1971 and 1973.

**TVR Grantura I, 1960**
The TVR Grantura I coupé being cornered energetically by John Wadsworth at Silverstone. Only 100 Mark I Granturas were made, with the option of Ford Anglia, Coventry Climax or MGA engines. He is pursued by an Austin A40.

126-bhp engines, five-speed gearboxes and a top speed of 115 mph. Despite their advanced design they were always cheaper than the Elan: 1973 prices were £2,370 for the Europa compared with £2,467 for the Elan Sprint and £2,841 for the Elan Plus 2. Europa production ended in 1975, after 9,230 had been made.

The Lotus was the most successful 1950s make to begin life as a kit car, and with Ginetta, Marcos and T.V.R. the only one still to be in business in 1986. There were, however, many others, encouraged by the tax loophole whereby Purchase Tax (thirty-three per cent) was not levied on cars sold in kit form. This fortunate state of affairs lasted until 1973 when Purchase Tax was replaced by Value Added Tax on which no such concessions were allowed. The best kit cars were well-designed machines suitable for serious competitions while other firms merely supplied fibreglass body shells for fitting to a customer's usually rather tired Austin or Ford chassis. Among the most popular with sporting drivers was the Buckler which was actively campaigned by its designer, Derek Buckler, from Reading, Berkshire. All the 500 Bucklers supplied between 1949 and 1962 had tubular frames and independent front suspension, but there was considerable variety in the bodies which were narrow with cycle-type wings or all-enveloping, in fibreglass or light alloy, while engines were mostly Ford, BMC or Coventry-Climax. Fairthorpe of Chalfont St Peter, Buckinghamshire, made light two-seater sports cars powered by Standard Ten, Triumph Vitesse, Ford Zephyr or Coventry-Climax engines. They could be had as complete cars as well as kits, and the marque lasted into the mid-1970s, latterly as a closed coupé only. Another simple and reasonably priced sports car was the Turner from Wolverhampton which used the mechanical elements of the Austin A30, and later the A35, in a ladder-type frame with trailing-arm rear suspension and fibreglass body. The earliest models could achieve 80 mph (129 km/h), probably 85 (137) with the 948-cc A35 engine and over 90 (145) when fitted with a light-alloy crossflow head by Alexander Engineering. The fastest Turners were those fitted with the 1,098-cc Coventry-Climax FWA engine, made from 1959 to 1966 and good for 100 mph (161 km/h). About 660 Turners were made between 1955 and 1967 – many were exported to the United States and to South Africa, and their overall impact on motor sport in Britain was small.

A larger-production kit car was the TVR, whose familiar squat shape lasted in production from 1958 to 1979. Practically always seen as a closed coupé, the Blackpool-built TVR was made in a bewildering variety of forms, with at least seven different engine options by Coventry-Climax, BMC, British and American Ford. They ranged in size from the 997-cc Ford Anglia to the 4,950-cc Ford V8, the latter in the Tuscan. Some V8-powered TVRs were sold on the American market under the name Griffith – after the American distributor Jack Griffith.

Other kit makes which continued in production alongside complete cars included the Welsh-built Austin- and Ford-powered Gilbern coupé, the East Anglian Ginetta which progressed from Lotus 6-like stark two-seater to a sophisticated Ford V6-powered GT coupé, and the unique wooden-construction Marcos from Wiltshire. The latter two companies are still in business. There were several others, while at least thirty-five firms offered fibreglass bodies for second-hand chassis. All this activity was evidence of the tremendous enthusiasm for amateur motor sport which characterized Britain in the fifties and sixties. Most of the cars mentioned were raced or rallied, if only at club level, and owners had a great deal of fun without great expense.

We have so far only looked at the smaller British sports cars, even if some of them, like the TVR Tuscan, had pretty big engines. There were also numerous cars in the more expensive categories, generally with engines of more than 2½ litres. The first to appear after the war was the Allard which was a continuation of the 1930s Anglo-American hybrid theme. Sydney Allard had always favoured the 3,622-cc side-valve Ford V8, though he had only made about a dozen cars before the war. In mid-1946 he brought out his first production cars, which used the familiar engine in a simple chassis with divided-axle independent front suspension. The bodies were very striking, with waterfall grilles and long bonnets. The J1 sports two-seater was made in very limited numbers, but the L-type tourer and M1 drophead coupé sold 191 and 500 units respectively. The instantly recognizable styling, combined with excellent acceleration and the fact that there were no rivals, helped the Allard to sell well in the immediate postwar years. The best season was 1948 when 432 cars were delivered.

A true sporting Allard appeared in 1949. This was the J2 which had a De Dion rear axle and coil springs, with a very simple doorless body and cycle-type wings. For British purchasers a 3,917-cc 140-bhp Mercury V8 was usually fitted, but many J2s were shipped engineless across the Atlantic to be fitted with Cadillac, Lincoln or Oldsmobile engines. This 'motorcycle on four wheels' could do 110 mph (177 km/h) even in its 'mildest' form, and with the big American V8s 150 mph (241 km/h) was possible. A Mercury-engined J2 was third at Le Mans in 1952, while Cadillac-engined cars were first and third at Watkins Glen in 1950 and second in 1953.

Though striking to look at and good performers, the Allards were a trifle crude by early 1950s' standards, and once William Lyons had launched his Jaguar XK120 at the 1948 London Motor Show, they stood little chance. Production dropped to 132 in 1952 and 123 in 1953, and only forty-four were made thereafter before the end in 1957.

**Allard J2, 1951**
This car has the 3,917-cc Mercury V8 engine, an enlarged Ford V8, but many J2s were fitted with more powerful Cadillac or Oldsmobile engines.

**TVR S2 Vixen, 1969**
The 1969 TVR S2 Vixen has the same basic shape as the Grantura, but the Ford 1600 engine was now standardised. Servo brakes and an all-synchromesh gearbox were features of this model.

**Allard J2, 1951**
A 1951 Allard J2 in action at the Prescott hill climb.

The XK120 made an even bigger impact than its predecessor, the S.S.100. It really only came about because Lyons planned an all-new saloon with twin-ohc engine, and wanted a test-bed for this engine so that all the problems could be ironed out before the car went on the market. He therefore planned a limited production of 200 sports cars as test-beds – with the spin-off of providing some welcome publicity. Two engines were tested, a 2-litre four and a 3½-litre six, but only the latter went into production, under the name XK120.

The 3,442-cc engine developed 160 bhp which enabled the car to exceed the 120 mph (193 km/h) implied in its name. A special version with undershield reached 132.6 mph (213.4 km/h) in Belgium, and regular production cars submitted for Road Tests by British journals exceeded 124 mph (199.5 km/h). Other features of the car were torsion-bar independent front suspension, a four-speed transmission with synchromesh on the three upper speeds, and a light alloy body on an ash frame. After the first 200 cars, the body was changed to pressed steel. Today the aluminium cars are more highly favoured as they are less prone to rust, but they are obviously rare and very expensive.

The XK120 made a tremendous impact on a car-starved postwar Britain. With its sleek lines and outstanding performance it must have triggered off more daydreams and schoolboy fantasies than any other car. It was also remarkably good value; at only £1,263 it was less than half the price of a contemporary 2-litre Ferrari, but this was immaterial to most Britons as ninety-two per cent of XK120s went for export anyway. As soon as he saw the tremendous demand generated by the new car, Lyons abandoned his plan for a limited production run and made the XK120 part of his regular line. In October 1950 it was joined by the similarly-engined Mark VII saloon, and in 1951 came the C-type sports/racing derivative which won the Le Mans 24-Hour Race that year and set the pattern for Jaguar's phenomenal successes in competitions of the 1950s. The XK120 itself earned a very good sporting reputation, including wins in the 1950 Tourist Trophy race in Ireland, and in several European rallies. A total of 12,078 XK120s was made, of which 7,631 were roadsters, 2,678 coupés, and 1,769 convertible coupés. Some of the latter had automatic transmission. They were succeeded by the XK140 in 1954, but the twin-cam engine was continued for many years. As well as sports cars and sedans it powered limousines (Daimler Vanden Plas), ambulances, armoured cars and racing hydroplanes.

**Jaguar XK120 roadster, 1951**
From its slim radiator shield to the sweeping rear lines, the XK120 was an elegant design, especially in its roadster form, here shown, without side windows.

KHP 678

**Jaguar XK120, 1951**
A Jaguar XK120 in driving tests at the finish of the 1952 Eastbourne Rally.

In the light of more recent cars, the XK120 can be criticised on account of its heavy steering and inadequate brakes, but in its time it was an outstanding sports car. Its successors the XK140 (1955–7) and XK150 (1957–61) have never had quite the charisma of the original, though they had numerous improvements, such as rack-and-pinion steering on the 140, and disc brakes on the 150. Power was increased to 190 hp on the 140 (210 bhp on special-equipment cars) and 250 bhp on the 150 which, from 1959, had a 3.8-litre engine.

After a twelve-year production run the XK was superseded in March 1961 by the E-type. This used the XK150's 3.8-litre engine but was otherwise all-new, with a combined monocoque/multi-tube chassis, all-independent suspension and a sleek, aerodynamic body which owed a lot to the D-type sports/racing Jaguar of the 1950s. (Incidentally, there was never an A- or a B-type Jaguar; the C-type of 1951 was so named because it was the Competition model of the XK120, and the letters D and E followed naturally. It remains to be seen if there will ever be an F-type.) The E-type was initially available as a two-seater only – open roadster or closed coupé – but in 1966 came a 2 + 2 coupé, with an extra 9 in (229 mm) in the wheelbase and a proper rear door for luggage. In 1965 the 6-cylinder engine was enlarged to its final size of 4.2 litres, and given an all-synchromesh gearbox for the first time. Power output was 265 bhp, giving a top speed of 152 mph (244.5 km/h) for the coupé, which was always faster than the roadster, due to its better aerodynamics.

The Series II E-type came out for 1969; power steering was now optional and there were minor styling changes, but the car was tailored to meet increasingly severe emission controls in the United States, which resulted in a reduction in power. By 1970 these cars delivered only 171 bhp. To overcome this problem Jaguar brought out a brand-new 5.3-litre V12 engine, a version of which had been tried out in the mid-engined XJ13 sports/racing car, of which only one was built, in 1966. The new V12 had only one camshaft per block instead of the two of the XJ13, but it still developed 272 bhp which restored the E-type to something like the performance it had enjoyed in the sixties, while still meeting emission regulations. The Series III E-type could be distinguished by its crosshatch radiator grille. It was available as a roadster or 2 + 2 coupé; power steering was now standard and a Borg-Warner automatic gearbox was optional, as was air conditioning on the coupé. The engine was the first volume-production V12 since the Lincoln of 1948; just as the XK120 engine had been tried out on a sports car before going into a saloon, so the V12 proved

**Jaguar E-type, 1961 (*over*)**
This is an early model, with 3.8-litre engine.

itself in the E-type before being put into the XJ6 four-door saloon in June 1972, to make the XJ12. Not that the E-type was a mere test-bed, for more than 15,000 Series III cars were made before the model was phased out early in 1975. The last fifty cars were painted black and carried a dashboard plaque to identify them. They could be said to be instant collectibles from the moment the last one left Coventry. Total production of all E-types was 72,507, compared with 30,334 XKs made over a slightly shorter period. This indicates the greatly increased market for sports cars brought about by growing prosperity in the industrialized countries. The E-type had more rivals than its predecessors, but like them it was always excellent value.

Aston Martin was in a different price bracket from Jaguar, and even in the 1950s was more of a grand tourer than a sports car. This distinction has become increasingly marked over the last twenty-five years. A handful of Aston Martin DB1 2-litre 4-cylinder drophead coupés were made between 1948 and 1950, but with the David Brown takeover of Aston Martin in 1947 came an excellent 2.6-litre twin-ohc 6-cylinder engine which W.O. Bentley had designed for Lagonda. A fastback coupé powered by this engine ran at Le Mans in 1949, and a modified version went into production in 1950 under the name DB2. In addition to the two-seater coupé styled after the Le Mans car, a drophead version was available. They were not cheap, at £1,915 for the closed coupé and £2,043 for the drophead, but as Aston Martin only made a handful of cars per week they were able to sell all they made. With an eye to the American market the earlier DB2s had steering-column gearchange, but this move away from the sports car image was not welcomed, and was soon abandoned. Although the engines were complex, maintenance was aided by the fact that the entire bonnet/wings/nose assembly hinged ahead of the wheels, giving unrivalled access.

In 1953 came the DB2/4 which had two additional (very small) seats and a hatchback. The 116-bhp Vantage engine, which was available on DB2s, was standard on the DB2/4, and was replaced in 1954 by a 2.9-litre version. This restored the performance lost by the extra weight of the 2/4's body, and top speed was 120 mph (193 km/h). The series was

**Aston Martin DB1**
The Aston Martin 2-litre was designed by Claude Hill before the company was bought by David Brown, and was then given the designation DB1. Only 15 were made. This one is competing at Le Mans in 1949. A private entry by Robert Lawrie, it finished eleventh.

444 NHT

**Aston Martin DB2, 1952**
An Aston Martin DB2 competing in an Aston Martin Owners' Club race at Silverstone in 1954.

**Aston Martin DB2/4, 1953**
An Aston Martin DB2/4 hatchback coupé.

progressively developed through the Mark II and III DB 2/4, before being replaced in 1958 by the larger-engined DB4. This had a 240-bhp 3.7-litre engine giving a top speed of 140 mph (225 km/h) and a 0 to 60 mph (96 km/h) time of around 8.5 seconds. Brakes were power-operated discs all round and the DB4 was now a full four-seater. At £3,755 it was one of the most desirable high-speed touring cars of its day, but was it a sports car? The four-seater saloons and convertibles would not qualify by many people's definition, and were not really suitable for racing in any form. However, there was a short-wheelbase version, the DB4 GT which went on sale in October 1959.

The DB4 GT had 5 in (127 mm) less wheelbase, 200 lb (90.5 kg) off the weight and a 267-bhp engine with a 12-plug head and triple Weber carburettors. When John Bolster tested it for *Autosport* in 1961 he recorded 152 mph (244.5 km/h) and 0 to 60 (96 km/h) in 6.4 seconds. Once again Aston Martin had a GT car suitable for track as well as road, and it was campaigned with great success by such drivers as Stirling Moss, Roy Salvadori and Innes Ireland. A total of seventy-four 'standard' DB4 GTs were made, but there was an even rarer version with body by Zagato. This weighed 100 lb (45 kg) less, and the engine delivered 314 bhp gross. Its styling was controversial, most people would think less attractive than the DB4 GTs, which were themselves styled in Italy by Superleggera Touring. 'Brutishly handsome' was one appellation, and as fair as any. Only nineteen DB4 GT Zagatos were made, but the theme was revived in 1986 for a limited-production coupé of which just fifty are to be made at a price of £87,000.

After the DB4 GT was withdrawn in 1963, Aston Martins put on more weight and moved away from the true sports-car market. Automatic transmission was optional from 1970. The DB5 and 6, DBS and V8 cars were, and are, nevertheless, magnified fast tourers.

One make on which automatic transmission would have been unthinkable was Frazer-Nash. The little Isleworth firm had no BMWs to sell in the immediate postwar years, so they built a series of sports cars, mostly in their prewar image of stark, functional machines for the sportsman. The power units were the 2-litre BMW-derived engines that were being built by the Bristol Aeroplane Co. for their coupés. The first production postwar Frazer-Nash was originally called the High Speed, but after taking third place at Le Mans in 1949 they were renamed Le Mans Replica. The 6-cylinder 2-litre engine had inclined overhead valves operated by a single camshaft, the same design that was first used on the 1937 BMW 328. It developed 120 bhp in original form, and 140 bhp in the later Mark II version. Transmission was by a four-speed gearbox, with synchromesh on all speeds but first, and the chassis was a tubular steel frame. It was very light, turning the scales at 1,500 lb (680 kg) and had a top speed of over 120 mph (193 km/h). Equally important was its simplicity and reliability, which meant that it was no problem for a private owner to maintain the car that he raced, and there was no need for the company to provide a customer tuning service.

The Le Mans Replica was sold in many countries, including the United States, Sweden, Italy and Portugal, and competition successes poured in from 1950 onwards. Among the most notable was Franco Cortese's victory in the 1951 Targa Florio, the only time a British car won the gruelling Sicilian mountain race, and Stirling Moss' victory in the British Empire Trophy, also in 1951. In 1952 Harry Grey and Larry Kulok won the Sebring Twelve-Hours Race. In hill climbs and rallies it was equally at home: Winterbottom and Duff winning a Coupe des Alpes in the 1951 Alpine Rally in the same car that had run at Le Mans a few weeks earlier. Imagine Derek Bell's Porsche 962 competing in a rally today!

In 1952 competition from more specialized sports/racing cars such as the Connaught and Cooper-Bristol led Frazer-Nash to introduce the Mark II Le Mans Replica, with more powerful engine, and lower and lighter body. With this car Ken Wharton came second in the 1952 Jersey Road Race, behind a C-type Jaguar, but the day of the amateur who maintained and drove his own car to meetings was coming to an end, certainly in major events, though the Le Mans Replica continued to give a good account of itself in club events for many years. The last Mark II was made in 1953, and thereafter Frazer-Nash concentrated on road-going sports cars with full-width two- and three-seater bodywork.

The first full-width Frazer-Nash had, in fact, preceded the Le Mans Replica. This was the 1940 Mille Miglia BMW converted to right-hand drive and given a Frazer-Nash badge and radiator grille. It was shown at the 1948 London Show, but was dropped in favour of the Le Mans Replica. Several varieties of full-width coachwork were fitted to Frazer-Nashes in the years 1950 to 1957, including the Targa Florio with sidescreens, the Sebring, which was a full-width successor to the Le Mans Replica, and a fixed-head coupé. All these used

XOU 3

**Frazer-Nash Le Mans Replica, 1950**

versions of the Bristol engine, but a roadster was proposed with a 4-cylinder 2.6-litre Austin engine (this was dropped by Leonard Lord in favour of the Austin-Healey), and the last two coupés were powered by a 3.2-litre BMW V8. None of these achieved the competition success of the Le Mans Replica – of the eighty-four Frazer-Nashes made after the war, thirty-four were Le Mans Replicas. A.F.N. Ltd began importing Porsches in 1954, and the German cars rapidly took over from the native product, just as BMW had twenty years earlier.

Another make to use the Bristol engine was A.C. This company entered the postwar market with a saloon and tourer powered by the old 1,991-cc six which had first seen the light of day in 1918. In 1953 this went into an all-independently sprung open two-seater sports car called the Ace. This had a tubular frame designed by John Tojeiro who had used a similar design in a few M.G.- and Bristol-engined sports cars made under his own name in his small factory at Royston, Hertfordshire. The Ace's body looked not unlike a Ferrari, and with a top speed of 103 mph (165.5 km/h) the car had quite an appeal to the sportsman who wanted something more economical and distinctive than an XK120. Also, the Ace had the advantage of being readily available on the home market. A closed coupé called the Aceca was added in 1954, and two years later the Bristol engine was used in both cars, though the old A.C. unit was continued as an alternative until 1963. The Bristol developed 120 bhp and gave the Ace a top speed of 120 mph (193 km/h). Between 1957 and 1960 it did particularly well in American club racing, winning the SCCA (Sports Car Club of America) E production class in 1957, 1958 and 1959. To give the Ace-Bristols more effective opposition they were moved into Class D in 1960 and into Class C in 1961, when previous winners had been of the calibre of Ferrari GT, Mercedes-Benz 300SL and Porsche Carrera. Once again an Ace-Bristol won, driven by Pierre Mion. In Britain Ken Rudd won the 1956 Autosport Production Sports Car Championship in a very early Ace-Bristol. A specially prepared car finished eighth at the Le Mans in 1958, and the following

**Frazer-Nash, 1950**
This Le Mans Replica was photographed in competition trim at Aintree.

**Frazer-Nash Mille Miglia, 1952**
One of the rare Frazer-Nashes with all-enveloping bodywork, this is a 1952 Mille Miglia taking part in the MCC National Rally.

year a standard model won its class, being driven to and from the circuit, which was already becoming an uncommon thing to do.

In 1961 the supply of Bristol engines dried up, and A.C. turned to the 2.6-litre Ford Zephyr, originally installed by Ken Rudd as an option. This was very suitable to tuning, and Rudd offered five stages from the 85 bhp basic up to 170 bhp. *Motor Sport* recorded a top speed of 123.8 mph (199.2 km/h) in a road test. Untuned, the Ford-engined Ace was £400 cheaper than the Ace-Bristol and, as even the most expensive Stage Five tune-up cost only £225, these last Aces were something of a bargain.

The most exciting period of A.C.'s history began in 1961 when the American racing driver Carroll Shelby, no doubt impressed by the Ace's showing in SCCA events, decided that an even better car could be made by installing an American-built Ford V8 engine. At first a 4.2-litre unit was used, but after seventy-five cars had been made this was replaced by a 195-bhp 4.7-litre; in American terms this had a capacity of 289 cubic inches, and the car became known as the Cobra 289. In 1965 the largest Ford engine, the 7-litre 427-cubic inch V8 could be installed as well, this car being called the Cobra 427. An output of 400 bhp was easily available, and with tuning, it was closer to 500 bhp. The chassis was strengthened and slightly heavier than that of the Ace, but with that amount of power, performance could hardly help being shattering. The 289 had a top speed of 138 mph (222

**A.C. Ace, 1956**
This had quite an advanced chassis, with twin-tube frame, front and rear independent suspension via a transverse-leaf arrangement, and centre-lock wire wheels.

**A.C. Ace, 1956**
A 1956 A.C. Ace competing at Prescott.

**A.C. Shelby Cobra 427, 1965**
Few cars exhibit sheer power in their appearance more than the Cobra. Note the enormous rear tyres needed to transmit up to 500 bhp to the road.

km/h) and 0 to 60 mph (96 km/h) in 5.5 seconds, while the 427 had a top speed in excess of 165 mph (265.5 km/h) and a 0 to 60 (96 km/h) time of 4.2 seconds.

Carroll Shelby entered teams of Cobras in all the main European sports car races in 1964 and 1965, and although suffering more than their share of misfortunes, they won the GT Championship in both years. The 1965 winner was the Daytona coupé which was not available to the public. Cobras also dominated SCCA Class A racing in the United States between 1963 and 1969. They were discontinued when Carroll Shelby became involved with the Ford GT 40 and also began building the Shelby-Mustang 350. Cobra production was 560 of the 289 and 510 of the 427. It has proved a popular subject for replicas, both in kit form and as a complete car.

Another Anglo-American hybrid which Carroll Shelby had a hand in initiating was the Sunbeam Tiger, sometimes nicknamed 'the poor man's Cobra'. Shelby had seen a Sunbeam Alpine, an attractive sports car that deserved more power than the Rootes Group could give it. The 78-bhp, 1,785-cc engine which was basically an enlarged Hillman Minx unit was replaced by the same 4.2-litre Ford V8 that went into the early Cobras. After building one prototype Shelby handed the project over to Ian Garrard, Rootes' Sales Manager in California. It received the blessing of Rootes management in England, and with a stiffened frame but similar external appearance to the Alpine, the car went into production as the Sunbeam Tiger in 1964. Top speed was 118 mph (190 km/h) and 0 to 60 (96 km/h) acceleration 9.5 seconds, compared with 95 mph (153 km/h) and 14 seconds for the

**A.C. Shelby Cobra 289, 1963**
One of the two Cobra 289s entered by A.C. Cars for the 1963 Le Mans Race, with aluminium hard top. Stirling Moss was team manager, and this car was driven by Ninian Sanderson and Peter Bolton into seventh place, behind six Ferraris.

**Daimler SP 250, 1960**
A 1960 Daimler SP 250 with detachable hard top.

Alpine. At £1,446 it was reasonable compared with the Cobra 289 at £2,732 (1966 prices). The Tiger was current from 1964 to 1966, and American buyers could have the 289 engine from 1967 to 1968.

The only other British sports car to use a V8 engine was the Daimler SP250. Made from 1959 to 1964, it was a curious departure from Daimler's traditions, though there had been a roadster on the Century chassis in 1954. The SP250 was an all-new design, with a 140-bhp 2½-litre ohv V8 engine designed by Edward Turner who had recently come to Daimler from the Triumph motorcycle firm. The curiously-styled two-seater body was made of fibreglass which did not match ideally with the rather flexible and lightly braced chassis. Later models to the B specification (1961–3) had stiffer frames. The SP250 was raced successfully at club level in Britain and the United States, where it was twice raised to a higher class, as the A.C.-Bristol was. A number were also used by British police forces. The engine was later used in the Jaguar Mark II hull in the Daimler V8-250 saloon.

**Daimler SP250, 1960**
A 1960 Daimler SP 250 competing in a club race at Brands Hatch.

# Europe

No single European country produced the variety of sports cars made in Britain, and indeed the whole of continental Europe built fewer in terms of numbers. No manufacturer attained the half million production totals of M.G., yet some of the finest and most roadworthy machines came out of European factories in the 1950s and 1960s.

France, which had made so many magnificent machines in earlier years, contributed little to the sports-car scene, particularly in the larger classes. The once great firms of Delage, Delahaye, Hotchkiss and Talbot all restarted production after the war, but with *grands routiers* rather than competition sports cars. Admittedly a 3-litre Delage was second at Le Mans in 1949 and a 4½-litre Talbot won there in 1950, but these were special competition cars not sold to the public. While production of these four makes ran into several hundred each, Bugatti made no more than ten of a warmed-up Type 57 with new body and choice of manual or Cotal electromagnetic transmission. Its price of 3,000,000 francs, 50 per cent more than a Type 135 Delahaye, was enough to deter even the loyalest Bugattiste.

Salmson, which had made no sports cars since the 1920s, came up with an interesting GT coupé in the Italian style. This was the 2300S which used the well-tried 2.3-litre twin-ohc four in a channel-section frame with tubular cross members, and torsion-bar independent front suspension. The two-door body was styled by Eugene Martin and built by Chapron. These Salmsons could reach 118 mph (190 km/h), and had a number of rallying successes. These included class victories in the 1954 Tulip, Lyons-Charbonnières and Alpine Rallies, and fifth overall in the Liège-Rome-Liège. One ran at Le Mans in 1956 complete with full upholstery and a radio. Production of the 2300S ran from 1953 to 1956, by which time 227 had been made, including a few open two-seaters.

The only supporter of the old Salmson/Amilcar tradition was Germain Lambert who built a handful of traditional small sports cars from 1948 to 1952. He abandoned the independent suspension and front drive that had characterized his prewar cars, opting for beam axles and leaf springs, semi-elliptic at the front and quarter-elliptic at the rear. His cars were powered by the old 1,100-cc Ruby engine of which Lambert must have amassed a small stock, for Ruby were no longer in business. He had a number of successes in the Bol d'Or races in the early 1950s, but could not keep going with *une production artisanale* and closed his doors in 1952.

The most significant French sports cars of the 1950s had no links at all with prewar tradition. They were derived from quantity production saloons, the Dyna-Panhard and 4CV Renault. Panhard themselves produced a sports version of their 750-cc flat-twin front-wheel-drive Dyna, which they called the Junior, but the best known Panhard-derivative was

**Salmson 2300S, 1955**
Despite its Italian lines, the Salmson coupé was designed and built in France.

**Salmson 2300S, 1955**
One of the rare open versions of the Salmson 2300S, this two-seater ran unsuccessfully at Le Mans in 1955, and was subsequently shown at the Paris Salon, but never went into production.

the D.B. made by Charles Deutsch and René Bonnet. They built a streamlined coupé using the 750-cc Dyna engine, replacing it in 1955 with a fibreglass coupe powered by the enlarged (850-cc) Dyna engine. This gave a remarkable maximum speed of 96 mph (154.5 km/h), or more with a supercharger. Most production D.B.s were coupés, but open models were made for racing in which the marque was very successful. An open D.B. won the 1954 Tourist Trophy outright, and they won the Index of Performance at Le Mans, which allowed for engines of small capacity, in 1954, 1956, 1959, 1960 and 1961. D.B.s also had class wins in the Mille Miglia, Nürburgring 1000-Kilometre, and Sebring 12-Hour races.

In 1961 the partnership was dissolved, Deutsch joining Panhard as a technical adviser, while Bonnet made a few Renault-powered small cars in the former D.B. factory at Champigny-sur-Marne. One of these, the mid-engined Djet coupé, was taken over in 1965 by the rocket firm, Engins Matra of Romorantin. Renamed the Matra Djet, this was made with Renault engines of 70, 94 or 105 bhp, being joined in 1967 by a more comfortable four-seater coupé, the M. 530. This used a German Ford V4 engine but lacked the performance of the Djet. None of the Matras made the impact that the earlier D.B.s had

**D. B. Rallye 750 cc, 1954**
D.B. 750-cc Rallye coupé, seen taking part in the round-the-houses speed trial at the end of the 1954 Monte Carlo Rally. This steel-bodied coupé was rarer than the fibreglass version offered from 1955 onwards.

**Renault Alpine 1600S, 1972**
A 1972 Renault Alpine 1600S, of the type which won the 1973 World Rally Championship.

done, for there was less competition in the 1950s, and the little D.B.s were among the most exciting cars that a young Frenchman could buy.

A few other companies followed D.B.'s recipe of a flat-twin Panhard engine in a sporting coupé, though with much less success. They included Arista with a steel roadster body or a fibreglass coupé, the R.E.A.C., designed in Casablanca and built at Champigny-sur-Marne, the Marathon which carried its engine at the rear, and the German Dyna-Veritas.

Of the Renault-based cars, the best known was the Alpine. This reached the market later than the D.B., but by the late 1950s was the only serious rival to the flat-twin from Champigny. The first Alpine was a small two-seater fibreglass coupé built by rally driver Jean Rédélé whose father was the Renault concessionaire in Dieppe. He operated from his own works in Dieppe, but from the beginning he was supported by Renault which found it useful to have an unofficial competition department which could test its components yet not lay the nationalized company open to the charge of wasting money on competition work. Rédélé started well by winning his class in the 1955 Mille Miglia, so he christened his little coupé the Mille Miles. Engine options included 21-bhp 845-cc and 38-bhp 904-cc Renaults, the latter giving a top speed of 103 mph (166 km/h).

A convertible was added in 1957, and the Alpines were steadily improved during the 1960s. A 77-bhp 998-cc engine was available in 1961, and by 1964 a Gordini-tuned Renault R8 gave 87 bhp from 1,108 cc. The late 1960s saw the final development of the original Alpine coupés, the most powerful of which had 115-bhp twin-cam 1300 engines giving a top speed of 127 mph (204 km/h). These made first-class rally cars, and among victories between 1968 and 1973 were the Coupe des Alpes, Three Cities, Italian, Acropolis and Monte Carlo Rallies. In 1973 they won the World Rally Championship. For customers who were not so competition-minded, the larger but lower-stressed 92-bhp 1½-litre Renault 16 engine was available. Backed by Renault's international connections, the Alpine was made in several foreign countries, including Spain, Bulgaria, Mexico and Brazil.

As might be expected in a defeated and divided country, sports-car production in Germany was slow to get going. BMW did not make a car again until 1952, and then it was a bulky five-seater saloon. However, the excellent 328 engine provided the basis of several sports and racing cars in the lean and austere 1940s. The best-known sports car was the Veritas, made by two former BMW employees, engineer Ernst Loof and salesman Lorenz Dietrich. They set up their business at Hausern in Bavaria, part of the American Zone where manufacture of cars over 1 litre in capacity was forbidden. They therefore offered a rebuilding service, saying in effect to customers, 'Give us your BMW engine, gearbox and transmission, plus DM 35,000, and we will make you a Veritas sports car'. The engine was completely rebuilt, with modified cylinder head, larger valves and newly ground crankshaft, and a slab-sided aerodynamic body was provided.

Few cars were 'made' at Hausern, and in March 1948 Veritas moved to Messkirch in French-controlled Baden, where there were no restrictions on car manufacture. The early Veritas models were competition sports/racing cars, as well as open-wheel Formula 2 racing cars, but in 1949 Loof was asked for a car with some comforts for road use. This was the Komet two-seater coupé, joined later by the Saturn 2 + 2 coupé and the Scorpion convertible. The bodies were made by the well-known coachbuilder Spohn of Ravensburg, and the engines were modified BMW or a new 1,988-cc single-ohc six designed by Erik Zipprich and built by Heinkel. This was available in various stages of tune from 100 to 140 bhp and the cars were handsomer than the early Veritas. Unfortunately there was insufficient capital to develop the engine, and the discontent of many customers was one reason for the eventual failure of Veritas. Another was competition. In the late forties a Veritas was the only sports car a German could buy: by 1952 Porsche was becoming well established; also there was more chance of acquiring an imported car. Veritas closed after only seventy-eight cars had been made, though Ernst Loof set up a new company at the Nürburgring where he made a further twenty cars with wider bodies, still by Spohn. Dietrich signed a deal with Panhard whereby he bought Dyna-Panhard chassis which he clothed with bodies by Baur of Stuttgart, selling them under the name Dyna-Veritas.

The origins of the Porsche were really no less humble than those of Veritas. Ferdinand Porsche was imprisoned by the French who thought he had helped Hitler's war effort a little too enthusiastically, though he had never joined the Nazi party, and had no great respect for Hitler himself. During his two-year imprisonment, his son Ferry worked on the design of a

**Veritas, 1948/49**
An early Messkirch-built Veritas competition two-seater, from 1948 or '49. As photographed it is in racing trim, with the passenger seat blanked off, and only the driver has a head fairing behind him.

**Porsche 356B, 1962**
One of the first Porsche 356 coupés, built at Gmund in 1949.

small Volkswagen-based sports car. From the VW came an engine with modified cylinder heads, transmission and suspension. Different were the space-frame chassis and the body, a sleek aluminium sports two-seater. On the first prototype the engine was mounted ahead of the rear axle in what has come to be the classic mid-engined position, but on the production cars the layout was reversed, with the engine behind the axle in the same position as in the Volkswagen 'Beetle'. This enabled the space behind the seats to be used for luggage, and it was argued that with the engine further away the interior of the car would be quieter.

The prototype and first fifty production cars were made at a sawmill in the small Austrian village of Gmünd, where Porsche had retreated from the bombing of Stuttgart in 1944, but in 1950 the company moved back to Stuttgart, and production proper started in the Reutter coachbuilding factory. The 356 now had a steel body and a platform chassis. The VW engine was gradually enlarged and developed, to 1,286 cc (44 bhp) in 1951, to 1,488 cc (60 bhp) for 1952, and to 1,582 cc (95 bhp) in 1955. The original VW crash gearbox was replaced by a Getrag synchromesh transaxle in 1952.

Although its handling could catch out the unwary, particularly the sudden switch from understeer to oversteer in fast cornering, the 356 was one of the most popular sports cars of its era, and was widely used for SCCA club racing in the United States. Its first international success was to win the 1,100-cc class at Le Mans in 1951, and in the world of rallying victories included the 1952 Liège-Rome-Liège, the 1952 Lisbon and 1957 Alpine Rallies. The competition 550 won class honours at Le Mans, the Mille Miglia and Carrera Panamericana in 1954.

**Porsche 356B, 1962**
By 1954 the 356 was a familiar sight, yet the body lines had changed little from the prototype. This British-registered car is taking part in the London Motor Club's Little Rally of 1956.

36653

**Porsche 356B, 1962**
The 356B was made from 1959 to 1963 in coupé and cabriolet form. Engine size was 1,582-cc but tuning gave a variety of outputs from the 60-bhp *Damen* (ladies) model to the 90-bhp Super 90.

The classic Type 356 was a two-seater coupé, but cabriolets and roadsters were also made. The 4-camshaft Carrera engine was developed for racing, and in 1956 this unit was installed in the 356 body to make the Carrera coupé. In its final 2-litre form this could reach 130 mph (209 km/h), though 115 mph (185 km/h) was about the limit for the more common twin-cam 1.6-litre Super 90. Like its cousin the VW Beetle, the 356 was gradually improved over the years so that the last models had scarcely a single component that had not been changed, yet the overall appearance was little altered. Major improvements were a restyled front end with raised headlights and bumpers in 1959, and disc brakes in 1963 on the Type 356C. When production ended in 1965, a total of 76,303 had been made. In 1964 Porsche brought out the first really new model since they started, the 911. The engine was still rear-mounted, air-cooled and horizontal, but it was now a flat 6-cylinder of 1,991 cc. In its original form with two triple-choke carburettors it gave 130 bhp, but this was increased to 170 bhp on the 911S, and with a 2,195-cc capacity, power went up to 180 bhp. Dual-circuit disc brakes were provided on all four wheels, and the 2 + 2 coupé body had a family resemblance to that of the 356, though it was larger and roomier. The standard gearbox was a five-speed manual, though a Sportomatic semi-automatic four-speed was available on some 911s.

The 356 was dropped in 1965, but its 1,582-cc engine was used in the 911 body shell to make the 912, of which 30,745 were made from 1965 to 1969. Other variants on the 911 theme were the 911S with high-compression engines and forged alloy pistons, the 911E which had a longer wheelbase and 2,195-cc 155-bhp engine, and the 911T, the tamest of the family with carburettor rather than fuel injection, and 110 bhp from the 1,991-cc engine, 130 from the 2,195-cc.

Although Porsches were now building highly specialist sports/racing cars for top-class events like Le Mans, the 911s had a long career in club racing and also in rallies. In America they won the under 2-litre class Trans-Am Championship in 1967, 1968 and 1969, but the increase in engine size to over two litres then put them out of the running. They dominated Group 5 racing in Britain, and won the Monte Carlo Rally in 1968, 1969 and 1970. (A Turbo, developed from the 911, would win again in 1978.) Other rally victories included the 1967 Tulip, Geneva and Lyons-Charbonnières and the 1970 Swedish. Despite the relatively high price of all 911s, they have sold in larger numbers than any other

Continental sports car; from 1965 to the end of 1983 nearly 254,000 were sold not counting Turbos, and a 3,164-cc version is still made in 1986. Body styles were limited to three, the coupé, the full convertible (since 1982), and the Targa-top convertible which had a permanent roll bar fixed in a loop over the passenger compartment.

In 1969 a joint exercise between Porsche and Volkswagen produced the VW-Porsche mid-engined sports cars. These were intended to boost VW's image and lend the magic of the Porsche name to a cheaper range of cars. There were two models in a similar body shell, the 914/4 powered by an 80-bhp fuel-injected flat-4 VW 411 engine, and the 914/6 which used the flat-6 Porsche engine in its 110-bhp 911T form. There was also a competition version, the 914/6 GT with tuned 911 engine which finished sixth overall and won the GT class at Le Mans in 1970. This was the basis of the 916 which used a 2,341-cc flat-6 and was planned as a direct competitor to the Ferrari Dino. However, it was found that this would be more expensive than a 911S to make and the project was dropped after about twenty 916s had been made.

The body shell of the VW-Porsche was a curious-looking two-seater, styled by Gugelot Design to look like neither a VW nor a Porsche. They succeeded in this aim, but most people thought it ugly, with a little passenger compartment halfway between front and rear of a slab-sided body. The engine was mid-mounted, which should have given better handling than the rear-engined 911s, but as the great majority had the less powerful VW engine this was not of much importance. The 914/4 did not please Porsche enthusiasts, but it sold pretty well, nevertheless – 107,722 between 1969 and 1975. In contrast, the 914/6 was too close to the 911 in price (DM 19,000 compared with DM 19,970 for a 911T) and was withdrawn in 1972 after only 3,332 had been sold.

A VW-based sports car which looked not unlike the open Porsche 356 was the Austrian-built Denzel. Made in Vienna from 1948 to 1960, it used VW engines bored out to 1,281 cc and 1,488 cc, the latter developing 85 bhp. Top speed was 105 mph (169 km/h) and the Denzel's performance compared very well with the contemporary Porsche 356, with the advantage that the open body could seat three, side by side. Driven by their constructor Wolfgang Denzel and others, the cars did well in national events, winning the 1954 Austrian Alpine Rally, but never made much mark on the international scene.

The only two German manufacturers in the large sports car category were BMW and Mercedes-Benz, and of these only the latter were raced. BMW did not revive the 328, although the 326 2-litre engine went into their first postwar saloon, the 501 launched in 1952. In 1954 a brand-new 2.6-litre V8 engine went into this body shell, and it was a development of this engine which powered BMW's first postwar sports car, the Type 507, which was launched at the Frankfurt Motor Show in September 1955.

The enlarged V8 had a displacement of 3,168 cc giving 150 bhp in the 507 and 140 bhp in the 2 + 2 coupé known as the 503. It was a pushrod overhead-valve unit with a single camshaft in the neck of the V, and aluminium block and heads. Twin Zenith 32 carburettors were used. The transmission was a 4-speed all-synchromesh by ZF, and front suspension was independent by torsion bars. Top speed was 124 mph (199.5 km/h) and 0 to 60 (96.5 km/h) acceleration took 8.8 seconds.

The striking two-passenger body was the work of Count Albrecht Goertz who was asked to produce design studies by Max Hoffman, New York distributor of BMWs and many other fine cars. He took them to BMW in Munich and they were accepted without question. Goertz worked closely with technical director Fritz Fiedler who had designed the prewar BMW 328 engine, and the whole project was completed in ten months.

Purchasers of the 507 included Prince Rainier of Monaco and the kings of Greece and Morocco, but the car was not a best-seller. It had the misfortune to run concurrently with the Mercedes-Benz 300SL which outperformed it and, particularly in gull-wing form, was more glamorous and exciting. In price the cars were pretty close, the BMW costing from DM 26,500 to DM 29,950 during its three-year life span, and the Mercedes DM 29,000 for the gull-wing coupé and DM 32,500 for the roadster. Production of the 507 ended in 1958 after just 252 had been made. They are now highly priced collector's items especially in the United States where there is a club particularly devoted to the model.

Since the demise of the 507, BMW have never produced an open sports car though many of their saloons and coupés have been developed to give a very high performance.

Mercedes-Benz re-entered motor sport dramatically with their 300SL (3 litres, Sport, Leicht [Nimble]) which used a much-modified version of the engine used in the 300 saloon and 300S roadster. The 6-cylinder single-ohc engine was inclined at an angle of 45° to fit

**BMW 507, 1958 (*over*)**
This was BMW's answer to the Mercedes-Benz 300SL. It had a V8 engine with 150 bhp.

5 BMW

**Mercedes-Benz 300SL, 1951**
The original competition version of the Mercedes-Benz 300SL, first tested in November 1951 and announced to the press in March 1952.

under the very low bonnet. The chassis was a multi-tube space frame with slim and absolutely straight tubes, none of which had to withstand bending or torsional stresses. Obviously a closed car made entirely of this construction would not allow any access for the passengers, so a compromise was made, with very deep sills and upwards-opening gull-wing doors which became the best-known features of the cars. The hydraulic servo brakes worked in finned drums, and like most Mercedes-Benz cars since 1932 they featured all-independent springing with swing axles at the rear.

The three team cars had a tremendously successful 1952 season, finishing second and fourth in their first outing in the Mille Miglia, first in the Swiss Grand Prix, first and second at Le Mans and 1-2-3-4 in the Nürburgring 1,000-Kilometre Race. First and second places in the Carrera Panamericana brought the cars to the attention of American enthusiasts.

The 300SL might have remained a competition car pure and simple had it not been for the enthusiasm of the New York City Mercedes importer Max Hoffman, who encouraged the makers on what must have seemed a risky exercise by placing an order for a thousand cars. Introduced in 1954, the production 300SL had a redesigned body, strengthened frame and Bosch fuel injection in place of the three Solex carburettors of the competition cars. Power output went up from 175 to 215 bhp, and top speed was 140 mph (225 km/h), with 150 (241) attainable with the highest available gearing. A total of 1,400 gull-wing coupés were made between 1954 and 1957, when they were replaced by an open roadster with conventional doors. These were made until 1961 (1,858 built), the last models having disc brakes. However, it is the gull-wing which is the classic and most coveted 300SL; a tribute to this is the fact that a California company is currently building fibre-glassbodied replicas with 6-cylinder Chrysler engines.

In 1955 Mercedes-Benz produced the 300SLR which used an enlarged version of the 2½-litre straight-8 Grand Prix engine in an open two-seater body. With an output of 300 bhp and top speed of 180 mph (290 km/h), it was strictly a competition car, winning practically all the seasons' major sports car events. It would almost certainly have won at Le Mans, but the team was withdrawn after Levegh's car had crashed into the crowd, killing the driver and more than eight spectators. None was sold to the public, but chief engineer Rudi Uhlenhaut drove a gull-wing coupé version of the SLR.

The Daimler-Benz company also made a 'poor man's 300SL' in the shape of the 190SL, a roadster of similar shape with 105-bhp, 1,897-cc 4-cylinder engine. It was really more of a promenader than a sports car, for a top speed of 105 mph (169 km/h) and 0 to 60 (96 km/h) in 14 seconds was not particularly exciting for a 2-litre car in the late fifties. However, it sold

**Mercedes-Benz 300SL, 1955 (*over*)**
This is a British-registered car, but like all 300SLs, it has left-hand drive. The angle at which the engine was canted prevented a conversion to right-hand drive.

on its looks, and 25,881 found customers between 1955 and 1963. It was replaced by the 6-cylinder 230SL, a more angular design made in hard-top as well as roadster form, and this led to a whole series of SL models, the 250s and the 280s, 350s and 450s. Attractive high-speed tourers though they were, none of these was properly a sports car.

**Mercedes-Benz 300SL, 1955**
Driving compartment and operation of the 300SL's gull-wing doors.

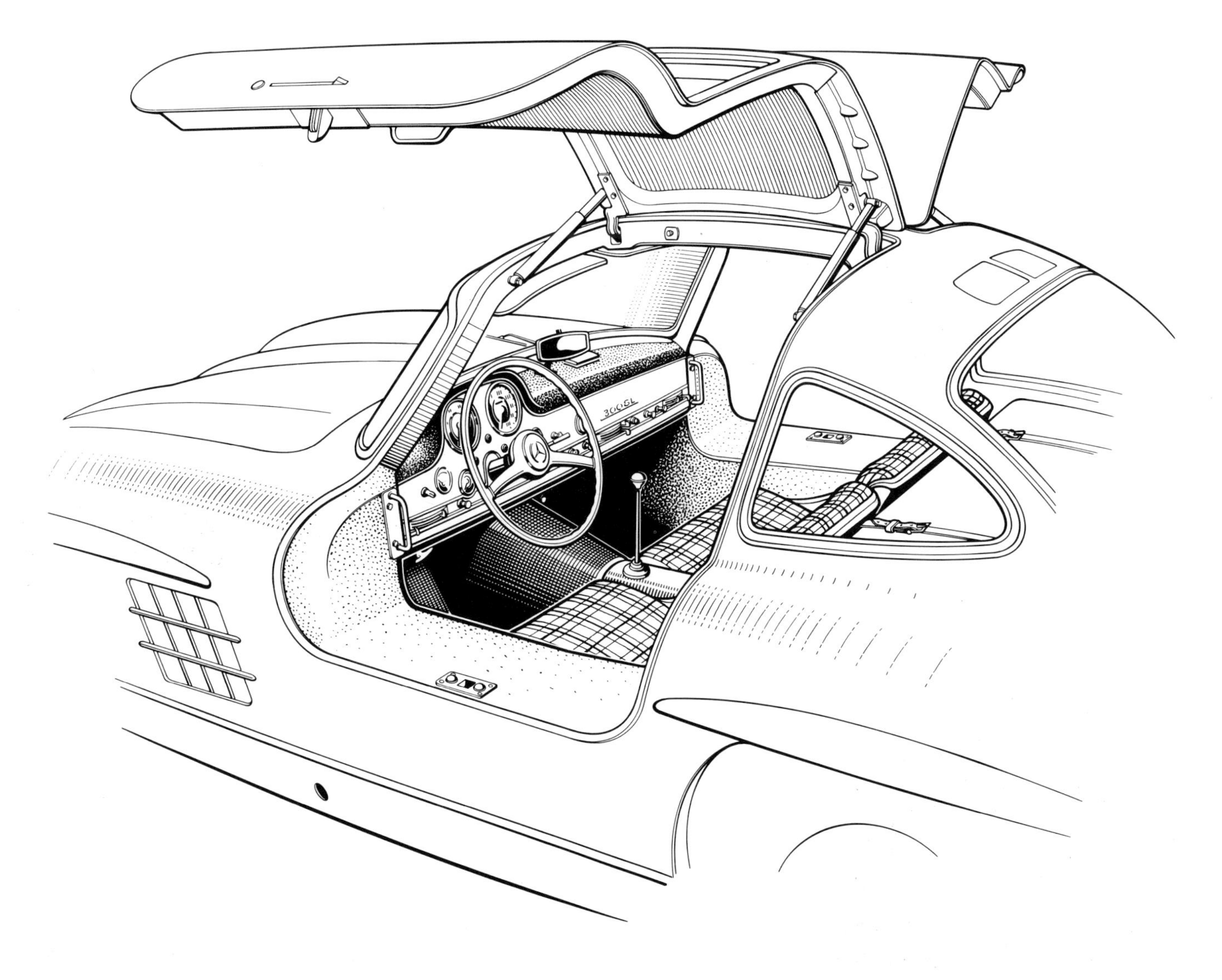

GB
WT 48

RGO 28

**Mercedes-Benz 300SL, 1956**
Two production models of the 300SL, photographed at Prescott in 1957. The absence of bumpers on the right-hand car give it a much lighter appearance.

In Italy the postwar years saw a remarkable renaissance of sports cars, and the fifties were far more interesting than the thirties had been. The renaissance took place on two fronts, the Fiat-based small sports car and the complex expensive machinery put out by Ferrari and Maserati. Alfa Romeo became a volume manufacturer and produced several sporting derivatives of their mass-produced saloons.

Fiat were early in the field with an attractive coupé derived from the 1100 saloon. The 1,089-cc engine was tuned to give 51 bhp and with a neat coupé body styled by Pininfarina the 1100S was capable of 95 mph (153 km/h). They took second and third places in the 1947 Mille Miglia, but were expensive (more than the basic price, without Purchase Tax, of an XK120 Jaguar), and only 401 were sold. Fiat's next sports car was even more expensive, and a complete breakaway from previous practice as it used a brand-new, 1,996-cc V8 engine developing 115 bhp. This compared well with the 110 bhp produced by the V12 Ferrari 166 of nearly the same capacity. The Fiat's cylinders were mounted at the unusual angle of 70°, instead of the more familiar 90°, in order to fit under a narrow bonnet.

The attractive two-seater coupé body was a multi-tubular frame covered with sheet steel, welded to a tubular steel-chassis frame. The suspension units were those of the Fiat 1100 saloon, coil springs, wishbones and anti-roll bar at front and rear. The four-speed gearbox had synchromesh on all forward speeds, quite unusual in the early 1950s. The standard bodies were made by Fiat, but Ghia and Zagato made a few coupés, and the engine was used in some Siata coupés, these having five-speed gearboxes and Vignale bodies.

Fiat never intended the 8V to be a big seller, and its body/chassis design did not lend itself to manufacture in large numbers. A total of 114 were made in three years, and its only major sporting success was to win the Italian GT Championship in the 2-litre class in 1954. O. Capelli finished fifth in the 1952 Targa Florio, and the 8V chassis and suspension were used as the basis for Fiat's experimental gas-turbine car of 1954.

During the 1960s Fiat took the sports car more seriously than they had ever done before. They had made an open two-seater based on the new 1100 during the 1950s, and in 1959 used a 1½-litre twin-cam engine developed by OSCA in the 1100 platform frame. This was the 1500S made to 1962, when it was replaced by the 1600S which was continued until 1966. There were also parallel 1500 models which used the ordinary pushrod-ohv Fiat 1500 engine. Girling disc brakes were available on both models from 1961, and the last 1600S cars had a five-speed gearbox. As with the MGA, the twin-cam Fiats were rarer than the pushrod models.

In 1961 Fiat brought out a sports coupé version of the 6-cylinder 2300 saloon. This 2300S has been described as a poor man's Ferrari (not too poor, though), and had a 135-bhp twin-carburettor engine which gave the four-seater coupé a top speed of 120 mph (193 km/h). As might be expected, there were disc brakes all round, and the car was well equipped with items such as electrically operated windows.

Fiat's rather belated answer to the Spridget was the 850 Spyder of 1965, a Bertone-styled open two-seater derived from the 850 saloon. The 843-cc engine was replaced by a 52-bhp 903-cc unit in 1968, and in this form the Spyder could touch the 100-mph (161-km/h) mark if one risked revving the engine up to 7,000 rpm. The 850 Spyder sold well in the United States and Canada, as did the coupé version which was made in large numbers, 380,000 compared with 140,000 Spyders.

There were also sports models of the 124, again in coupé and Spyder form. They had five-speed gearboxes on the later models (1969 onwards), and the Spyder with 2-litre fuel-injection engine was made for the American market up to the end of 1985. More exciting were the Fiat Dinos, which used the four-camshaft V6 Ferrari Dino engine in unitary hulls by Bertone (coupé) and Pininfarina (Spyder). Top speed was 130 mph (209 km/h), and if they were always somewhat overshadowed by the 'genuine' mid-engined Ferrari Dino, they were 25 per cent cheaper. Five-speed all-synchromesh gearboxes were found on all Dinos. About 7,500 were made, between 1967 and 1973; up to 1969 engine capacity was 1,987 cc, thereafter 2,418 cc.

Just as interesting as Fiat's own sports cars were those made by small companies using components from the 'Colossus of Lingotto'. Some of these, such as SIATA, had started before the war when they tuned the 500 Topolino, but the majority were phenomena of the fifties. One of the best known, and the longest lived, was the Abarth, creation of Austrian-born Carlo Abarth. After working with Piero Dusio on the abortive Cisitalia Grand Prix car, Abarth set up his own company to make silencers and tuning kits. In 1950 he launched the

**Fiat 8V coupé, 1952**
Like most of the 114 8Vs made, this has a factory-built body. It is one of the second series, which had different headlamp arrangements.

**Fiat Dyno, 1967**
Spyder and coupé versions of the Fiat Dino, powered by a V6 Ferrari engine. Pininfarina made the spyder bodies and Bertone the coupés.

ZONA OSPEDALIERA

first car to bear his name, a Fiat 1100-based coupé capable of 114 mph (183.5 km/h). One of these finished sixth overall in the 1950 Mille Miglia. Thereafter he built a great variety of Fiat-based sports cars, initially front-engined, but when the rear-engined 600 became available in 1955 Abarth really came into his own.

Two lines of development took place under the Abarth name: tuned versions of Fiat saloons which retained the basic body shell, and coupés with outside coachwork. Abarth

**Fiat-Abarth 1100, 1961**
A Fiat-Abarth 1000 bialbero (twin-cam) coupé. The light alloy body is by Zagato.

**Fiat-Abarth 850, 1967**
This Fiat Abarth has a similar appearance, but is powered by a smaller twin-cam engine of 850 cc. It is awaiting its turn at the Mittholz-Kandersteg hill climb in Switzerland in 1968.

ordered the latter from a variety of coachbuilders, particularly Allemano, Bertone, Boano, Ghia, Serena and Zagato. Abarth worked wonders with the small Fiat saloon: his hottest 500 was tuned to give 38 bhp and 87 mph (140 km/h) from an engine which in standard form produced 15 bhp and was good for 53 mph. The most dramatic of all was the OT1600 – this consisted of an 850 body shell with front-mounted radiator into which was fitted a 154-bhp twin-cam Abarth 1600 engine. Top speed was 137 mph (220.5 km/h).

The coupés used Fiat 500, 600 and 1100 engines, always rear-mounted and often enlarged in capacity. Some were based on the rear-engined Simca 1000 which appeared in 1961. These, again, had enlarged engines of 1,100 cc or more, and top speeds up to 143 mph (230 km/h). Like most Abarths they were very expensive for their size: a Simca-Abarth 1300 cost nearly double the price of an E-type Jaguar. They were also noisy and no fun to drive in city traffic, but their road-holding and performance endeared them to many. Abarth had countless successes in racing and hill climbs, in particular winning their class in the Nürburgring 500-Kilometre Race every year from 1960 to 1964, and again in 1966. The name ceased to appear on cars in 1971, but the Abarth expertise was retained by Fiat for tuning their successful rally cars in the 1970s.

The Abarth pattern was followed, more or less, by at least eight other Italian manufacturers. The 1946 Cisitalia coupé was a beautiful little car, setting the pattern for Italian GT cars for years to come. The Pininfarina body was chosen by the New York Museum of Modern Art in 1951 as one of eight cars showing excellence as works of art. A Fiat 1100 engine in 50- or 60-bhp forms gave it a top speed of 105 mph (169 km/h). Not many were made before Cisitalia's reorganization in 1949, and later cars from this Turin company were less attractive. Cisitalia finished by making coupé versions of the Fiat 600 up to 1961.

Moretti and OSCA also made lively small sports cars in the 1950s, though they both began by building their own tiny high-revving twin-cam engines, before turning to Fiat-based machinery. OSCA's twin-cam engine was used by Fiat in their 1600S sports cars made from 1959 to 1966.

Alfa Romeo built a larger number of sports cars in the postwar era than they had ever done before, thanks to a Marshall Plan-financed expansion which turned them from specialist makers of expensive cars to mass producers of quality saloons, most with above-average performance. They began postwar production with the prewar 6C-2500, now with steering-column gearchange and updated styling. Most were saloons or

**Alfa Romeo Giuletta Sprint Coupé, 1956**
Powered by a 1,290-c.c., twin-ohc 4-cylinder engine producing 65 bhp, the styling is by Bertone. This was one of the best small Italian cars of the 1950s.

**Alfa Romeo 1900, 1955**
The body on this model is by the Italian coach-builder Zagato. In the background a 1981 Alfa Romeo GTV 2.0.

cabriolets, but there was also a Super Sports variant with three carburettors and a top speed of 105 mph (169 km/h). The 130-mph (209-km/h) 6C 2500 Competizione was not a catalogue model, and only three were made.

In 1950 Alfa Romeo broke new ground with the 1900, a unitary-construction four-door saloon powered by a 1,995-cc twin-ohc 4-cylinder engine. Coupé and cabriolet models were made, but of more interest to the sportsman was the smaller Giulietta introduced in 1954. Intended as an answer to Fiat's 1100TV and Lancia's Appia, the 1,290-cc twin-cam Giulietta appeared as a two-door coupé about six months before the four-door saloon, while there was also an open two-seater spyder version. All had excellent road-holding and brakes, and well-spaced gear ratios. Top speed of a 'standard' 80-bhp Giulietta coupé was 105 mph (169 km/h) and the 90-bhp twin-carburettor Veloce could exceed 110 mph (177 km/h). They were deservedly popular all over Europe and in the United States. Production lasted from 1954 to 1962, during which time 27,141 coupés and 17,096 spyders were made. Of these, 5,854 had the more powerful Veloce engine.

The Giulietta was succeeded by the Giulia which had a larger engine of 1,590 cc in 92- or 112-bhp form, and similar body styles. Early models had disc brakes on the front wheels only, but from 1966 discs were employed all round on the GT Veloce. The next step was a further increase in capacity to 1,779 cc on the coupé, while the spyder was restyled by Pininfarina in 1966 and renamed the Duetto. In 1967 the larger engine went into the Duetto as well, and this was enlarged still further in 1970 to 1,962 cc. This model, known as the Spyder Veloce, has remained in production ever since – one of those evergreen designs, like the Fiat 124 Spyder, which have outlived all their competitors such as the MGB.

In common with Alfa Romeo and many other car makers, Lancia revived their prewar designs in 1946. These were the excellent Aprilia saloon and its smaller sister, the 903-cc Ardea. In 1950 the Aprilia was replaced by the Aurelia, similar in concept being a four-door saloon of above-average performance and handling, powered by a 1,754-cc V6 engine. A year later came an enlarged engine of 1,991 cc which went into the Aurelia B.21 sedan and a fastback two-door coupé, the B.20. The body was built by Pininfarina; Lancia supplied a platform chassis and the coachbuilder used over 100 hand-beaten panels welded together to form a monocoque construction. Top speed of the first series B.20 was 100 mph (161 km/h), but in 1953 came the third series with 2,451-cc engine developing 118 bhp and giving a speed of 115 mph (185 km/h). This was in turn replaced by the sportiest Aurelia of all, the 1954 fourth series with De Dion rear axle, which gave it more neutral handling than previous models. This was the first Lancia to have left-hand drive, the Italian factory being the last to abandon the tradition whereby quality sports cars had right-hand drive, regardless of the fact that the rule of the road had always been to drive on the right. The four-speed transaxle was controlled by a steering-column gearchange, but the purchaser could have a floor change made by Nardi who would also supply a hotter camshaft enabling the engine to develop 145 bhp. The classic B.20 was still a fastback coupé, but Pininfarina also made a convertible, the B.24.

The Aurelia B.20 had a very fine competition record in both racing and rallying. It was the last car capable of winning its class at Le Mans, which it did in 1951, and still being a practical machine for road use. In the 1951 Mille Miglia Giovanni Bracco and Umberto Maglioli came second behind a much more powerful and expensive Ferrari and ahead of another Ferrari, while third-series cars won the 1953 Liège–Rome–Liège and 1954 Monte Carlo Rallies.

The 1954 B.20 represented the high-water mark of the Aurelia coupés, for the fifth series of 1956 had a milder camshaft and only 110 bhp, while weight was increased because of a new gearbox and other improvements. The final, sixth, series (1957/8) was a more comfortable touring car than any of its predecessors but the sparkling performance was no longer there. Production of the B.20 ended in June 1958, after 2,568 had been made.

The Aurelia's successor was the Flaminia, a five/six-seater saloon which had its spyder and coupé variants by Touring and Zagato, but they were grand tourers rather than sports cars. Lancia enthusiasts had to wait until 1966 before another truly sporting car appeared. This was the coupé version of the front-wheel-drive Fulvia saloon, originally with an 80-bhp 1,216-cc V4 engine, but in its final form with a 1,584-cc unit delivering 118–130 bhp. Fiat's takeover of Lancia in 1969 provided a welcome injection of capital, and Lancia were able to field a works rally team of Fulvia HF coupés which won the World Rally Championship in 1972. They also helped the marque to win the 1974 Championship, together with the Beta

TXT 25

**Lancia Aurelia B.20, 1955 *(left)***
All in all, 2,568 of these fast and comfortable coupés were built, in six different series.

**Lancia Aurelia B.20, 1953**
A Lancia Aurelia B.20 3rd Series in the 1954 Monte Carlo Rally. A team mate of this car, driven by Louis Chiron and Ciro Bassadonna, won the rally that year.

coupé and the Stratos. Obviously the Fulvia HF bought from the dealer did not have the power or performance of the works rally cars, but they shared a number of features such as aluminium panels and plexiglass windows. A five-speed gearbox was featured, and top speed was 115 mph (185 km/h). Just 7,102 HF coupés were built, between 1966 and 1972, compared with 160,000 of the ordinary Fulvia coupés. These mostly had the same factory-built notchback bodies as the HF, but some wore fastback Zagato bodies.

More than any other make, the postwar Italian sports-car renaissance was symbolized

**Lancia Aurelia B.20, 1953**
A Lancia Aurelia B.20 in a 1954 production car race at Silverstone, leading Ken Wharton's Daimler Conquest.

**Lancia Aurelia B.24, 1954**
A Lancia Aurelia B.24 spyder by Pininfarina. The absence of bumpers indicates that this is a prototype.

by Ferrari, the full-blooded cars with the Prancing Horse mascot which have dominated sports-car and Grand Prix racing for just on forty years. The name Ferrari was celebrated in motor sport long before any cars bore it proudly on their bonnets. Born in 1898, Enzo Ferrari began his racing career in the 1920s, and from 1930 to 1937 he ran the very successful Scuderia Ferrari team of Alfa Romeos, which effectively took the place of a works team. When he parted from Alfa one of the terms of the agreement was that he should not use his name in racing for at least four years, so the first cars of his own manufacture, which were built in 1940, carried the name Auto Avio Costruzione. Only two of these were made, and the first Ferrari, in name as well as in all other respects, appeared in December 1946. This had a 1½-litre V12 engine designed by Giaochino Colombo, with one overhead camshaft to each bank, five-speed gearbox, tubular frame and independent front suspension by transverse leaf springs. Known as the 125, this was made as a sports and as a racing car, differing little except for the wider body and road equipment of the former. Their first race took place in May 1947 at Piacenza, and Ferrari's first wins were gained later that year at Forli and Parma by the veteran driver Tazio Nuvolari. For 1948 the engine size was increased to 1,994 cc, and the model name changed to 166 (Ferrari model numbers were taken from the capacity in cubic centimetres of a single cylinder). This was only made as a sports car, because the prevailing Grand Prix regulations limited supercharged racing cars to 1½ litres. One of these early 166s won the 1948 Targa Florio, the marque's first major victory, with Clemente Biondetti at the wheel. They were known as the Corsa Spyder, and only about ten were made before they were replaced by the Mille Miglia named in honour of Biondetti's win in the 1948 race. This was similar mechanically, but had a more civilized all-enveloping body by Touring. One of these won the first postwar Le Mans race, in 1949, driven by Luigi Chinetti; closed cars were also made; of a total of about forty-two second series 166s made between 1949 and 1953, a dozen were coupés.

Like Bugatti, Ferrari did not always abandon an old model when a new one appeared, so there was a three-year overlap while the 166 was still being made alongside newer models. These were essentially enlargements on the same theme, the 2,340-cc 195 and the 2,562-cc 212, introduced in 1950 and 1951 respectively. These had five-speed gearboxes, the engine being so flexible that a 212 could move away from 10 mph (16 km/h) in top.

Maximum speed was 120 mph (193 km/h), and 0 to 100 mph (161 km/h) took 22.5 seconds.

These early Colombo-designed cars were very small, the 166 wheelbase being shorter than that of a T-series M.G. A new larger series began with the arrival of designer Aurelio Lampredi in 1951. He produced the big V12s aimed at the American market, the 4,102-cc 342, 4,522-cc 375 and 4,962-cc 410 Superamerica, the latter giving 340 bhp at 6,000 rpm. The final development of this line was the 500 Superfast, whose 4,962-cc engine gave 400 bhp, and propelled a two-seater coupé at up to 170 mph (273.5 km/h). Only thirty-seven of these were made, between 1964 and 1966.

Glamorous though they were, the big Lampredi-designed cars could never hope to sell in serious numbers, so in 1953 he brought out a 3-litre version to replace the original Colombo-designed cars. This was the 250 Sport with open spyder bodies and a choice of four- or five-speed all-synchromesh gearboxes, followed by the 250 Europa – a two-seater coupé with 200 bhp. Only four speeds were available in this car which, in 1956, evolved into the 250GT, one of the best-known Ferrari models. This combined traditional Ferrari performance with a comfortable interior and accommodation for four passengers. The standard coachwork was by Pininfarina, and it was joined in 1959 by the 250GTB with shorter wheelbase and a Scaglietti body which was strictly a two-seater. The 250GT was made until 1964 when it was replaced by the 275GTB with five-speed transaxle, all-independent suspension and dual-circuit servo disc brakes. Also strictly a two-seater, this was made from 1964 to 1966 in coupé and convertible form. It was further improved in the GTB4 which had dry-sump lubrication, six Weber carburettors and a top speed of 165 mph. Only 289 of these were made, from 1966 to 1968. Ferrari now had one of the fastest road cars in the world, and it seemed unlikely that it could be improved on, but in 1968 came the ultimate development of the long line of front-engined Ferraris.

**Auto Avia Costruzione 815**
The first car built by Enzo Ferrari, although it did not carry his name, was the Auto Avio Costruzione Tipo 815, powered by a 1½-litre straight-8 engine using two Fiat 508C heads on a specially cast block. Two were made, one of which is seen here on test in February 1940. They led their class in that year's abbreviated Mille Miglia, though neither completed the course.

The GTB4 Daytona had an all-new body, styled by Pininfarina and built by Scaglietti. The production run consisted of 955 coupés and fifty open spyders. The engine was a new four-camshaft V12 of 4,390 cc which developed 352 bhp. The basic chassis layout was retained, including the rear-mounted five-speed gearbox, but the wheel tracks were wider. The Daytona was a very beautiful car with an awe-inspiring performance. In second gear it could exceed most of the world's speed limits at 86 mph (138.5 km/h), while it could top 140 mph (225 km/h) in fourth and 175 (281.5) in fifth. It is difficult to quote precise maximum speeds for these ultra-fast cars, but the Daytona was probably at least as fast as the more celebrated Lamborghini Miura. With its incredible performance went refinement and an amazingly flexible engine.

The only way such a car could be further improved would be to make it still faster, but Ferrari preferred to break the mould and bring out a brand-new design for his next super-car. This was the mid-engined Berlinetta Boxer, announced in 1973. For three years it was made alongside the Daytona, until the latter was dropped in 1974, after 1,005 had been made.

**Ferrari 166 Inter, 1949**
A 1949 Ferrari 166 Inter 2-litre coupé, body by Carrozzeria Touring of Milan.

**Ferrari 212, 1952**
The same family as the 166, this is a 212 coupé of 1952 with 2½-litre engine and five-speed gear-box.

**Ferrari 250 GTB Berlinetta, 1960**
The short-wheelbase Ferrari 250 GTB with Scaglietti body.

Throughout the period under discussion, Ferrari had been winning countless sports-car races, some with specially designed competition cars which are outside the scope of this book, others with near-standard machines such as the 250GT. This model did particularly well in the Tour de France, a 3,100-mile (4,988-km) circuit of the country which included special stages on several of the most famous tracks and hill climbs. After six consecutive wins between 1957 and 1962 with the Europa or 250GT, Ferrari became aware of the competition from cars like the Aston Martin Zagato and the lightweight E-type Jaguar. In order to remain competitive in the sports car class (the Worlds Sports Car Championship was for GT rather than open cars from 1962), Ferrari brought out the 250GTO (Grand Turismo Omologato) for 1963.

Strictly speaking, for a car to be Omologato (homologated) a minimum of 100 had to be built, but Ferrari made only forty GTOs. They got round the rules by saying that the GTO was a mildly modified version of the short-wheelbase 250GT, of which several hundred had been made. The main difference was a new body shape styled by Ferrari themselves (the 250GT was a Pininfarina design) with a tiny oval radiator grille and a long nose for aerodynamic efficiency. The triple-carburettor engine gave 290 bhp, compared with 220 or 240 bhp (according to tuning) for the 250GT, although some GTs were fitted with the GTO engine. The top speed of a GTO was around 160 mph (257.5 km/h). It was very popular with drivers such as Innes Ireland, Michael Parkes and Graham Hill, all of whom praised its untemperamental engine and overall controllability. Among its more impressive successes were second overall at Le Mans in 1962, victories in the 1963 and 1964 Tours de France, and in the 1962 and 1963 Tourist Trophies.

By the mid-1960s Ferrari was aware that there was a gap in its range of cars which needed to be filled. The large and powerful front-engined V12s were very expensive, but

they had nothing with which to meet the challenge of Porsche whose 911S was selling extremely well. Their answer was the Dino 206, later 246GT, which had a complicated ancestry. Enzo Ferrari's son Alfredino died at the age of twenty-four in 1956, but he had already begun to work on a 1½-litre V6 engine to be used in the company's Formula 2 racing cars. These went into action in 1957 and had a very successful career; in modified form this engine won Mike Hawthorn the Formula 1 World Championship in 1958. They were considered too expensive and complex power units to manufacture in any numbers, so a simplified version, re-worked by Franco Rocchi, was chosen for the 166P prototype of

**Ferrari 250GT, 1958**
The celebrated Ferrari 250 GT, known as the Tour de France after six consecutive wins in this event, from 1957 to 1962. This is a 1958 model.

**Ferrari 365 GTB4 Daytona, 1972 (*over*)**
One of the fastest front-engined road cars ever, the Ferrari GTB4 Daytona had a top speed of 175 mph (282 km/h). This is a 1972 coupé.

DAYTONA

6 PEV

**Ferrari GTO, 1962**
A Ferrari GTO at Le Mans in 1963. This is the Beurlys/Langlois car which finished second.

**Ferrari GTO, 1962**
A 1962 Ferrari GTO coupé.

1965. (Ferrari always thought of the Dinos as a separate line of cars from the other models, and chose a new numbering system – the first two figures represented the engine size in decilitres, and the last the number of cylinders.) In 1966 the 166P became the 206S and was used for competition work, but meanwhile Pininfarina had produced a styling exercise at the 1965 Paris Salon, clothing the 206S in a beautiful low two-seater coupé body. At the following year's Turin Show came the second version, closer to the production model in appearance, with faired-in headlamps and the scoops running rearwards from the doors, which helped to cool not the engine but the brakes.

The 1967 Formula 2 regulations stipulated that the engines had to be derived from those used in production cars, and this spurred Ferrari to put the Dino engine into production. However, they could not make enough to meet the regulations on their own, so arranged to have the engine made for them by Fiat and used in a front-engined Fiat sports car which also bore the name Dino. Apart from anything else, this was the first co-operation between the two companies that led eventually to a permanent link. The Ferrari Dino 206 carried its 1,987-cc 180-bhp V6 engine just behind the cockpit, mounted transversely, driving through a 5-speed gearbox. The engine was of all-alloy construction and so was the body, which was built by Scaglietti to the Pininfarina design. It was a beautiful car, but although it handled better than the Porsche it lacked the power to see off the German car. Its successor, launched in 1969, was the 246GT, whose larger engine (2,418 cc, 195 bhp) had a cast-iron block. The body was now made of steel, with aluminium panels, and was 3.7 in (94 mm) longer, although the cars looked very similar. Performance was improved, with a top speed of 148 mph (238 km/h), and although the Dino was more temperamental than the Porsche it had, and has, a devoutly loyal following. In 1973 the GTS model was added to the range, with a detachable Targa top.

**Maserati 3500 GT, 1960**
A Maserati 3500 GT with spyder body by Vignale.

Ferrari's great rival on road and track was Maserati, the Modena-based company which gained a new lease of life when they were taken over by the Orsi family in 1947. Before the war the handful of road-going Maseratis made were street-legal versions of racing cars, but Adolfo Orsi wanted to make proper road cars, and at the 1947 Geneva Show he launched a two-seater coupé powered by a 1½-litre single-ohc 6-cylinder engine derived from that of the company's voiturette racers. It had a tubular chassis and neat, functional body-style by Pininfarina. With 65 bhp and 95 mph (153 km/h) it was not a match for the Ferrari 166, but in fact more were sold – sixty Maseratis compared with about forty-two Ferraris. The original A6 was replaced by the 2-litre A6G in 1950, but Maserati were once more heavily involved with Grand Prix racing, and only sixteen of the 2-litre cars were made.

Between 1950 and 1957 virtually no road-going Maseratis were made, though sports/racing cars such as the 2-litre A6 GCS and 3-litre 300S did well on the circuits. In 1957 appeared the first of a new range of production cars with 3,485-cc twin-ohc 6-cylinder engines, the 3500GT. With 230 bhp, top speeds in the region of 140 mph (225 km/h) were possible in considerable comfort. Standard bodies were a coupé by Touring and a spyder by Vignale, but a number of special bodies were made as well on a chassis that sold about 2,000 units between 1957 and 1964. Much more expensive and rarer was the 5000GT which used a four-camshaft V8 engine derived from that of the 450S sports/racing car in a 3500GT chassis. Although listed from 1959 to 1964, the 5000GT was not really a production car. A few were assembled as and when customers ordered them, and the total made has been estimated at thirty-two or thirty-seven. Top speed was 170 mph (273.5 km/h), and the later models had Lucas fuel injection. Bodies were various, mostly coupés by Allemano. Among the select group of customers for the 5000GT were the Shah of Iran, the Aga Khan and Gianni Agnelli, head of Fiat.

The 3500GT's successors were the shorter-wheelbase Sebring coupé (1962-66) and the Mistral coupé or spyder (1964–70). These had the 3,485-cc engine to start with, followed by 260-bhp 3,693-cc and 275-bhp 4,014-cc. Automatic transmission was optional. Parallel with these was a series of V8-powered cars, the Ghibli two-seater coupé or spyder which was Maserati's answer to the Ferrari Daytona, the Mexico four-seater coupé and the Quattroporte (four-door) saloon. The Ghibli was one of the fastest cars of its period, with a top speed of 170 mph (273.5 km/h). Made from 1967 to 1973, the Ghibli sold 1,274 units. The last Maserati of the 1960s was the Indy, also using the big V8 engine but a pioneer in being the first Maserati to have unitary construction. The body was a Vignale 2 + 2 coupé and top speed was 156 mph (251 km/h).

Although selling in reasonable numbers, Maseratis lacked the glamour of Ferraris, perhaps because after about 1960 they had no racing triumphs to back them up. However, the 1960s saw a new Italian make which never raced at all, yet had tremendous charisma – the Lamborghini. It is rare for a new make of car to come into the limelight and hold its position for more than a few years, to become a household name. Lotus did it in the fifties

**Lamborghini Miura, 1966**
This was first shown at the Geneva Salon in 1966, and it quickly became a classic. Both ends could be tilted up, to provide easy access at the front to the spare wheel and front suspension, and at the back to the transversely placed 3.9-litre V12 engine.

and the most striking newcomer of the sixties was undoubtedly Lamborghini. Ferrucio Lamborghini was a successful manufacturer of farm tractors and central-heating equipment who realized his dream of becoming a car maker in 1963 with the launch of his 350GTV. This was a Gran Turismo coupé powered by a 270-bhp 3½-litre four-overhead-camshaft V12 engine designed by Giotto Bizzarini, who soon left the project to return to his own design studios. This engine was later enlarged to just under four litres and this was the power unit that went into the car that came to be called the Miura.

This had a somewhat unusual background in that the chassis was built, unknown to the boss, by three Lamborghini employees, Gianpaolo Dallara, Bob Wallace and Paolo Stanzini, in their spare time. It was a welded box-section structure with coil independent suspension all round, in which the V12 engine was located transversely. Power was

**Lamborghini Islero, 1968**
The Islero had a 4-litre V12 engine and a 2 + 2 seating arrangement. It was lavishly equipped, with electrically powered windows and air-conditioning. The later S version had 350 bhp under the bonnet.

**Maserati Ghibli, 1970**
Maserati had been making sports and racing cars since 1926, often with custom-built coachwork. This magnificent Maserati Ghibli spyder has coachwork by Ghia.

transmitted to the clutch by a pair of spur gears, and thence to a 5-speed gearbox. From there another pair of gears transmitted power to the differential. This chassis met with Lamborghini's approval and went on exhibition at the 1965 Turin Show. By the Geneva Show the following March it had acquired a body designed by Marcello Gandini of Bertone, and was given the name Miura after a celebrated Spanish breeder of fighting bulls, Eduardo Miura. At first considered as a one-off show car, the Miura attracted many serious enquiries from would-be customers, and Lamborghini decided to put it into production.

The first car was delivered to its owner in March 1967, and 108 Miuras were sold that year. The next year, the first of full production, 184 cars were delivered, and the Miura was on its way to becoming a legend. The original version had a top speed of 173 mph (278.5 km/h), and this was increased to just short of 180 mph (289.5 km/h) on subsequent models. Road-holding was exceptional and the Miura was remarkably untemperamental, suffering little from the plug-fouling or irregular idling often associated with exotic machinery. Customers included Canadian Grand Prix sponsor Walter Wolf, who has owned several subsequent Lamborghinis, and a number of pop stars, as well as wealthy enthusiasts on both sides of the Atlantic.

In January 1969 an improved model, the Miura S, was announced. This had a more powerful engine giving 375 hp, with air conditioning and electrically operated windows as options. Two years later came the final development, the Miura SV with wider rear tyres to cope with the still greater power resulting from different cam timing, modified carburettors and bigger inlet valves. Output was now 385 bhp at 7,850 rpm, and top speed 179.8 mph (289.3 km/h). Most of the bugs had been ironed out by this time, and the SV was, and is, the most desirable of all the Miuras. It remained in production for a little more than twelve months, as it was to be succeeded by the even more dramatic Countach. Total production of Miuras was 765.

Outside the main car-producing European countries few sports cars were made. In Spain a brief but brilliant comet flashed across the scene in the shape of the Pegaso. This was designed by Wilfredo Ricart and built by ENASA, the government-owned Barcelona company who were, and still are, Spain's largest makers of trucks and buses. Ricart's design was immensely complicated, with a four-camshaft V8 engine featuring dry-sump lubrication and sodium-cooled exhaust valves. This was the first use of twin camshafts per block in a road-going car, earlier examples being purely racing engines by Mercedes-Benz, Miller and Novi. Ferrari did not use this design for a road car until the GTB4 Daytona of 1968. The gearbox had five indirect speeds without synchromesh, and was mounted on the rear axle. In its original form, as shown at the 1951 Paris Salon, the 2½-litre engine developed between 165 and 225 bhp according to tune, but later versions were enlarged to 2.8 and then 3.2 litres. The latter could be supercharged, when output was claimed as 350 bhp. From about 1955 Ricart simplified his engines, using pushrod V8s of 4, 4½ or 4.7 litres, the largest giving 300 bhp.

Pegaso bodies were mostly by outside coachbuilders, although early models had factory bodies, a neat 2 + 2 coupé something like a Ferrari 166, and a convertible. These were more restrained than the subsequent creations by Saoutchik. Later Pegaso chassis were shipped to Milan to be bodied by Touring, but this made them very expensive, and the final cars were Spanish-bodied by José Serra. Pegasos were raced on rare occasions, but their brakes were inadequate for their weight, and the company did not keep up with the latest technology such as disc brakes. Commercial vehicles claimed most of their attention and finance, and the Pegaso car was dropped in 1958 after about 100 had been made. Of these, only four were later pushrod Z.103 models.

Although their rally drivers and cars have scored innumerable successes, Sweden has never been renowned for its sports cars. However, both its leading manufacturers have made sports cars during the period under review. Saab were first in the field, with an open two-seater derived from the 3-cylinder 93 saloon. Only six of these were made, in 1956, and they were intended for racing, with no production in mind. The 748-cc engine and transmission were turned round, compared with the saloon, so that the engine was behind the front wheels. This gave better weight distribution as the two-seater steel/light-alloy monocoque was much lighter than the four-seater saloon.

The 1956 car was christened the Sonett, and this name was revived ten years later when Saab launched a GT coupé based on the 841-cc 96 saloon. By now the company had a worldwide reputation for their rally cars, thanks to the successes of Erik Carlsson, his wife

**Pegaso Z.103, 1957**
The exotic Pegaso sports cars, with their complicated V8 engines, were built at the old Hispano-Suiza factory in Barcelona. This is one of the four Z.103s built with more simple pushrod V8 engines.

P
B-105377

Pat Moss, Ove Andersson, Simo Lampinen and others. American dealers in particular asked for a more sporting car than the 96, so Saab commissioned two design studies for a GT coupé on the 96 floorpan. Elements of both designs were included in the production version, which was later restyled by the Italian, Sergio Coggiola. Initially the 60-bhp 841-cc Saab 3-cylinder engine was used, giving a top speed of 105 mph (169 km/h), but from autumn 1967 the German Ford 1,498-cc 65-bhp V4 which powered the saloons was adopted on the Sonett as well. For 1971 the larger 1,698-cc V4 was used on the Sonett III which remained in production until 1974. Most went to North America, and it was the increasingly strict emission and safety regulations there which caused Saab to abandon the Sonett. Of the total of 10,219 made, 8,351 were Sonett IIIs.

Volvo did not have Saab's rallying background, and the P1800 (1961–72) was perhaps more of a sporting coupé than a true sports car. It was based on the Amazon saloon but had a totally new two-seater body styled in-house by Volvo. As the company was short of factory space, body production was contracted out to Pressed Steel in England, and the cars were assembled by Jensen at West Bromwich. The original 1,778-cc engine gave 100 bhp and 105 mph, but in 1969 it was increased to 1,985 cc and given fuel injection. This boosted output to 125 bhp. By this time all production was undertaken in Sweden.

The P1800 had quite a following in Britain where it received welcome publicity as the personal transport of the Saint, hero of a long-running television series. Variants included the P1800S (1963–69) with dual-circuit braking and 2-litre engine on the last models, the P1800E with fuel injection, and the 1800ES (1971–73) which was a sporting estate in the Reliant Scimitar GTE fashion. Total production of the P1800s was 41,407 coupés and estates.

**Saab Sonett, 1956**
Only six of this model, which was intended to be a racing car, were ever built. With a glassfibre body, the complete car weighed just over 1,000 lb (500 kg) and was powered by a two-stroke, 3-cylinder engine with a top speed of 100 mph (160 km/h).

**Volvo P1800, 1961** ***(opposite top)***
The "other" Swedish sports car, this became popular especially in Britain and the USA. Over 47,000 were built. This is an early version, assembled at the Jensen factory in England.

**Volvo 1800ES, 1972** ***(opposite below)***
From 1971 to 1973, the P1800 sports car was available as a kind of station wagon, with a large glass hatch at the back. A total of 8,077 of this version were built.

FKW 138

**Saab Sonett V4, 1967**
The Sonett sports car had a two-stoke 3-cylinder engine in the beginning, but in 1967 it got a V4 engine which took up so much space that the bonnet had to be given a characteristic "bump".

P80294

# The United States of America

The sports-car boom in the United States was sparked off by imported cars such as the M.G. TC, Allard J2 and Jaguar XK120, leading to the giants of Detroit taking a serious interest in the subject from the mid-1950s onwards. Before that, a number of enthusiasts had entered the fray, in particular Briggs Cunningham, the millionaire sportsman who had many successes in ocean yacht racing. His ambition was to see an American car win at Le Mans, and between 1950 and 1955 he built some very fast and exciting cars, although he never saw his dream come true. The nearest he got was third in 1953 and 1954. The competition Cunninghams had tuned Chrysler V8 engines, and this unit also powered the few street Cunninghams which were known as C3s. They had attractive fastback coupé bodies by Vignale of Italy and a top speed of 145 mph (233.5 km/h). Having the bodies built in Italy made the cars initially very expensive, and at $9,000 the C3 found only twenty-six customers in 1953 and 1954.

There were numerous other American sports cars made in small numbers in the 1950s – perhaps the best known was the Kurtis, built at Glendale, California. Frank Kurtis had made Indianapolis-type racing cars since before the war, and his sports cars built between 1949 and 1958 were specialized machines intended for competition rather than road use. They had light, open wheeled two-seater bodies and the engines were supplied to the customer's choice, mostly Cadillac or Mercury. The nearest to a regular road car was his roadster of 1950 with slab-sided body, but after thirty-six had been made the design was sold to Earl Muntz and subsequent cars were marketed under the name Muntz Jet. The Excalibur J and Woodill Wildfire used the Kaiser Henry J 2.6-litre 4-cylinder engine, while a still smaller engine of only 726 cc powered the tiny Crosley Hotshot. No beauty, the Hotshot was likened to a bath-tub on wheels, but it could do 75 mph (120.5 km/h) and had some success in the smallest class of SCCA racing.

**Cunningham *(below and opposite, top)***
Two of the Cunninghams entered at Le Mans in 1953. The open car, No. 1, was driven by Briggs Cunningham and Bill Spear, finishing 7th, while the coupé, No. 3, was driven by Charles Moran and John Bennett into 10th place. Their team mates Phil Walters and John Fitch were best placed, with third.

**Chevrolet Corvette, 1953 *(below)***
The Chevrolet Corvette's first European appearance was at the 1953 Paris Salon. Though the car was attractive to look at, its 3½-litre 6-cylinder engine did not set the Seine on fire.

**Chevrolet Corvette, 1961 *(over)***
By 1961 the Corvette had been developed into a fine performer. On the most powerful models, 0–60 (96.5 km/h) took 5.9 seconds, compared with 11 seconds for the 1953 car. The sculptured sides and dual colour scheme were Corvette features from 1956 to 1962.

The Chevrolet Division of General Motors had never been associated with glamour or performance cars of any description until the launch in 1953 of the Corvette. Originally a General Motors Styling show car and the brainchild of Harley Earl, this was not only America's first sports car from a major car producer, but also the world's first car with an all-fibreglass body. It was a very attractive-looking two-seater but with only 150 bhp from the lightly tuned stock Chevy six engine (the old Cast Iron Wonder which had been introduced in 1929), and a two-speed automatic transmission, it was hardly a great performer. In 1956 the new 255-bhp V8 engine was installed in the Corvette, and a three-speed manual transmission was also available. Thanks to the work of Chevrolet engineer Zora Arkus-Duntov, outputs built up steadily, and by 1962 the 5,358-cc unit with fuel injection was giving 380 bhp. The following year came the Sting Ray which, apart from the engine,

**Ford Mustang, 1966**
The enormously successful Ford sports car in fastback coupé version, with 2 + 2 seating.

was an all-new car. The body was completely restyled and in addition to the roadster there was a striking split-window fastback coupé. Suspension was all-independent, by coil springs at the front and by transverse leaf spring and lower wishbones at the rear. The latter was inspired by earlier competition Corvettes developed by Arkus-Duntov. The wheelbase was 4 in (102 mm) shorter, rear track 2 in (51 mm) narrower and frontal area was reduced by 1 $ft^2$ (0.09 $m^2$). Weight distribution (front axle figure first) was 48/52 compared with 53/47 for previous Corvettes. Ride and handling were significantly improved. With the most powerful engine option giving 360 bhp, top speed was 147 mph (236.5 km/h).

Chevrolet now had a sports car which could compare well with European competition, and at a sensible price of $4,037 for the roadster and $4,252 for the coupé. This was reflected in sales which were over 21,000 in the Sting Ray's first year, compared with the best figure of 14,500 for any previous year. The Sting Ray was steadily developed during its five-year lifespan, notably in 1965 when disc brakes were fitted and engine displacement went up to 6,490 cc. This became 6,997 cc in 1966 when 425 bhp was developed, giving 0 to 60 (96.5 km/h) acceleration in less than five seconds, and a theoretical top speed with the 3.08 rear axle of 170 mph (273.5 km/h). Most powerful of all was the L88 competition engine of 1967/8 which developed a staggering 560 bhp.

The Sting Ray name disappeared in 1968, to be revived as one word on the new Stingray for 1969. Although the Stingray sold very well, the favoured car of the Corvette connoisseur will always be the Sting Ray of 1963 to 1968. Corvettes were continued throughout the 1970s and up to the present day. By 1985 sales had exceeded 750,000.

Ford's answer to the Corvette was the Thunderbird, introduced for the 1954 season. With a 198-bhp 4¾-litre V8, the Thunderbird was a good 10 mph (16 km/h) faster than the Corvette, and was in the eyes of most people a better looking car with a clean-lined two-seater body and, in 1956, a rakish rear-mounted spare-wheel cover. In its first year the Thunderbird sold 16,155 units, more than double the total number of Corvettes up to that year. A hardtop with distinctive portholes behind the windows was available on 1956 models, and for 1958 the Thunderbird was made into a four-seater and whatever claim it had to being a sports car was lost. Chevrolet was tempted to reply with a four-seater Corvette, but wisely resisted, so retaining the character of their sports car.

Ford's next contender in the sporting-car stakes was the Mustang. Launched in April 1964, this was promoted as a personal car for the young, or young-in-heart driver rather than as a sports car. Ford was aiming at a wide market, and their initial approach was seen

**Corvette Sting Ray, 1966**
The classic Corvette, here with side exhausts.

**Ford Thunderbird, 1956** ***(over)***
Ford's two-seater sports car, with the characteristic ventilation ports in the hardtop. These were on the 1956 model, which also had an external reserve wheel.

1956
MAR
Virginia
81
ONE 56

to be wise when the Mustang became the third most popular car in the United States within five months of its appearance. Half a million were sold in eighteen months, and the 1½ millionth was delivered in June 1967. It was certainly the right car at the right time, cashing in on the growing interest in sporting motoring without being too noisy and uncomfortable. Within two years, though, one could buy a Mustang which was very much a sports car.

The Mustang was initially offered with a choice of a pretty tame 121-bhp 2,781-cc six, or a more powerful 271-bhp 4,727-cc V8. The latter was the famous '289' (289 $in^3$) engine used in the earlier Shelby Cobras, and it was Carroll Shelby who took the Mustang in hand and made a fine performance car out of it. He ordered the 289 engine from Ford's San José, California, plant with certain modifications such as stiffer, stronger con rods and crankshaft, and his own design of camshaft. They were then delivered to Shelby's plant near Los Angeles airport where the engine was further developed, with a four-barrel Holley carburettor and improved exhaust manifolding. Handling was improved by stiffer anti-roll bars, new steering arms and modified rear suspension. The rear seat was replaced by a shelf, and a fibreglass bonnet replaced the metal one. Externally the Shelby Mustangs could be distinguished by a thin blue stripe running between front and rear wheel arches incorporating the letters and figures G.T. 350, and two wide blue stripes running from the front of the bonnet over the top and down the trunk to the rear bumper. In standard form a GT 350 gave 306 bhp, but Shelby soon brought out the Competition Prepared version with 350 bhp. About twenty-five of these were sold, and they became SCCA B Production Class champions in 1966 and 1967. Production of GT 350s was only 562 in 1965, but the following year 2,378 were sold, including 936 bought by Hertz Rent-A-Car. Customers for these had to be over twenty-five, with a clean licence, and rates were $17 per day and 17 cents a mile. Most of the Hertz cars, apart from the very earliest, had automatic transmissions whereas the regular GT 350 came with a four-speed manual transmission.

In 1967 the GT 350 was joined by the GT 500 which offered such refinements as a rear seat, air conditioning, and power steering and brakes. This had the larger 428-$in^3$ (7,014-cc) engine, necessary in view of the increased weight, and performance was on a par with the smaller cars though they were not competitive in racing as their size took them into the class dominated by the Shelby Cobra. Late in 1967 Shelby lost his lease on the Los Angeles airport site, and subsequent Shelby Mustangs were built in the Ford plant, up to 1970 when they were dropped.

Ford's most dramatic sports car of the 1960s was the GT 40, developed with the express purpose of beating Ferrari at Le Mans. As it was designed as a competition car for track use it is beyond the scope of this book, but in fact thirty-one street versions of the GT 40 were built. It was an Anglo-American project, with development initiative changing from one side of the Atlantic to the other with confusing speed. Although the engines came from America, as did the body design, most GT 40s were built by Ford Advanced Vehicles Ltd at Slough, Buckinghamshire. All the street versions were Slough-built – the 4.7-litre engine was detuned from 390 to about 330 bhp, and greater cockpit comfort provided, including adjustable seats. The right-hand gearchange was moved to a central position. These GT 40s were capable of 165 mph (265.5 km/h), and sold for £6,428 in 1966. A model with great comfort was built by the Swiss specialist car maker Franco Sbarro, selling for 110,000 Swiss francs, or £9,130 ($16,000) at the 1967 rate of exchange. The GT 40 became an instant classic, and examples of both street and track models command very high prices today. However, for those who cannot afford an original, a South Wales company, K.V.A. of Swansea, make a replica.

Chevrolet's answer to the Mustang was the Camaro which began life in much the same way, as a sporty personal car with a choice of engine from 140-bhp 3.8-litre six up to a 375-bhp 6½-litre V8. These were the 1967 models, and apart from the adoption of the Corvette's front disc brakes later in 1967, no major changes were made until 1970 when the completely restyled '1970½' models were announced. These had a wider range of engine options, from a 4.1-litre six through four 'small-block' V8s of 5.7 litres to two big-block V8s of 6,573 cc which developed 375 bhp. The high-performance model was the Z-28, distinguished by a full-width rear spoiler, stripes on body sides and boot top, and strengthened suspension. Disc brakes, rather surprisingly, were still on the front wheels only.

The Pontiac Division's version of the Camaro was called the Firebird, and development followed that of the Chevrolet pretty closely. The equivalent of the Z-28 was the Trans Am, named after the Trans-American series of stock-car races organized by the SCCA. On the

**American Motor Corporation AMX, 1968**
When AMC released its new AMX coupé, it was the first two-seater American sports car to be series-produced since the Ford Thunderbird was turned into a luxury four-seater in 1958.

1970 Firebird Trans Am, the 6½-litre engine gave 345 bhp at 5,400 rpm, top speed was 135 mph (217 km/h) and 0 to 60 mph (96.5 km/h) took 5.4 seconds. Transmission was a four-speed box with Hurst floor shift. Roll bars and staggered shock absorbers were designed in the light of the previous two years' experience in Trans Am racing, which had not in fact been very successful despite the presence of the talented Jerry Titus in the team. The fibreglass front air dam and rear spoilers were based not on wind-tunnel testing, as one might have expected, but by running on a dry lake. Production of the 1970½ Trans Am was 3,196 cars, and they are generally regarded as the high point of the Firebird range. Later Firebirds, and Camaros, although dramatic in appearance, were gradually downgraded in power due to emission controls and the need to conserve fuel.

Cars in the Mustang/Camaro class were nicknamed 'pony cars', possibly because the first was a Mustang, but the name was also appropriate to a light, smaller-than-standard machine. Two of America's smaller manufacturers also entered this class: American Motors and Studebaker. The American Motors Javelin was a four-seater coupé with a choice of engines up to a 280-bhp 5.6-litre V8, giving a top speed of 119 mph (191.5 km/h). It was introduced in 1967 for the 1968 season and was joined in February 1968 by the AMX, a shorter-wheelbase two-seater coupé. This came with three engine options, 4.7, 5.6 or 6.3 litres, the latter giving 315 bhp and a top speed around 135 mph (217 km/h). American Motors secured the services of Land Speed Record holder Craig Breedlove to promote the AMX, and with a specially prepared car he achieved 175 mph (281 km/h), and 0 to 60 mph (96.5 km/h) in 6½ seconds. Another 'special' with a rumble or dickey seat was called the AMX-R and was used as a pace car at Trans Am races, though American Motors did not campaign the AMX in these events. They were, however, widely used for drag racing. A total of 19,134 AMXs were made from 1968 to 1970, with 1969 being the peak year for production.

The Studebaker Avanti was a forerunner of the pony car, as it appeared in 1962, two years before the Mustang. It was the idea of Sherwood Egbert, the new President of Studebaker, who wanted to give the flagging company a new dynamic image. The car was not all-new, there was neither the time or money for that, and it had a Lark convertible frame and the standard Studebaker 4.7-litre V8 engine. The body was new, however, and very striking with its razor-edged front fenders, jacked-up tail and complete absence of a

**Studebaker Avanti**
The first Avanti came in 1963 and was the last model to be presented by Studebaker before the company ceased automobile production.

radiator grille. (The air scoop was concealed under the front bumper.) The body was made of fibreglass. The engine developed 240 bhp in standard form, giving a top speed of 124 mph (199.5 km/h).

In order to publicize the Avanti's performance, Egbert had a special car prepared with which Andy Granatelli broke twenty-nine stock car records at Bonneville in October 1962. His best flying kilometre was covered at 168.24 mph (270.69 km/h) – faster than any other American stock car at that date. The following year Granatelli returned to Bonneville with an even more powerful Avanti, whose twin-supercharged engine developed an incredible 575 bhp. Not much streamlining was needed as the Avanti body was so slippery anyway, but the rear wheels were enclosed. The car was christened 'Due Cento' (Italian for Two Hundred) as they hoped to top 200 mph (322 km/h), but its best figure was 196.62 mph (316.36 km/h).

Unfortunately the Avanti did not move so quickly in the showrooms, largely because production difficulties delayed its appearance, and many of those who ordered an Avanti in late 1962 and early 1963 cancelled and bought Corvettes instead. A total of 3,834 were built in 1963, and only 809 in 1964, by which time Studebaker were nearly through as car makers. In that year they transferred production to their Canadian plant, but the Avanti did not make the journey across the border. It was not the end of the design, however, for in 1965 two South Bend Studebaker dealers, Leo Newman and Nathan Altman, bought the rights to the car and put it into small-scale production in a part of the Studebaker plant, using Corvette engines.

A new type of car that appeared in America in the 1960s was the replicar, with styling based on the interwar classics but with modern running equipment. Their status as sports cars is rather ambiguous and they have mostly appealed to the self-publicist rather than to the enthusiast. Until the fuel crisis of the early 1970s, their large V8 engines gave them a very exciting straight-line performance, but since about 1974 they have been downsized like all American cars, and performance has suffered. The best-known 1960s replicars were the Excalibur, built by stylist Brooks Stevens and based fairly loosely on the Mercedes-Benz SS, and Glenn Pray's Auburn 866, a close replica of the 1935 Auburn speedster. The Corvette-powered Excalibur had a top speed of 130 mph (209 km/h) in its fastest form, while the Auburn used the same 7-litre Ford V8 as the Cobra 427, and could do 135 mph (217 km/h).

# Japan

The rise of the Japanese motor industry was well under way by the 1960s, though it had not yet reached the point where it outproduced the United States. (This happened for the first time in 1980.) Sports cars did not play a large part in the Japanese industry until the late 1960s, when the Datsun 240Z burst upon the world. Most of these were made after 1969, and will be covered in the next chapter.

The first Japanese sports car to reach Europe was the little Honda, which began life in 1962 with a tiny twin-ohc 4-cylinder engine of only 360 cc, developing 33 bhp at the remarkable engine speed of 9,000 rpm. On early models, the rev counter read up to 14,000 rpm! A five-speed gearbox transmitted power to the differential, whence drive was by chains to the rear wheels. This was perhaps understandable as it was the first car from a motorcycle maker. Gradually the engine size grew to 492, 606 and finally 791 cc, which was the model that reached Europe in 1968. By that date the gearbox had four speeds, and the chains were replaced by a conventional hypoid rear axle. Known as the S.800, the little Honda was made as an open two-seater or a GT coupé. It did not sell as well as the makers hoped, only 1,350 finding buyers in Britain. The high-revving engine was somewhat fragile, the gearbox had to be used a great deal, and to a public spoilt for choice with open sports cars such as the M.G. Midget, Triumph Spitfire, and Fiat 1600S, its appeal was limited. It was dropped in 1970, and Honda have never made a sports car since, though their current CRX coupé comes quite close.

**Honda S.500, 1963**
This is the 492-cc version that was sold only in Japan. It had a four-stroke, 4-cylinder engine with overhead camshafts and five gears.

# CHAPTER FIVE

# THE SPORTS CAR AT BAY 1970-85

'In the sixties it all started to go wrong for the motoring enthusiast', wrote Graham Robson, one of the most discerning commentators on the motoring scene. Certainly the seeds were sown for a dramatic decline in the number and variety of sports cars over the next decade and a half. In 1965 overall speed limits were introduced in Britain for the first time since 1930, and enforced much more rigorously than the outdated 20 mph (32 km/h) limit had been in the twenties. Britain was followed by Holland in 1968 and France in 1973, until by the late 1970s Germany alone lacked an overall speed limit, and this applied only to the *Autobahnen*. Most damaging of all to the sports car was America's adoption of a nationwide 55 mph (88.5 km/h) limit in 1965, followed by the Clean Air Act of 1968, which imposed such strict emission controls that outputs of all cars sold in the United States were drastically cut. A 'federalized' MGB of 1976 had no better performance than an MGA twenty years earlier, and European cars in their highly tuned form just dropped out of the American market altogether.

This had a very damaging effect on European sports-car builders who depended on the American market, and this meant all those who built in quantity. It was possible for a small firm like Ginetta or Alpine to survive by making less than a thousand cars a year, mainly for their home market, but M.G., Triumph, Alfa Romeo and Fiat were not viable as sports cars unless they sold at least 50% to the United States.

The other factor which militated against the traditional open sports car was that the public everywhere were turning away from the open car. The improved performance of family saloons, particularly the high-performance versions which almost every manufacturer was offering by the late seventies, meant that one no longer had to put up with wind-in-the-hair motoring if one wanted to travel quickly. Open cars were fun in the fifties because overall speeds were not so high, and 50 to 60 mph (80 to 96 km/h) felt very fast indeed in an open, firmly sprung M.G. Midget or Austin Healey. By 1970, when a motorway network covered most of Europe, cruising speeds of 90 mph (145 km/h) or more were possible (legislation permitting), but this was much less fun in an open car, particularly when it involved breathing in diesel fumes from the growing number of heavy trucks.

From being the typical sports car, the open two-seater has become a minority vehicle, a fun machine to be taken out on weekends and holidays rather than used for everyday transport. However, it is by no means extinct, and there has been something of a revival in the last few years, just as the convertible has made a comeback in America, after several years of absence from the market.

**Alfa Romeo 2000 Spider Veloce, 1975**
One of the evergreen sports cars, the Alfa Romeo Spider Veloce 2000 has been made with little change since 1970 (the body dates from 1966) to give today's enthusiasts a taste of traditional open-air motoring. This one dates from 1975.

## Traditional Configuration

Of the open cars available during the 1970s, several were old stagers kept alive, paradoxically, by a small but continuing demand in the United States. These included the Alfa Romeo Spider Veloce, a 1970 design which is still in production in 1987, and has become available again on the British market, though not from the regular Alfa Romeo importers, and the Fiat 124 Spider. From 1982 to the end of 1985 this was assembled and marketed by Pininfarina, and in the United States it was sold as a Pininfarina rather than as a Fiat. The Italian giant has taken the same step with the X1/9 mid-engined sports car which they handed over to Bertone in the same way.

In Britain the Jaguar E-type was discontinued in 1975; of the last fifty E-types made, forty-five were open roadsters. Despite being starved of development money by British Leyland management, which favoured Triumph as a sports car maker, M.G. continued the Midget and MGB throughout the decade. Both received ugly black plastic bumpers at front and rear to meet American safety requirements in 1974, the year in which the Mark III Midget was introduced. This had the Triumph Spitfire 1500 engine and gearbox which gave the Midget a top speed of over 100 mph (161 km/h) for the first time.

The Spitfire itself was continued to 1980, and the TR6 to 1976, but Triumph's new sports car for the seventies was the controversially styled TR7, launched in 1975. This used a smaller engine than the TR6, a 1,998-cc 8-valve four derived from the 16-valve unit used in the Dolomite Sprint. The 4-speed gearbox was also a Dolomite unit, but later TR7s had the 5-speed box of the Rover SD1. The body was a monocoque construction with generous overhang at front and rear, so that although the wheelbase was 3 in (76 mm) shorter than the TR6, the TR7 was 2½ in (64 mm) longer overall. The styling has been described as wedge-shaped, squat or dumpy, and few could be found who would have called it attractive.

The TR7 was an unlucky car from the start, production being delayed by strikes, and being moved twice, from Speke on Merseyside to Coventry and then to Solihull. The first sixteen months' production, from January 1975 to May 1976, was exported, although the American market was never more than lukewarm about it. A top speed of 109 mph (175 km/h) was not very exciting for a 2-litre sports car in the mid-seventies, although performance improved with the arrival of the 120-mph (193-km/h) 3½-litre V8 TR8 in 1980. This was made only for export, although a few right-hand-drive TR8s were made for evaluation on British roads. However, by 1980 the BL management was disenchanted with sports cars, and the whole range was dropped in 1981. Most TR7/8s were hardtop coupés, but a convertible TR7 was available from 1979. Total production of the TR7 was 112,368 and of the TR8 2,722.

One of the last classic front-engined, rear-driven open sports cars was the Jensen-Healey, designed to capture the market of the old Austin-Healey 3000. It was thought up by Kjell Qvale, the American importer of Jensens who bought the company in 1971, and designed by Donald Healey. The engine was a 140-bhp 1,973-cc Lotus 16-valve twin-ohc 4-cylinder, the four-speed gearbox was made by Chrysler UK and Vauxhall Viva suspension was employed. The body was a clean but anonymous design, much prettier than the TR7, but rather lacking in character. A top speed of 120 mph (193 km/h) and good fuel consumption should have pleased many customers, but the Jensen-Healey arrived at the wrong time, only a year before the 1973 energy crisis. Also the early engines gave trouble and the bodies rusted too easily. Even before the parent Jensen company closed down in 1976, the Jensen-Healey's sales were flagging. In all 10,926 were made, all open two-seaters, apart from 474 2 + 2 'sports estates' in the style of the Reliant Scimitar GTE.

The Reliant itself was more of a GT than a sports car, being made in 2 + 2 coupé form from 1965 to 1970, then as the GTE sporting estate, with a convertible model being added to the range in 1982. All these Scimitars were powered by 3-litre Ford V6 engines. Reliant discontinued them at the end of 1985, but there were plans by a group of Nottingham businessmen to revive production in a separate factory. In October 1984 Reliant brought out their new Scimitar, the SS-1. The designation was not intended to evoke William Lyons' prewar S.S., but simply stands for Small Sportscar 1. This was a car to fill the gap left by the M.G. Midget, a simple open two-seater sports car with no frills. Power came from a choice of Ford engines, 1300 or 1600, giving 69 or 96 bhp. With production running at 2,000 per

**Triumph TR7, 1975**

The turbocharger, which employs the exhaust gases to drive a turbine to boost power, has become increasingly popular since the early 1970s. It is used on the high-performance versions of family saloons and hatchbacks, as well as on sports cars.

year, Reliant's annual contract accounts for about one day's production from Ford's Bridgend factory. The fibreglass body was designed by Michelotti. Top speed of the SS-1 1600 was 111 mph (179 km/h), and 0 to 62 mph (100 km/h) took 10.3 seconds. With 'hot hatchbacks' like the Golf GTi recording 118 mph (191 km/h) and 9.7 seconds, these figures were not all that impressive, and in order to improve the SS-1's performance a

**Reliant SS-1 1800 Turbo, 1986**
A Reliant SS-1 1800 Turbo with optional hard top.

**Morgan 2 + 2, 1985 *(over)***
This particular car has the Fiat 4-cylinder, twin-ohc, 1,585-cc engine, with five forward speeds.

turbocharged version was launched at the beginning of 1986. This used a 1.8-litre Nissan Silvia engine and five-speed gearbox. Output was 135 bhp and top speed is raised to 128.2 mph (206.3 km/h); 0 to 60 mph (96 km/h) takes only 6.8 seconds. This should make the SS-1 a more competitive sports car, even at the British price of £9,750, compared with £8,070 for the Ford 1600-powered car.

The alternatives to the Reliant in 1986 are all more expensive, the Morgan (£9,861 for the 4/4, and up to £14,834 for the Plus 8), the Panther Kallista (£9,850–£11,100) and the Naylor TF 1700 (£16,233). Morgans have evolved gradually over the years, with no dramatic innovations; indeed if there were any revolutionary changes the legendary waiting list would probably shrink sharply! At the time of writing the waiting list is about eighteen months, and Peter Morgan would start worrying if it fell to less than six months. Production is about nine cars per week from a workforce of 120. The 4/4 used the Ford 1600 engine during the seventies and the Escort or Fiat twin cam, both 1600s, from 1982. Some cars had alloy bodies which were lighter and more expensive, but the appearance has remained quite unchanged.

The Rover V8-powered Plus 8 has also remained unchanged in appearance though power has gone up from 150 bhp in the seventies to 193 bhp on the latest cars using the Rover Vitesse engine. This has a top speed of 122 mph (197 km/h) and 0 to 60 (96.5 km/h) takes only 5.9 seconds, though the hard ride means that such speed is only bearable on the smoothest of surfaces. Like 4/4, the Plus 8 can be had with steel- or aluminium-panelled body, while the frame is still the traditional ash wood of the 1930s.

The Morgan's continuing success in an uncertain market for open cars has brought forth a number of rivals. Panther West Winds Ltd was formed in 1972 by Robert Jankel, his first product being the J72, a replicar in the style of the prewar S.S.100 which, appropriately, used Jaguar running equipment. The 3.8- or 4.2-litre six was used at first, and from 1974 the customer could have the 5.3-litre V12 at a cost of £9,500 compared with £5,695. The drag imposed by the sweeping wings, square radiator and enormous head-lamps limited top speed, which was around 115 mph (185 km/h) for the six and 125 (201 km/h) for the V12. Most Panther customers were not sporting-minded, so three gears were quite adequate.

**Panther J-72, 1972**
Bob Jankel's first venture into the replicar market was the Panther J-72, loosely styled on the S.S. 100. This is an early model, dating from 1972.

**Panther Kallista, 1986**
The current Panther Kallista is available with 1.6- or 2.8-litre Ford engines, including a fuel injection version of the latter. All have five-speed gear-boxes.

PANTHER

B620 VWU

**Naylor TF 1700**
The Naylor TF 1700 is a very faithful replica of the MG TF.

About 300 J72s were made between 1972 and 1981, but a move down-market in 1976 brought increased sales. The new car was the Lima, a thirties-styled two-seater powered by a 2.3-litre Vauxhall Magnum engine, with transmission, suspension and underpan also courtesy of Vauxhall. (Later Limas had a separate tubular frame.) It was aimed at the Morgan buyer, costing £4,499, compared with £2,984 for the 4/4 and £3,978 for the Plus 8. The Lima was more successful saleswise than the earlier and more expensive Panthers, with about 1,200 finding buyers between 1976 and 1982. After running into financial problems, Panther was taken over by the Korean shipbuilder Young C. Kim who replaced the Lima with the Kallista. This was similar in appearance, but the Lima's fibreglass body was replaced by a pressed alloy one and engines were Fords, a 1600 four or 2.8-litre V6. Chassis and bodies were imported from Korea, and the price was reduced from £6,455 to £5,850 for the 1600. The Kallista was, and is, a more enjoyable car to drive and more viable for the makers. It is now the only Panther made, though the all-new mid-engined Solo is planned for 1987, and sales (up to mid-May 1986) total 858. Panthers have not played much of a sporting role, though Mike Hinde's Lima won the 1979 RAC National Production Car Championship.

The latest recruit to the open two-seater revival is the Naylor TF 1700, in appearance a very faithful replicar of the M.G. TF 1700, powered by a British Leyland O-series 1.7-litre 4-cylinder engine. Gearbox and rear axle are also by BL. Points that distinguish the Naylor from the M.G. are revised suspension including coil springs in place of leaves at the rear, and disc brakes on the front wheels. The 77-bhp engine gives the Naylor a top speed of nearly 94 mph (151 km/h) and 0 to 60 (96.5 km/h) in 11.8 seconds, not outstanding but the car is aimed at the buyer who seeks 1950s-style motoring with 1980s components and easy availability of spares, rather than sheer speed. Constructor Alistair Naylor has had many years' experience in restoring M.G.s and his cars are beautifully built. Unfortunately their current price of £16,233 means that one is paying a lot for one's nostalgia – an original TF in tip-top condition would be cheaper, and for the performance lover, so would a Morgan Plus 8.

**Caterham Super Seven Sprint**
For exciting open-air motoring at a reasonable price, no car can beat the Caterham Super Seven Sprint.

For the hardy enthusiast who wants 'motorcycle-on-four-wheels' performance, Caterham Cars took over the Lotus Super Seven when it was dropped by its original makers, and have made their own version ever since. It has a tubular space-frame chassis, doorless aluminium-alloy body and coil springs all round. Ford engines are used, the most powerful current one being the 170-bhp 1700 with twin Weber carburettors. This gives the simple and light (1,210 lb/550 kg) Caterham 1700 HPC BDR remarkable acceleration, 0 to 62 mph (100 km/h) in under 5 seconds. The weaker 1600 with 150 bhp needed 9.5 seconds to reach 80 mph (130 km/h). The model is less impressive in its maximum speed as its period shape is hardly aerodynamic. About 120 mph (195 km/h) is the limit. However, for road-hugging fun on a fine day (or for the real stoic, on any day) the Caterham is unbeatable. Sales have averaged ninety per year since the current S.3's introduction in 1973. A Dutch company, Donkervoort, make a very close copy with five-speed gearbox and 2-litre engine called the Super Eight.

The Cobra has attracted numerous replicar makers, mostly in kit form, but a very authentic built-up version is made by CP Autokraft Ltd of Byfleet, Surrey, working from premises inside the old Brooklands Track. They began in 1972 by rebuilding existing Cobras, and ten years later made their first cars from scratch. These had similar chassis made on the same jigs, aluminium-alloy bodies and fibreglass mouldings for the bulkhead and footwells. A number of improvements have been made to the cockpit, which is 4 in (102 mm) wider and 6 in (152 mm) longer than the original, but as builder Brian Angliss says, these are the sort of developments that A.C. might have done themselves had they continued production. At first, the cars were aimed at the American market, and like the Allards of old were shipped engineless across the Atlantic. However, the 5.8-litre Ford V8 with which they were fitted gave only 170 bhp in its federalized form, so performance was hardly up to the original Cobra's standard. Later models have been prepared for German and Saudi Arabian customers – in these the 5.8-litre engines, factory-installed and free of

**Chevrolet Corvette Stingray, 1980**
The Chevrolet Corvette is another evergreen traditional sports car. This is a 1980 Stingray.

emission controls, give 320 bhp, and the remarkable acceleration figure of 0 to 62 mph (100 km/h) in 4.9 seconds. By agreement with A.C., Autokraft can call their cars A.C. Mark IVs, and in August 1986 Ford at last granted them permission to use the name Cobra, sign of an increasingly close relationship between Autokraft and the Ford Motor Company. In 1987 the Mk IV received a 4.9-litre Ford V8 engine. The new A.C. Ace was presented in 1986. It is a 2 + 2, four-wheel-drive, front-engined sports car.

A remarkable survivor from the sixties is the Chevrolet Corvette. During a decade in which the muscle cars waxed, waned and disappeared, the powerful Corvette carried on with little change, apart from an inevitable reduction in engine size as the big V8s were not available any more. The big-block 7.4-litre unit was dropped after 1974, and the last convertible was made in 1975, because of concern about roll-over legislation, and also lack of demand. In 1983 the Corvette was completely restyled, with a forward-tilting alligator bonnet, removable roof panel and hatchback rear window. The body was still in fibreglass, brakes were Australian-made Girling discs all round, and the engine was a 203-bhp 5.7-litre fuel-injected V8. Power went up to 230 bhp in 1985 and from January 1986 a convertible model was once again available. Top speeds of the current Corvettes are: convertible, 140 mph (225 km/h); coupé, 146 mph (234 km/h).

From the foregoing it would seem that there were still a good number of open sports cars around between 1970 and 1985. However, in quantities made they were vastly outnumbered by the closed sports car, either two-seaters or 2 + 2s. They fall conveniently into two groups, the traditional front-engined rear-driven cars, and those with engine behind the driver, mostly ahead of the rear axle (mid-engined) although two distinguished makes, Porsche and Alpine, were genuinely rear-engined.

In sheer numbers the make which led the field was Datsun with their 240Z and its successors. Introduced in 1969, this was a two-seater coupé powered by a 2.4-litre 6-cylinder engine with single overhead camshaft. It developed 151 bhp at 5,600 rpm, but

**Datsun 24OZ, 1972**
Datsun sports cars in this series are the most numerous in the world, followed by MGB. Shown here in a hill climb, in Super Samurai tuned form.

JPK 4K

**Datsun 240Z coupé, 1972**

Many traditional European sports cars could not be modified to suit the American safety and pollution standards introduced in the mid-1970s, except at astronomical costs, so they were discontinued. Datsun produced a completely new design with these restrictions in mind, and thus made a direct breakthrough in this important market.

was later tuned to give considerably more power. The gearbox was a five-speed all-synchromesh unit, and the suspension was independent all round, with MacPherson struts and anti-roll bar at the front. The body/chassis was of integral construction.

The 240Z was a conventional design for its time, and had none of the glamour of the exotic mid-engined sports cars with twin overhead-camshaft engines, but it soon became clear that it was a good example of the right car at the right time. The big Austin-Healey 3000 had recently ceased production, being forced out of the important American market by safety legislation, and Nissan's engineers saw to it that there could be no complaints about their car from the bureaucrats in Washington. The 240Z soon took off on the American market, being in many ways a logical successor to the Austin-Healey, with more modern lines which some likened to those of the E-type Jaguar. John Morton's 240Z took the Class C production-car championship of the Sports Car Club of America in 1970, and many other racing successes followed, although the great majority of the cars sold in the United States got no nearer a race track than the spectators' car park. In international events a 240Z won the 1971 East African Safari, driven by Edgar Herrmann, and the cars were raced in a number of European events.

In 1973 the 240Z became the 260Z with engine size increased to 2,565 cc, but power output was now only 126 bhp, due to emission regulations, and the 125 mph (201 km/h) obtainable on the 240Z was no longer possible. As so often happens with successful designs, the Z series put on weight as the years passed, and enthusiasts generally consider that the first models were the best. A 2 + 2 version of the 260Z followed, and in 1978 they were replaced by the broader and heavier 280ZX with 2,753-cc engine, also available as a 2 + 2, and later as an open, Targa-topped model. On the American market automatic transmission was available on the Z series from the early 1970s, but not in Europe. Total production of the 240Z/260Z models from 1969 to 1978 was 622,649, with a further 414,358 of the 280ZX made up to the end of 1983. The current successor to the 280 ZX is the 190-bhp 3-litre 300ZX, while Nissan also make a smaller sporting coupé, the Silvia/Gazelle (the 200ZX in the USA), with standard 1.8-litre single-ohc turbocharged engine and optional twin-ohc 2-litre engine, the latter developing 144 bhp.

The other Japanese make to attract a lot of attention with their sports cars was Mazda who have been the only company in the world to make a commercial success of the Wankel rotary engine. They first tried this in a limited-production sports car, the 110S, made from 1967 to 1972. This was a good-looking two-seater hardtop coupé with a 116-mph (186.5-km/h) top speed from its twin-rotor power unit. Good-looking though it was (William Boddy, editor of *Motor Sport,* described it as the Lotus Elan of Japan), Mazda only intended it as a test-bed for the new engine which was later installed in family sedans as well as sports coupés. Mazda's competition début took place in 1969 when R-100 coupés came fifth and sixth in the Spa 24-Hour Race, being beaten only by Porsches.

The RX-7 sports coupé was introduced in the Spring of 1978. It had a Wankel twin-rotor engine, each with a displacement of 573 cc, but this is equivalent to a conventional engine of 2,292 cc, with a power output of 115 bhp. Top speed of this attractively styled coupé was 119 mph (191.5 km/h), with 0 to 60 mph (96.5 km/h) acceleration in 9.6 seconds. Maximum safe engine speed was 7,000 rpm, and in order to avoid expensive blow-ups Mazda installed a buzzer which warned the driver when 6,800 rpm was reached. The wind-tunnel tested body had a very low drag coefficient of 0.32, though this is not so good at night as the raising of the headlights from their covers in the wings increases the drag coefficient by 6 per cent.

For those seeking greater power and performance, several firms provided turbocharged versions of the RX-7. The first of these was Elford Engineering run by former British racing driver Vic Elford. Their Garrett AiResearch turbocharger increases power to 160 bhp giving 140 mph top speed. Even more powerful is the Motorspeed RX-7; this develops 200 bhp, with a top speed of 145 mph (233.5 km/h) and 0 to 60 (96.5 km/h) acceleration in 6.2 seconds. The RX-7 has been very successful on the race track: the team entered by Tom Walkinshaw won the British Saloon Car Championship in 1981 and 1982, and the 1981 24-Hour Race at Spa in Belgium, where Wankel-engined Mazdas first competed in 1969. In the United States Jim Downing's RX-7 won the American GTU Driver Championship of 1982.

The RX-7 sold extremely well, nearly 500,000 to the end of 1985, but faced with very strong competition from Porsche and their countryman Mitsubishi, Mazda have brought out a revised and more powerful RX-7 for 1986. Capacity is increased to 654 cc per rotor,

equivalent to 2,616 cc under the new rating for rotary engines. This used to rate them at twice their actual capacity, but the new and more realistic multiplication factor is 1.8. Power is now 150 bhp at 6,500 rpm, and top speed 132 mph (212.5 km/h). A new body makes the RX-7 look very like a Porsche 928.

Other Japanese makes to enter the very competitive sports coupé market include Mitsubishi, Subaru and Toyota. Although they made sporty-looking four-seater coupés in the seventies, Mitsubishi's first really high-performance car was the Starion. Introduced in 1982, this was a powerful hatchback in the manner of the old Datsun 240Z. The 168-bhp 2-litre single-ohc was turbocharged, a speciality of Mitsubishi who offer it on all their range, there was a 5-speed gearbox and disc brakes all round. Top speed was 133 mph (214 km/h), but in 1985 an intercooler added to the turbocharger boosted power to 180 bhp and added an extra 4 mph (6.5 km/h) to the maximum speed. Other traditional sports coupés have been offered by Toyota with their Celicas which come with a wide variety of engines from a 1.6-litre four to a 2.6-litre six, the latter a rally winner for several years in twin-cam form. In 1985 the Celica was given front-wheel drive and a completely new body shell. These models have a 133–185-bhp 16-valve 4-cylinder engine of 2 litres, giving a top speed of 140 mph (225 km/h). *Motor* magazine described the Celica as 'the best front-wheel-drive chassis' when they road-tested it.

The most powerful current Toyota sports car is the Supra 3000GT, a rear-drive four-seater hatchback powered by a 3-litre twin-ohc six which develops 204 bhp in export version, but for the home market an intercooler is used which gives 230 bhp. Even with automatic transmission the 3000GT has been timed at under 7 seconds for 0 to 60 mph (96.5 km/h), and with the manual box, which will be available on export models, the performance should be still better.

**Mazda RX7, 1981**
A 1981 Mazda RX7 driven by Win Perry, winner of the 1981 RAC Tricentrol British Saloon Car Championship.

**Mazda RX7, 1982**
A 1982 Mazda RX7 turbocharged by Elford Engineering.

Subaru have built four-wheel-drive road cars for longer than any other manufacturer, and in 1985 they built their first sports car, the XT Turbo coupé. This has the same 1.8-litre flat-4 engine as Subaru's saloons and estate cars, and other features, such as the electronically controlled air suspension for variable ride height, hint at its off-road origins. The four-wheel-drive is part time, and for town work and low-speed manoeuvring front drive only is engaged. Top speed is an acceptable 124 mph (199.5 km/h), but the XT is too much of an off-roader dressed up as a sports car to stand comparison with the RX-7, the Toyotas or Porsches.

**Porsche 944 Turbo coupé**

The best-known European traditional sports coupé is the Ford Capri, introduced in 1969 and finally withdrawn from production in December 1986. Ford conceived it as a European Mustang, a 2 + 2 personal car with a wide range of engine options. These ranged from a very tame 61-bhp 1300 to a 140-bhp 3-litre V6 on the Mark Is, but the really high-performance Capris were the RS2600 built in Germany and the RS 3100 built at Halewood, Merseyside. (Capris were made in both countries until 1977 when production was concentrated in Germany.) The RS models were really homologated specials to allow Ford to go racing, and road models were rare. Two hundred of the RS 3100 were made, with bored-out 3-litre engines giving 148 bhp and over 120 mph (193 km/h). Racing versions used a Cosworth conversion of the V6 engine with four overhead camshafts and 3.4 litres, giving 400 bhp.

The Capri Mark II with opening hatchback arrived in 1974, and 1978 saw the Mark III, restyled and with four headlamps. The same wide range of engines was available, the 3-litre car being good for 118–120 mph (190–193 km/h). For 1982 the 1300 was dropped and the 3-litre engine replaced by a fuel-injection 2.8-litre giving 160 bhp and 125 mph (201 km/h). This continues as the flagship of the range, apart from the Tickford Capri prepared by Tickfords, the coachbuilders. This was much more than a Capri with skirts and air dams, though it had these as well, for it had an IHI turbocharger and Garrett intercooler which extracted 205 bhp from the 2.8-litre engine, giving a top speed of 140 mph (225 km/h). Brakes and suspension had also received attention, and the rear axle had a limited-slip differential. Interior fittings were to a very high standard, and the doors were opened by a remote hand-held button. Prices started at £17,220, compared with £10,599 for the standard Capri 2.8i.

In 1975 Porsche made a complete break with their air-cooled rear-engined tradition when they announced the front-engined water-cooled 924. This had begun as a project for VW-Audi to replace their poor-selling 914/916 models, but it never carried anything but the Porsche badge. It was something of a cocktail, having a 1,984-cc single-ohc version of an Audi engine which would later be used in the Volkswagen LT van. The front suspension was similar to that of the VW Golf, and brakes came from the VW K70. The gearbox was mounted on the rear axle, mostly five speeds, although there were some basic-specification cars with four speeds, and some automatics. The 924 handled excellently and reached a new market, costing less than the cheapest rear-engined Porsche.

The main drawback of the 924 was lack of power, only 125 bhp, but this was rectified on the turbocharged version which came out in 1978. This had 170 bhp, and a top speed of 140 mph (225 km/h). Not all that many were made, 12,115, compared with more than 122,000 924s up to the models of 1985, because the Turbo's role was taken over by the 944 in 1981. This had a new Porsche-designed 2½-litre single-ohc slant-four engine which gave 173 bhp and 137 mph (220.5 km/h) maximum speed. With a turbocharger this went up to 158 mph (254 km/h), and 0 to 60 (96.5 km/h) in 5.9 seconds, making it faster than the 4.7-litre V8 928S and only slightly slower than the 911 Turbo – still the yardstick against which the performance of Porsches, and most other cars, is measured. When *Motor* tested the 944 Turbo in the summer of 1985 they found it unsurpassed in performance, steering and roadholding – comparing it with the rear-engined 911 they said 'If you're man enough to tame it (the 911) the chassis is more rewarding than any other, and few would deny the prestige attached to the timeless shape of those three evocative figures, 911. But consider a car that has all of its pace and more, the economy and refinement of a quick family saloon, space in the back for kids, and handling of the very highest order that doesn't bite back. That car is the Porsche 944 Turbo, the runt that became a prince.'

Before either the 924 Turbo or 944 appeared, Porsche produced what they intended to be the ultimate high-performance front-engined car, the 928. This had a 4,474-cc V8 with one camshaft per bank of cylinders and a choice of five-speed manual or three-speed automatic gearboxes, the latter bought from Mercedes-Benz. The four-seater hatchback body bore some family resemblance to the 924, but was wider and squatter – less attractive, but more aggressive which was perhaps appropriate to its performance. Denis Jenkinson, the widely experienced continental correspondent of *Motor Sport,* considered it the ideal high-speed mode of transport when it was introduced, but diehard Porsche enthusiasts thought that no car should bear the name unless it had a rear engine, and what was worse, even with 240 bhp, the 928 could not outperform a 911 Turbo. Capacity went up to 4,664 cc on the 928S and 928S2, the latter being capable of over 150 mph (241 km/h) and a 0 to 60 (96.5 km/h) figure of 6.5 seconds. This is still inferior to the 944 Turbo which

**Saab 900 Cabriolet, 1986**
Saab's sporty image was underlined by the introduction of a cabriolet version of the 900, powered by a 16-valve turbocharged engine.

costs some £11,000 less. However, for 1987 the 928S4 has a 320-bhp 4,957-cc engine with four valves per cylinder. This gives a top speed of 168 mph (270.5 km/h). Production of the original 928, which was dropped in 1982, was 17,710.

One of the most successful rally cars in recent years is the Audi Quattro, which introduced four-wheel drive to the rally world, and led to the Group B supercars such as the Lancia Delta S4, Peugeot 205 Turbo 16 and Metro 6 R4. But while these are strictly competition cars, and were banned after the 1986 season due to a number of fatal accidents, the Quattro rally cars are closer to the production models. The idea originated as a result of tests in Scandinavia involving a group of Audi saloons and a Volkswagen Iltis four-wheel-drive utility vehicle. It was soon clear that the latter, with a less powerful engine, easily ran away from the saloons which were driven from their front wheels only. Development engineer Jorg Bensinger and his boss at Audi, Ferdinand Piech, who is a grandson of the great Dr Ferdinand Porsche, decided that the next step should be a car with four-wheel drive. Thus was born the Quattro, a two-door 4/5-seater coupé on the floorpan of the 80 saloon and powered by a 2.2-litre 5-cylinder engine turbocharged to give 170 bhp. This engine overhangs the front axle, with the five-speed gearbox immediately behind the axle. Drive to the front wheels was through an integral differential as on the other front-driven Audis, while a two-piece propeller shaft and Iltis-derived rear axle took the drive to the rear wheels. A differential from the Volkswagen Polo provided differential action between the two axles. Disc brakes all round and power-assisted steering were both fed from a high-pressure hydraulic accumulator, fed in turn by an engine-driven pump.

Development work on the Quattro began in 1977, and the production car was launched at the 1980 Geneva Motor Show, alongside a similar-looking coupé with drive to the front wheels only. Production began in the late summer of 1980, and the Quattro made its first appearance in a major rally in the Monte Carlo the following January. Since then the Quattro's rallying performances have become legendary; it won the World Rally Championship for Makes in 1982 and 1984 with such leading drivers as Stig Blomqvist, Hannu Mikkola, Michèle Mouton and Walter Röhrl. By using a more powerful KKK turbocharger and a larger intercooler, power could be increased to as much as 370 bhp, although 340 bhp was as much as was needed for the rally cars. In 1984 a 'short Quattro' with wheelbase reduced by 12 in (305 mm) was introduced; 200 were to be made for rally homologation purposes. The extra work needed for this special model, and indeed for all Quattros, is reflected in these 1985 prices; DM 24,340 for the front-drive coupé, DM 75,915 for the Quattro coupé and DM 198,000 for the short-wheelbase Quattro Sport. Despite providing nearly 500 bhp in rallying guise the latter were not so successful, proving difficult to handle. The long-chassis two-valve-per-cylinder Quattro won twenty-one World

**Audi Quattro**
One of the most significant cars of the 1970s, the Audi Quattro which introduced four-wheel drive to rallying and to the every-day road car.

B925 DNH

Championship events in four years, the short-chassis four-valve car only two. Production occupied only a few months, but the 'long Quattro' is still made, with refinements such as anti-lock braking.

Before leaving the front-engined sports cars, it is worth mentioning that several other small production cars were, and are, made, mostly in Britain. These include the TVRs, whose most powerful model is a Rover V8-powered two-seater whose engine is enlarged to 4.2-litres, giving 300 bhp, and the Marcos Mantula with a variety of engines by Ford and Rover, and now, most powerful of all, the 190-bhp Rover Vitesse giving nearly 140 mph (225 km/h) and 0 to 60 (96.5 km/h) in 5.7 seconds. The Marcos can be had as a kit in various stages of completion, or as a complete car. The kit-car phenomenon as a whole will be covered later in this chapter.

In 1986 Aston Martin brought out their dramatic Vantage Zagato V8 coupé. While other Astons in recent years have been grand tourers rather than sports cars, the Vantage Zagato is strictly a two-seater with a hoped-for top speed around the magic 300 km/h (186.4 mph). The 5.3-litre Vantage engine is tuned to give 435 bhp. The two-seater body is styled and built by Zagato in Milan, as were those of the DB4 Zagato in 1961.

Ferrari limited production of their 308 GTO to 200 for homologation purposes, but Aston Martin, who have no intention of returning to racing, have chosen a production run of only fifty, to ensure exclusivity. This has made the Vantage Zagato an instant collector's car, and even at £87,000, all fifty were ordered within a few months of the model's announcement.

## Engine in the Middle

The trend towards the mid-engined sports car accelerated during the 1970s, and moved down-market from the supercars towards more affordable machines for the average enthusiast. The first company to make this move was Fiat with their X1/9, launched in 1972. This was based on a Bertone 'dream car' and the bodies were always made by the Turin coachbuilders. The engine was the 1,290-cc 75-bhp four, as used in the front-engined 128 Sport, mounted transversely behind the passenger compartment, and driving through a 128 gearbox. The body was styled in the wedge-shaped manner fashionable in the early seventies, but the car was not as fast as it looked, being good for no more than 100 mph

**Fiat X1/9**
The first reasonably priced mid-engined sports car, the Fiat X1/9 was launched in 1972 and is not due for replacement until 1988.

(161km/h). However, it handled superbly, and was sensibly priced. At £2,998 in 1976, it compared well with the M.G. Midget at £1,722 or the MGB at £2,353. It certainly couldn't outperform the latter, but to a public whose mid-engined envy had been fired by cars like the Lamborghini Miura and Ferrari Dino, it seemed very desirable. *Component Car* magazine described the X1/9 as 'very definitely at the soft end of the market' but cars at the hard end do not sell in large numbers, and sell the little Fiat certainly did, over 150,000 having been made up to the middle of 1986. The largest engine from the Fiat Ritmo (Strada in Britain), 1,498 cc and 85 bhp, was used from 1978 onwards, giving a top speed of 110 mph (177 km/h). Since 1982 the X1/9 has been badged as a Bertone rather than as a Fiat, assembly being undertaken in the Bertone factory. However, catalogues are still issued by Fiat. It has recently been announced that its successor, made entirely by Bertone, will have a front engine, driving the front wheels.

In many ways the car that takes off where the X1/9 finishes is the Toyota MR2. It scores by being a newer design, launched in 1984, and in its more powerful form has all the horsepower that the X1/9 needed to bring it out of the 'soft end'. Different-engined MR2s are aimed at clearly defined markets, the 83-bhp single-ohc 1.5-litre at the personal-car owner who might have bought one of the tamer Mustangs or Capris, and the 130-bhp twin-cam 1.6-litre at the keen sports-car driver. The MR2 (Mid-Ship Runabout, 2-seater) is Japan's first mid-engined sports car, and Toyota's first real two-seater sports car since the 1960s. As in the X1/9, which must have been studied very closely by Toyota's engineers, the engine is mounted transversely, driving through a five-speed gearbox, though a four-speed automatic is an option, even on the more sporty version. Handling is every bit as good as the X1/9, the Toyota's engine is quieter and above all more powerful, giving a top speed of 122 mph (196 km/h) and 0 to 60 (96.5 km/h) in 8 seconds, nearly two seconds better than its rival from Italy. On the debit side it is more than £2,000 more expensive in Britain, but a growing number of enthusiasts think the difference is worth paying.

The third current contender in the modestly priced mid-engined field comes from a surprising source. The Pontiac Fiero is made by one of the General Motors Divisions celebrated in the sixties for their successful stock cars, the GTO and the Firebird, but never associated with sports cars, as the Chevrolet Division has been. However, in 1979 Pontiac

**Toyota MR2, 1986**
A mid-engined coupé that has been successful in many countries, the version shown has a 1.6-litre engine.

**Pontiac Fiero**
America's only quantity-produced mid-engined sports car is the Pontiac Fiero, available with a 2½-litre four or 2.8-litre V6 engine.

decided to aim for the Mustang market with a stylish personal car. A front engine was considered first, but it would have made the bonnet line too high, so as GM had a reasonably small 4-cylinder engine, they took a leaf out of Fiat's book and located this transversely behind the passenger compartment. Development took a long time, and the Fiero was not launched until 1984. The engine was the 'Iron Duke', an unsophisticated pushrod ohv all-cast-iron unit of 2,475 cc which, with mandatory emission controls, developed an uninspiring 92 bhp. Top speed was only 97 mph (156 km/h), yet the Fiero took off on the American market, largely because the classic British sports cars like the MGB and Triumph TR7 were no longer available. However, enthusiasts lamented its lack of power to match its excellent handling, so in 1985 a 140-bhp 2,838-cc V6 was available as well, giving a 112-mph (180-km/h) top speed.

In Europe the mid-engined fashion spread to a number of manufacturers, the best known being the supercars from Ferrari, Lamborghini and Maserati. However, there were also several in a lower-price bracket, though well above the X1/9 or MR2 class. A.C. made a brave attempt at an up-to-date sports car to replace their large Ford V8-engined cars whose sales were badly hit by the oil crisis. Their ME 3000 was based on an independent design called the Diablo by Peter Bohanna and Robin Stables. As built by A.C. it had a 3-litre Ford V6 engine mounted transversely in a steel-perimeter chassis with a fibreglass body. It was a promising design, particularly when it was announced in 1973, but the company had many problems in gaining type approval, and cars were not available for sale until 1979. By this time the price had risen from an estimated £5,000 to £13,238, and the ME 3000 was facing tough competition from the Lotus Esprit. Handling was not ideal, and A.C. did not have the funds to develop the car as it deserved. Only eighty-two were made by the original company, and a further thirty by a new organization in Scotland in 1984. A.C. (Scotland) Ltd went into receivership just as a new Alfa-Romeo-powered sports car was due to be made, and it looked as if the A.C. name would disappear, except for the A.C. Mark II Cobra replica mentioned earlier, but in 1986 a new A.C. Ace was presented.

The Lotus Europa was made up to 1975, but Colin Chapman was planning a more expensive car. Though not cheap the Lotuses made up to the 1970s were aimed at the enthusiast who preferred to see his money go towards engineering rather than frills, and Chapman did not go after the Porsche or Ferrari market. However, with the difficult times of the early 1970s Chapman felt that expensive cars would be less susceptible to a depression than cheaper ones whose potential owners would be hit by unemployment. He therefore dropped the Elan and the Europa and brought out the front-engined four-seater Elite in 1975 and, a year later, the mid-engined two-seater Esprit. Both of these new models used a 1,973-cc 16-valve twin-overhead-camshaft 4-cylinder engine developing 160 bhp at 6,500 rpm. In the Esprit it was mounted in a backbone pressed-steel frame similar to that of the old Europa, and drove through a modified Citroën SM five-speed gearbox and final drive. The all-independent suspension was by coils, wishbones and anti-roll bar at the front, and by coils, transverse links, fixed-length drive shafts and radius arms at the rear. The body was designed by Giugiaro and originated as a show car on the Europa chassis, exhibited at the 1972 Turin Motor Show. Flip-up headlamps were featured, and the interior was more luxurious than on any previous Lotus.

Production began in 1976, and after considerable development work on both engine and suspension the Esprit was capable of its promised 140 mph (225 km/h). However, it did not really reach its peak until the introduction in 1980 of the turbocharged model with engine enlarged to 2,174 cc. This used a Garrett AiResearch T3 turbocharger which boosted engine output to 210 bhp at 6,000 rpm, and gave the car a top speed of 152 mph (244.5 km/h). At last Colin Chapman had a car to rival the Ferrari 308GTB, and subsequent improvements to suspension and, more important, to quality control at the factory, have made the Esprit Turbo an even more desirable possession.

In France Matra made the Simca-powered mid-engined Bagheera and Murena, while racing driver Jacques Ligier produced a small number of cars powered by the Citroën-Maserati V6 engine. The Bagheera, introduced in 1973, was unusual in having three-abreast seating, and an advanced specification included all-disc brakes. However, the engine was the 1.3-litre ohv four used in Simca's front-drive 1100 saloons, and did not give a very sporting performance. Later Bagheeras had a 1.45-litre 90-bhp engine, and were capable of 101 mph. The Murena, made from 1980, was restyled with a steel body in place

**Lamborghini Countach/Ferrari Testarossa**
The two leading rivals for the mid-engined super-car market, a 1982 Lamborghini Countach 400 and (*over*) a 1985 Ferrari Testarossa.

testarossa
B843 MPB

of fibreglass, a 5-speed gearbox, and frontal disc brakes only. A 93-bhp 1.6-litre Talbot engine gave the Murena a top speed of 113 mph (182 km/h), and when the 120-bhp ohc engine was fitted, the three-seater coupé was capable of 125 mph (201 km/h) and 0 to 60 (96.5 km/h) in 9.3 seconds. Although never officially imported into Britain, a few Murenas were brought in by an independent dealer, and were good value at £5,900.

The Ligier JS2 was an altogether more powerful machine, with top speed of 150 mph (241 km/h) from its 170-bhp 2.7-litre V6 engine, the same unit that was used in the Citroën SM coupé. In fact, the SM itself was assembled in Ligier's factory at Vichy, and this brought in more business than the JS2. Nevertheless, about 300 were made between 1972 and 1975, and they are still remembered with affection by French enthusiasts, who have had all too few native sports cars to enjoy in recent years.

The remaining mid-engined cars were all in the very expensive supercar bracket, and nearly all Italian. The exceptions were the Swiss-built Monteverdi Hai, a very limited-production Euro-American car powered by a 340-bhp 7-litre Chrysler V8, and with a claimed top speed of 180 mph (289.5 km/h), and the BMW M.1. This was a complete breakaway from previous BMW practice, and the only car from the famous Bavarian company not to have its engine ahead of the driver. In 1972 BMW produced a show car called the Turbo. This had a very low gull-wing coupé body with turbocharged 4-cylinder engine mounted transversely behind the seats. It was purely a design study with no question of production, but when, five years later, BMW were looking for a competition supercar to take over where the CSL had left off, they produced a design strikingly similar to the Turbo. Designated the E-26, and later the M.1, it had the 3½-litre 6-cylinder competition engine mounted in-line instead of transversely, and conventional rather than gull-wing doors. The plan was to use the 450-bhp engine for competing with Porsches in Group Four racing, with the possibility of an 800-bhp turbocharged version for Group Five. To be eligible for Group Four a minimum of 400 street versions had to be built, and as such a low-volume production run was difficult to fit into the mainstream at Munich, BMW looked around for an outside company to make the M.1 for them. The prototype had been developed with the help of Lamborghini in Italy, and they were given the contract for the production cars. However, they could not fulfill the contract due to their own financial problems, and a new arrangement was worked out whereby the fibreglass bodies and steel frames would be built by Ital Design in Turin, then taken by truck to a German coachbuilder, Baur of Stuttgart, who fitted the engine and completed the car. It was a complicated arrangement and one of the reasons for the high cost of the car (DM 100,000 or about £25,000 in 1981).

The M.1 did not do as well in competitions as its sponsors had hoped, though it gained fame by being used in the Procar series of curtain raisers to Grands Prix in 1979, with identical cars being driven by the Grand Prix contenders. This gave BMW useful publicity and helped to make use of the 400 cars, which were not selling well to the general public. In fact, 450 were made, the last one towards the end of 1981.

Ferrari built two lines of mid-engined cars in the 1970s, the Dino 246 and its descendants, and the 512 Berlinetta Boxer, or BB as it was familiarly called, the first 'full-size' Ferrari to have the engine behind the driver. The Dino 246 was replaced in 1973 by the Dino 308GT4 with a 255-bhp 3-litre V8 engine, 2 + 2 seating for the first time in this series, and a Bertone-styled body in place of Pininfarina's on the earlier car. Two years later came a new two-seater which was the true successor to the 246, the 308GTB. This had the same engine as the GT4 in a new body, once again Pininfarina-styled and built by Scaglietti. Top speed was 155 mph (249 km/h), and from 1978 a spyder was available in addition to the coupé. Pininfarina was also chosen as the stylist for the Mondial 8, the 2 + 2 successor to the GT4, which appeared in autumn 1980. The 308 engine received fuel injection in autumn 1982 and four valves per cylinder in 1983, the cars using this engine being known as the Quattrovalvole (QV).

The most dramatic development of the QV series was the GTO. Superficially resembling the 308GTB, it in fact shared hardly any components apart from the steel doors. The chassis was an all-new tubular space frame, 4 in (102 mm) longer in wheelbase and the same amount wider in track. The engine was basically similar to the 308QV, but the bore was reduced to bring capacity down to 2,855 cc. This was necessary because the engine was turbocharged; if the engine were any larger the 1.4 multiplication factor would put it outside the 4-litre unturbocharged class for racing. An important difference is that the GTO's engine is mounted longitudinally, not transversely, to allow space for the twin

**BMW M.1**
BMW's mid-engined sports car, seen here in front of three famous BMWs, the AM4 (rear), the 328 (next), and the 507 (nearest the M.1)

M WS 4235
DYE 910

turbochargers and better accessibility to the gearbox. The engine developed 400 bhp compared with 240 bhp. Although it was never fully tested by a magazine, the maker's claim of 0 to 100 km/h (62 mph) in 4.9 seconds and 187 mph (305 km/h) cannot be far out. The GTO was aimed solely at competitions, but 200 had to be made for homologation purposes. These were sold almost before the car was announced in 1984 – Britain's allocation was twenty cars, at a price of £73,000 each. At that time the contemporary BB512i sold for £50,699 and its rival the Lamborghini Countach for £54,950, so the GTO was indeed an extravagant purchase.

Ferrari's other supercar for the seventies was the 512 Berlinetta Boxer. For this they did not continue with the V12 power unit, but produced a new flat-12 engine derived from the 3-litre units of similar layout employed in Ferrari's Grand Prix cars. These horizontally-opposed engines were familiarly called 'boxers', hence the name of the new model (berlinetta is simply the Italian for coupé). The cylinder dimensions were the same as in the Daytona's V12 unit, giving a capacity of 4,390 cc, but power was higher, at 380 bhp. Four Weber carburettors were used, and each bank of cylinders had twin overhead camshafts.

The flat-12 was mounted in front of, and above, the final drive, while the clutch was behind it. Drop gears transferred the drive to a shaft into the five-speed gearbox, which was below the engine. Obviously such a layout was only possible with a flat engine. The rest of the car was conventional Ferrari, with a multi-tube chassis frame and all-independent coil suspension. The hydraulically operated disc brakes had vacuum servo assistance, necessary when braking a car from upwards of 170 mph (273.5 km/h). On today's speed-restricted roads it is difficult to obtain accurate top-speed figures for these high-performance cars; when *Motor* magazine tested the Boxer in 1975, they gave it an estimated maximum of 175 mph (281.5 km/h), the same as its rival the Lamborghini Countach. They also recorded a 0 to 60 mph (96.5 km/h) time of 6.5 seconds.

One could be forgiven for thinking that a car such as the Berlinetta Boxer would need little improvement, but in 1976 the engine's capacity was increased to 4,942 cc. Power output was in fact down, to 340 bhp, but this was achieved at a lower engine speed of 6,000 rpm, compared with 7,800 rpm for the original Boxer. Another important change (introduced in October 1981) was that the four Weber carburettors were replaced by Bosch K-Jetronic fuel injection, which is indicated by the small 'i' suffix in the car's name, Berlinetta Boxer 512i. The 512i was a distinctive car by any standards, but for those who craved even more originality, Koenig, the German tuning firm, offered a version with additional panels and a spoiler in fibreglass. Twin Rajay turbochargers boosted power to an incredible 653 bhp, giving the car a claimed top speed of well over 200 mph (322 km/h). Total production of all BBs was 2,323.

In the autumn of 1984 came the BB's successor, named Testarossa (Red Head) after a celebrated racing Ferrari of the 1960s whose cam covers were always painted red. The basic mechanical layout was similar, as was the engine size, but there were four valves per cylinder, and power was increased to 390 bhp. The body was completely restyled with distinctive slats in the body side channelling air into the radiator intake behind the doors. The Testarossa weighed 161 lb (73 kg) less than the BB, and top speed, as tested by the German magazine *Auto Motor und Sport,* was 181 mph (291 km/h). Its 0 to 60 (96.5 km/h) in 5.8 seconds was not record-breaking, and was exceeded by both Lamborghini's Countach and De Tomaso's Pantera, but the Testarossa's engine was exceptionally flexible, making it more of an all-purpose car than some of its rivals.

By 1970 Ferrucio Lamborghini had built up a reputation second to none for exotic and at the same time reasonably practical motorcars, led by the Miura, which in four years had become almost standard wear for pop stars and rich trend-setters all over Western Europe. Lamborghini knew that he could not stand still for he was in one of the most fickle of all markets, so after more than 700 Miuras had been made he brought out a new model which made its bow to the public at the 1971 Geneva Motor Show. When one of the Lamborghini employees first set eyes on it in the factory he exclaimed 'Countach', which in the Piedmontese dialect means 'Fantastic' or 'Incredible' and was adopted as the car's official name. It had a four-camshaft V8 engine generally similar to that used in the Miura, but enlarged to 4,971 cc and mounted longitudinally in the frame instead of transversely. This gave rise to its designation LP500 (Longitudinal Posteriore 5 Litri). The gearbox was ahead of the engine near the centre of the car, and the drive was taken from the gearbox's secondary shaft by a drop gear to a propellor shaft running rearwards to the final drive. The body was a Bertone design, and was a strikingly low and sleek two-seater coupé with

**De Tomaso Pantera, 1986**
More modestly priced than the Ferrari or Lamborghini, the De Tomaso Pantera offers a comparable performance. This is a current model photographed on the company's stand at the 1986 Geneva Motor Show.

doors that opened vertically by hydraulic jacks. A periscope mirror gave rearward vision. Many people thought it a mere design exercise like so many Italian-bodied cars that graced the motor shows, but Lamborghini worked on it for two years, and at the end of 1973 production models of the Countach began to appear.

They differed considerably from the Geneva Show car, having a tubular space frame in place of the prototype's semi-monocoque structure. This frame was built by Marchese of Modena, while the aluminium body was made by Lamborghini themselves. The engine was reduced in size to 3,929 cc, the same as in the Miura, but there were certain differences, such as the use of six horizontal Weber carburettors as against the four down-draught Webers of the Miura. The compression ratio was slightly lower, at 10.5:1 compared with 10.7:1, and power down from 385 to 375 bhp. Top speed of the Countach LP400 was quoted as 190 mph (305.5 km/h), the same as in the final Miura P400 SV, but this has never been officially confirmed by an independent road test, and it is likely that 175–180 mph (281.5–289.5 km/h) is a more realistic figure. *Motor*'s road test recorded a 0 to 60 mph (96.5 km/h) acceleration figure of 5.6 seconds, and 0 to 100 mph (161 km/h) in 13.1 seconds. Fuel consumption was 10 mpg (28 km/l), which meant that even with two huge tanks of 13.2 gallons (60 litres) each, the range between refuelling stops was only about 260 miles (418 km).

Early in 1978 a modified version, called the LP400S, became available. This was modelled on the special car made for Grand Prix sponsor and loyal Lamborghini customer Walter Wolf. It used the new wide Pirelli P-7 tyres, which necessitated wide wheel arches that somewhat spoilt the very clean lines of the earlier models. From 1982 onwards a 4,754-cc engine was available in the LP500 model, and this was enlarged still further in 1985 on the QV which followed Ferrari in having four valves per cylinder. The QV'S 5,167-cc engine gave 455 bhp and a 0 to 60 (96.5 km/h) figure of 4.8 seconds. However, the shape is less aerodynamic than the Testarossa's, and the QV'S maximum speed is about 8 mph (13 km/h) slower.

Alongside the Miura and Countach, Lamborghini made some smaller sports coupés, rivals to the Ferrari Dinos. These were the Urraco (1970–9), Silhouette (1976–7) and Jalpa (1981 to date). The Urraco was a 2 + 2, the others two-seaters, and all were powered by a

**Maserati Bora, 1973**
Made from 1971 to 1980, the Maserati Bora was the company's first venture into the mid-engined field. It was also the maker's first car under Citroën control. This is a 1973 model.

TED 637

transverse-mounted V8, initially of 2,463 cc, enlarged to 2,996 cc in 1974, and to 3,485 cc in 1981. The Silhouette was a Targa-top open two-seater (Lamborghini's first open car), and the Jalpa was similar but with the larger engine. Somehow these smaller Lamborghinis have not caught on to the same extent as the Miura and Countach, lacking the ultimate glamour of the supercars, yet being too expensive to compete with Porsches.

Two more mid-engined Italians in the same performance category as the Ferraris and Lamborghinis were the Mangusta and Pantera built by the Argentinian Alejandro de Tomaso. The great difference was that instead of complex 12-cylinder power units they used the straightforward ohv Ford V8. This made them substantially cheaper, but less desirable, and in addition there were serious handling problems with the Mangusta, which carried 68 per cent of its weight on the rear wheels. This rendered its excellent performance (155 mph [249.5 km/h] top speed and 0 to 60 [96.5 km/h] in 6.1 seconds, in 1967) less attractive and when Ford signed an agreement with de Tomaso by which they would market his cars in the United States through selected Lincoln-Mercury dealers, they insisted on a new design.

This appeared at the 1970 New York Motor Show in the shape of the Pantera (Panther). It was on the same general lines as its predecessor, but had better weight distribution (only 58 per cent on the rear wheels) and a pressed-steel monoque body/chassis which was cheaper to make than the tubular backbone frame and light-alloy body of the Mangusta. A 5.8-litre Ford V8 engine gave a top speed of 160 mph (257.5 km/h), and the interior was more luxuriously fitted out than the Mangusta's, with air conditioning as standard. The GTS model of 1973 with 350-bhp engine had a claimed top speed of 175 mph (281.5 km/h), putting it into the Ferrari BB class, but it was considerably cheaper because of the mass-produced engine. More than 4,000 had been sold by 1974 – well ahead of any of its all-Italian rivals.

In June 1974 Ford ended the agreement with de Tomaso because of a combination of the oil crisis and emission regulations. The Argentinian acquired Maserati in 1975 and continued to make the Pantera, still Ford-powered, in small quantities, as well as front-engined sedans and coupés. The current GTS Pantera uses a 5.8-litre 360-bhp engine, and the GT5/S features a full-width rear wing-type spoiler. A Lichtenstein-based tuning company, Saphier, offered Pantera with various stages of tune from a 450-bhp up to a twin-turbocharged model giving 650 bhp, a top speed of 189 mph (304 km/h) and 0 to 60 mph (96.5 km/h) in 3.8 seconds. In California, Hall Pantera of Bellflower are assembling Panteras from the large stock of components left over from the Ford operation, with engine options of 400, 475 bhp or more.

The introduction of Maserati's first mid-engined car, the Bora, coincided with the company's takeover by Citroën in 1969, the car using the French firm's complex hydraulic steering and brakes. The Bora was named after a strong north-west wind blowing from land towards the north Adriatic Sea; other Maseratis which borrowed their names from winds included the Ghibli, Khamsin and Mistral. The Bora's engine was the familiar 4.7-litre four-overhead-camshaft V8 which had powered front-engined Maseratis for several years, mounted in a two-seater body styled by Giorgetto Giugiaro and built by Maserati integrally with the chassis. Top speed with the 310-bhp engine was about 165 mph (265.5 km/h), slightly faster with the 320-bhp 4.9-litre engine used from 1976 onwards. The gearbox was a five-speed ZF transaxle. The Bora handled superbly and was remarkably quiet for a car of its class. It was said that one could hold an audible conversation while travelling at 150 mph (241 km/h).

In 1972 came the Bora's smaller sister, the similarly styled Merak powered by the Citroën SM 3-litre V6 engine. This was more compact than the V8, and as the Merak's wheelbase was the same, advantage was taken of the space saved to provide two extra seats, though they were small and of no practical use for adults. The 190-bhp V6 engine gave top speed of around 140 mph (225 km/h), but this went up to 153 mph (246 km/h) with the tuned SS version available from 1975 onwards. As well as having an additional 30 bhp, the SS was 100 lb (45 kg) lighter. There was also a 2-litre Merak for the Italian market where a car of this size enjoyed tax advantages. Lamborghini also offered a 2-litre Urraco for the same reason, but neither of these lower-powered cars sold well. Maserati made only 133 2-litre Meraks, compared with 1,401 of the larger models. The Bora was dropped in 1980, after 571 had been made, and the Merak in 1981. The next generation of Maseratis was the totally different front-engined 2-litre Biturbo. A competitor for the hotter BMW 3 series, it is not a sports car.

**Lancia Stratos**
Most pictures of the Stratos cars show them rallying, at which they were extremely successful, even if the driver had to have effective ear protection, as there was practically no insulation between the engine and the driver.

Lancia built two mid-engined designs in the 1970s, in great contrast to each other. The first, and the most exciting, was the Stratos, which began life as a Bertone styling exercise at the 1970 Turin Show and ended up by being the most successful rally car the company had ever made. The show car had a Fulvia 1600 engine mounted transversely, but when it was decided to make a competition car out of the Stratos more power had to be found. As Lancia and Ferrari were now both part of the Fiat empire they chose the Ferrari Dino 2,418-cc V6 engine as a power unit. In order to be homologated for rallying in the Group Four Special GT category, Lancia had to build 500 Stratoses in twelve months, and immediately put the car into production. It is thought that not more than 250 were actually completed, as the combination of the international oil crisis and higher taxes on larger-engined cars in Italy made the mid-seventies a bad time to sell a car such as the Stratos.

The car made its first rally appearance in the 1972 Tour de Corse. Sandro Munari and Mario Mannucci drove a works-prepared car with engine tuned to give 230 bhp instead of the 190 bhp of the regular Dino engine, and although they retired in this and in the Spanish Costa del Sol Rally they led the latter event and showed what the car should be capable of once it had been properly developed. The Stratos' first major win was the 1973 Tour de France, with Munari and Mannucci at the wheel, although at this time the Fulvia was still the main Lancia rally car. In 1974 a new 24-valve engine was available for the works rally cars, with power up to 240 bhp, and this year saw the beginning of the Stratos' remarkable career, with victories in the Neige et Glace, Sicilian, San Remo, Tour de Corse and Tour de France rallies, the leading drivers being Munari and Jean-Claude Andruet. Lancia were 1974 World Rally Champions, although some of their points had been scored by the Fulvia and Beta coupé. The Stratos helped the company to the World Championship in 1975 and 1976, Munari winning the Monte Carlo three times in a row: 1975, 1976 and 1977. The Stratos' run of successes continued through to 1970, though from 1978 onwards the Lancia Squadra Corse (Racing Team) was merged with Fiat's Squadra Corse Unificata. By the end of its career the Stratos had won fourteen World Championship Rallies and sixty-eight other international events. Lancia were World Rally Champions from 1974 to 1976, and fourth in the Championship in 1977. The leading drivers were Bernard Darniche, Sandro Munari and Tony Carello.

Less interesting was the Monte Carlo, a two-seater coupé which was originally intended to be a larger companion to the Fiat X1/9, coded X1/20. It had the 1,756-cc or 1,995-cc twin-ohc engine used in Lancia's front-engined Beta series, mounted transversely in a Pininfarina-styled integral-construction hull. Even with the larger engine top speed was no more than 120 mph (193 km/h), and the car's appearance seemed to indicate more. With the Stratos' Dino 246 engine the Monte Carlo would have been a real flyer, but then it would have challenged the Dino's own market, and what would have been the point of that?

For rallying purposes, the Stratos was replaced by the Rallye Coupé which looked a little like the Monte Carlo but, apart from the centre section, was a totally different car. The engine was mounted longitudinally, and although still of 1,995 cc, had four valves per cylinder and a supercharger to give 205 bhp in road form, or 325 bhp in works-team tune. The Rallye Coupé was strictly a homologation special, with no more than the mandatory 200 being made, the production run being completed in mid-1982. The Rallye Coupé's first major success was Walter Röhrl's 1983 Monte Carlo victory, and the team went on to win the World Rally Championship for Makes that year.

# Rear-engined Survivors

With the popularity of the mid-engined layout the rear-engined car became very much the odd vehicle out. In fact rear-engined sports cars were always rare birds, as it was argued that to have the heavy mass of the engine at the back of the car would cause it to swing out and lose traction when cornering hard. For this reason it was always said that a really powerful rear-engined car was a contradiction in terms, and the prewar Tatra V8 saloon was thought to be one of the most dangerous cars on the road. However, two makes of modern sports car have kept their engine in the back, and though handling problems can arise at high speeds, a combination of well-designed suspension and wide tyres has made them perfectly acceptable road cars. They are the relatively little-known Alpine and the world-famous Porsche 911.

By 1971 the little Alpine A110 had reached the end of its very successful career, and was replaced by the A310, a larger car with 2 + 2 seating and powered by a 1,605-cc Renault 16GTS engine developing 140 bhp. It had a five-speed gearbox and servo-assisted disc brakes, and in 1977 the 4-cylinder engine was replaced by the 2.7-litre V6 Douvrin power unit which was made by Renault and used in Peugeot and Volvo cars as well as in their own. In this form the Alpine A310 was capable of 133 mph (214 km/h), with 0 to 60 mph (96.5 km/h) acceleration in 7.2 seconds. The light-alloy V6 engine was mounted longitudinally behind the rear wheels, with the gearbox ahead of the engine, a layout shared with the De Lorean coupé which also used the Douvrin engine. The fibreglass body was bolted to a strong tubular-steel backbone chassis, and suspension was by upper wishbones and lower transverse links with coil springs and anti-roll bars, at front and rear. The 2 + 2 body provided very comfortable accommodation for two people, with the rear seats being suitable for two children, or two adults for short journeys. The original design incorporated disc brakes at the front only, a curious decision for such a high-performance car, but later models had discs all round.

**Porsche 911 Turbo**
The ultimate development of the Porsche 911 series, the Turbo, has been made without major change since its engine was enlarged to 3.3 litres in 1977.

Jean Rédélé's Alpine factory, at Dieppe, was taken over by Renault in 1977, and production of the cars increased somewhat during the 1970s, from around 300 to 400 per year in the previous decade to about 1,000. The A310 was highly thought of in France, but never became well known internationally as it was not exported widely. It was never available on the British or American markets.

For the 1985 season the A310 was replaced by a restyled coupé known as the V6 GT or V6 Turbo, depending on the engine. The GT had a 160-bhp 2,848-cc engine used in the Renault 25, and the Turbo a slightly smaller unit of 2,458 cc developing 200 bhp. The new body has one of the most aerodynamic shapes of any current car (drag factor of 0.30 for the Turbo and 0.28 for the narrower-tyred GT) and the Turbo's top speed is 155 mph (249 km/h).

Though still made at Dieppe, Alpines are now a recognized part of the Renault range, and are referred to as Renault Alpines. Exports of the V6 to Great Britain, under the name Renault GTA, commenced in the summer of 1986, and will reach the United States in 1987.

Porsche continued the development of the 911 during the 1970s, the 2.4-litre 911S

**Renault Alpine V6 Turbo, 1985**
The latest of the Alpines, the V6 Turbo replaced the A310 in 1985.

**Rinspeed Porsche Turbo R69**
Rinspeed Design's version of the Porsche Turbo has body styling inspired by the Ferrari Testarossa, and the retracting headlamps of the 944. Originally called the 969, it has been renamed the R 69 to avoid confusion with any future genuine Porsche models.

replacing the 2.2s in 1971. Over the next few years engine capacity was increased and tyres became fatter, necessitating the flared wheel arches which reached their peak in the Turbo. Larger engines were developed not so much to provide greater power, but to increase low-speed torque to make the cars more suitable for town work, and also to cope with the American emission controls.

In 1972 the name Carrera was revived for the 2,687-cc 210-bhp car, which was increased to 2,976 cc and 240 bhp for 1974. All Carreras had spoilers at the rear, as had many SCs (the 3-litre version of the 911) from late 1977 to customers' option. The most dramatic of the series appeared in October 1974. This was the 911 Turbo, known, confusingly, in America as the 930 which was the official factory designation. The KKK turbocharger boosted the 2,996-cc engine to 260 bhp and 153 mph (246 km/h) top speed, while the flared wheel arches and rear spoilers were larger than ever. In 1977 the Turbo's engine grew to 3,299 cc and 300 bhp, in which form it is still made today. With a top speed of just over 160 mph (257.5 km/h) and 0 to 60 (96.5 km/h) in 5.3 seconds it is the highest-performance Porsche made apart from the 928S 4, yet its fuel consumption of 15.9 mpg (5.6 km/l) is better than those of the Testarossa, Countach or Pantera. Although the newer front-engined 944 Turbo beats the 911 for refinement and ease of driving, the latter still has tremendous appeal to the enthusiast, and there is no sign of it going out of production yet.

Since 1982 Porsche has made a full cabriolet version of the 911SC, but this is not made in Turbo form. The perfectionist who wants a turbocharged cabriolet has to cross the frontier to Switzerland and call on Frank Rinderknecht's Rinspeed workshops in Zürich. Rinderknecht has made a speciality of improving various Porsche models, and his convertible Turbo, called the R39, has 928 front and rear panels. The price is 215,000 Swiss francs, compared with 110,000 Swiss francs for the 'ordinary' Turbo. Another Rinspeed conversion is the R69, a closed coupé with Ferrari Testarossa-style door slats feeding air to the rear engine, and retracting headlights from the 944.

The ultimate development of the 911 series, in effect a totally new car, is the four-wheel-drive 959, and the first deliveries were made during the summer of 1987. This car is described in Chapter Six.

# To Everyman his Kit Car

Before April 1, 1973 a car sold in component form, for the buyer to put together himself, had a considerable price advantage in Britain as Purchase Tax was not levied on the components. When Britain joined the EEC, Purchase Tax was replaced by VAT (Value Added Tax) from which components were not exempt. The overnight death of the kit car was prophesied, and it its true that makes such as Lotus, who had sold over 80 per cent of Elans in kit form, withdrew from the field and moved upmarket with their Elite and Esprit. However, some manufacturers continued, such as Arkley who made a fibreglass conversion on a Spridget base, and Dutton whose Lotus Seven-like sports car became the leader in the kit field.

Towards the end of the seventies more kit-car makers appeared, and within a few years they greatly outnumbered the manufacturers of complete cars. Between 1978 and 1986 well over 200 hopeful companies have appeared in Great Britain alone. Some fell by the wayside before they had barely established themselves, but a surprising number have survived – *Which Kit* published by *Component & Specialist Car* magazine lists eighty-seven models from fifty-four manufacturers in their Spring 1986 guide, and these are only the better ones. A good proportion are sports cars, or at least sporting in appearance, though their performance naturally depends on that of the donor car. This is the term used for the car whose mechanical elements are provided for the kit. The most popular of these are Mini, Ford Escort and Cortina, VW Beetle and Triumph Herald, with a growing number of up-market kits using MGB, Rover V8 or Jaguar power.

The growth of the kit-car phenomenon has been considerably boosted by the absence of small reasonably priced sports cars like the Spridget and Spitfire, and it is a valuable method of recycling engines and transmissions which still have years of service ahead of them, but whose unitary bodies have rusted beyond repair. Another factor has been the decline of Britain's engineering industry – quite a number of skilled engineers have invested their redundancy money in kit-car businesses. For those who want the individuality of owning a kit car but who lack the time and/or skill to assemble one themselves, several firms have sprung up who will do the whole or part of the job for the customer.

The variety of styles available in the kit-car world is enormous, from stark two-seaters vaguely resembling 1930s sports cars to Lamborghini Countach replicas. Among the most popular subjects for replicas is the Cobra, of which no fewer than twelve different manufacturers have appeared in Britain alone, with several more in the United States. Other replicas offered include the Jaguar XK120, C-, D- and E-types, Ford GT40, Porsche RSK and Squire. In America, as one would expect, the earlier Corvettes and Thunderbirds are popular subjects for replicas, but there are also kits resembling the Allard J2X, Auburn 851, Austin-Healey 3000, De Tomaso Pantera, Ford Model A, M.G. TD and TF and various Porsches.

The most successful kit cars are not so much replicas as roadsters in the style of the 1930s, or simple sports cars such as the Caterham Super Seven or the Duttons. Made since 1971, Tim Dutton-Woolley's cars used mainly Ford 1600, Triumph Spitfire or Spridget engines, though a few have had Alfa Romeo, Datsun, Fiat or Vauxhall power. They have evolved only slowly, because a simple open two-seater cannot be improved very much without spoiling its functional lines. About 4,000 of the B series and current Phaeton have been sold, a greater number than any other kit car. Dutton also offer an open 2 + 2, the Melos, as well as two closed models, the Sierra estate and the Rico saloon.

The N.G. is another successful kit car which provides very high performance in its Rover V8-powered TC, TD and TF. The TC is a two-seater and the TD and TF are 2 + 2s, the former with the TC's cycle-type wings and the latter with flowing wings. Top speed of a V8-powered TC is 135 mph (217 km/h) and 0 to 60 (96.5 km/h) takes 6 seconds. The 2600 Rover-six engine is also available, and for competition purposes there is the TCR with V8 engine tuned to give 215 bhp. There is now a series of races (at Castle Combe in Wiltshire) for kit cars, and with the TCR N.G. have competed successfully in the races sponsored by *Kit Cars & Specials* magazine. Their only serious rivals are the Marcos Mantulas.

Not all kit cars (or component cars as the industry prefers to call them) are open roadsters. Among closed models, the Mini-Marcos was made from 1965 to 1974 by Jem Marsh, and then by D. & H. Fibreglass Mouldings until 1981. It was a rather crude fibreglass two-seater coupé which could take Mini engines from 848 to 1,275 cc. In 1981 it gave way to the much more professional Midas, made originally by D. & H. and later by

**N.G. TF**
Introduced in 1984, the N.G. TF kit car offers four seats and will take a choice of MGB and straight-6 or V8 Rover engines. Kit price is £1,475 plus Value Added Tax.

Midas Cars Ltd. The body was restyled by Richard Oakes and Metro running equipment is now used, including the 93-bhp M.G. Metro Turbo which gives the little coupé a top speed of around 110 mph (177 km/h). *Component Car* voted the Midas Gold the most like a production car of all the kits in 1985. Another coupé is the Mini-powered mid-engined GTM which has been on the market since 1967, while the Hillman Imp-powered Irish-built Clan is a revival of the 1970s Clan Crusader.

The component car is certainly here to stay, and makes up in variety what it lacks in numbers (the 150 estimated British makes turned out only 3,000 cars in 1985). In price they range from the £345 Citroën 2CV-based Falcon S to the £17,250 GTD 40 Ford GT40 replica, all prices excluding VAT. Speeds vary from perhaps 65 mph (104.5 km/h) for the Falcon to 170 mph (273.5 km/h) for the Jaguar V12-powered Dax Cobra. The component-car industry may never ring alarm bells at Longbridge or Dagenham, but those who build and drive them are all people who love motoring for its own sake, in the tradition of sports-car owners since the beginning.

# CHAPTER SIX

# WHAT FUTURE FOR THE SPORTS CAR?

'Whatever happens, we may be quite sure that sports cars will continue to be built for those who demand something more than just transport from place to place – and a very good thing too.' John Stanford, *The Sports Car,* 1962.

'The sports car is a breed that is almost dead, and it has been killed off by progress.' Pat Mennem, writing in *Motor*, May 1986.

Can one steer a middle path between these two quotations, and find some grounds for prophesying a future for the sports car? Much depends on one's definition: Mr. Mennem's argument is that the days when one had to put up with discomfort in order to motor fast are over. He cited a journey from Monza to Buckinghamshire which he made in 1961 in an E-type Jaguar. He covered 876 miles (1,409 km) in a day, averaging just under 64 mph (103 km/h) from Milan to Calais, quite an achievement twenty-five years ago when France had not a single mile of motorway. 'But now', he went on, 'I hear that people are doing the same thing every day of the week in M.G. Metros, Golf GTis, Peugeot 205s and the like.'

It is certainly true that the hot saloons or hatchbacks, of which the pioneer was the Lotus-Cortina of 1963, do provide performance of a high order at a reasonable price. The Escort XR3i will accelerate from 0 to 60 mph (96.5 km/h) in 8.6 seconds, the Golf GTi in 8.1 seconds, the Fiat Uno Turbo in 8.3 seconds, figures which compare very well with smaller sports cars such as the Morgan 4/4 and Toyota MR2, both of which are more expensive. In a higher price range, the Mercedes-Benz 190E 2.3-16 offers a top speed of 140 mph (225 km/h) and 0 to 60 mph (96.5 km/h) in 7.4 seconds from a four-door five-seater saloon. Better performance, in fact, than from the two-door 2 + 2 Porsche 924S, though admittedly at a somewhat greater cost.

Where can the sports car find a place among this competition? In three quite distinct fields, it would seem. First, the simple traditional open two-seater such as the Caterham Super Seven or Morgan. These provide an element of fun and challenge that no closed car can give, and they make a statement about the owner's character, sporting and hardy, in the same way that a BMW is said to make a statement about his earning potential. Speed is not necessarily the first criterion now, though cars in the more powerful end of the market, for example the Morgan Plus 8, are certainly very good performers. It may never be a large market, though Lotus are pinning their faith to it with their forthcoming Toyota-powered X100 two-seater.

The second slot where the sports car is likely to thrive is the popularly priced mid-engined car such as the Toyota MR2 or Pontiac Fiero. Because of their weight distribution they handle better than any front-engined car, and are seen as the machine that a hot hatchback owner moves up to. And again, they make a statement, about discernment and driving ability. A new contender in this field is the Panther Solo, which starts production at the end of 1987. This was originally conceived as an MR2 rival, with Ford Escort power, selling for around £12,000 ($20,000) but the concept has moved up-market, and this now includes a 16-valve turbocharged engine and four-wheel drive. This has pushed the anticipated price up to about £25,000 ($40,000) so the Solo is no longer a popularly priced car. It is interesting as being the first completely modern car to come from Panther, though the traditionally styled, and much cheaper, Kallista will stay in production alongside it.

The third category which will undoubtedly flourish is the so-called supercar, priced from £25,000 ($40,000) upwards and incorporating the latest developments in high technology. Three cars in the development stage stand out in this field, and significantly two of these are Japanese. All three have four-wheel drive, and two steer through four wheels as well. The European contender is the Porsche 959, a development of the 911 using a twin turbocharged 2.8-litre engine producing 450 bhp at 6,500 rpm. Up to 4,000 rpm the exhaust gases are fed to one turbocharger only, which starts building up pressure at speeds as low as 1,200 rpm, reaching its full pressure at 2,000 rpm. Heavy use of the accelerator brings the secondary turbocharger into action, keeping the boost pressure on right up to the maximum of 6,500 rpm. Operation of the secondary turbocharger is electronic as is the suspension, which offers three damper settings: soft, normal and hard. The driver can choose these as he wishes at the start of the journey, but as soon as high speeds are reached, the electronic control automatically switches the dampers to a harder setting.

The 959's permanent four-wheel drive is variable according to driving conditions. Normally the balance of power is distributed 40/60 between front and rear wheels, but on hard acceleration out of a corner up to 80 per cent will be applied on the rear wheels. Other features of the 959 include a six-speed gearbox, ABS brakes, and power steering. When tested by *Top Wheels* magazine, the 959 produced an acceleration figure of 0 to 60 mph (96.5 km/h) in 4 seconds, and a speed of 175 mph (281.5 km/h). There was still power in hand at that speed, and the estimated maximum is 200 mph (322 km/h). For homologation purposes 200 are to be made, selling at a price of £155,000 ($255,000), and the makers claim that all have already been sold. In competition, they have already taken the first three

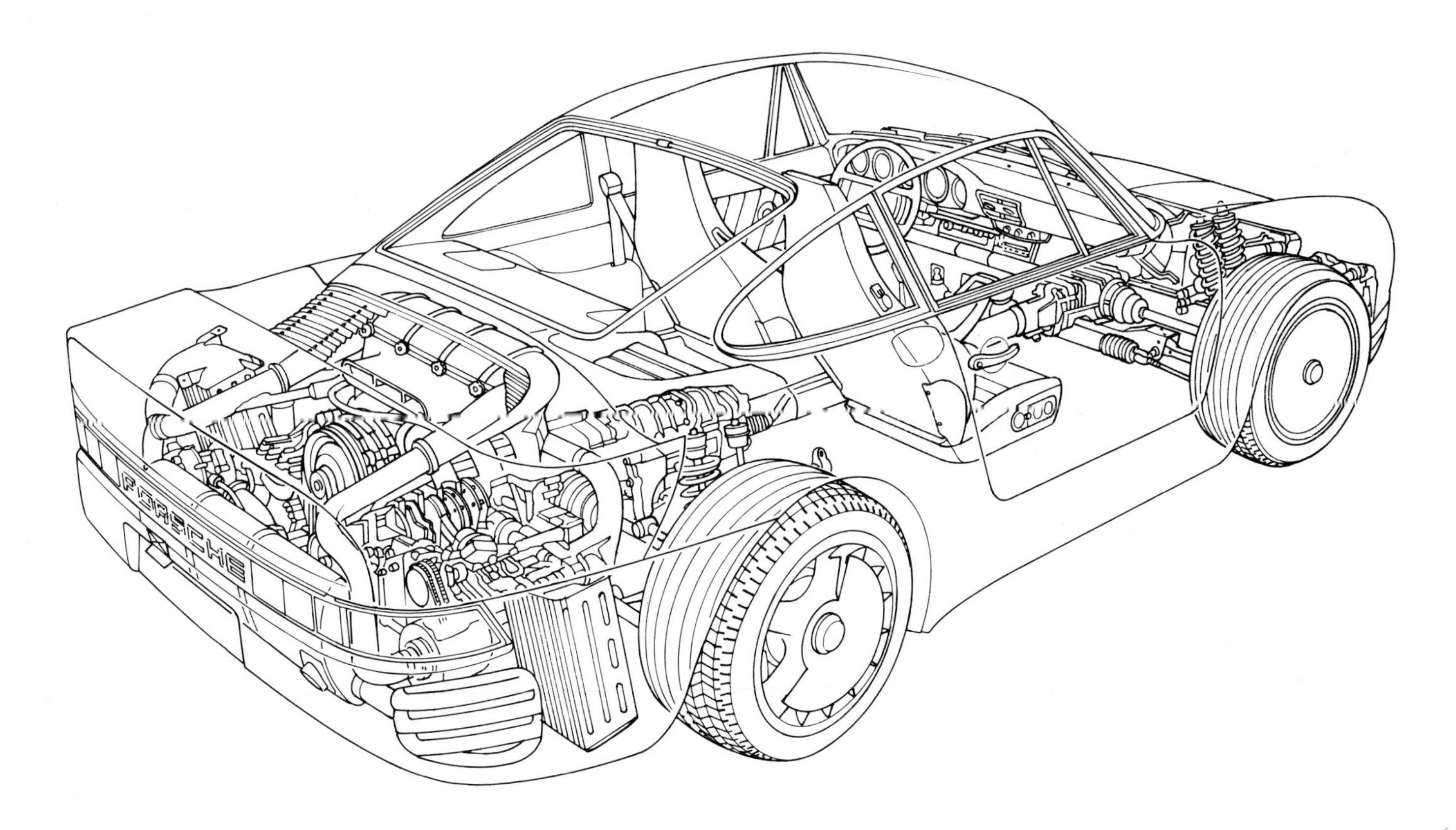


**Porsche 959**
Cut-away drawing of the Porsche 959.

**Nissan Mid-4, 1987**
Nissan Mid-4 prototypes, of which a number have been made for evaluation purposes and for exhibiting at motor shows around the world. Production cars, due in 1987, will have modified lines.

places in the 1986 Paris–Dakar Rally, but their future in European rallying is uncertain now that the Group B supercars are banned.

The Japanese four-wheel-drive car nearest to production is the Nissan Mid-4, Japan's first real supercar. It is appropriately named as it has four of many components – four valves per cylinder, four camshafts, four-wheel drive and four-wheel steering. The 3-litre V6 engine is based on that of the 300ZX, but has two overhead camshafts per bank, and develops a fairly modest 223 bhp. The drivetrain was developed by engineers from the Austrian Steyr-Daimler-Puch company (who make the 4 × 4 Mercedes-Benz G series estate cars) and provides a 33/67 front/axle split of power. Unlike the more complex Porsche 959, this is not variable. The rear-wheel steering turns the wheels hydraulically through 0.5 degrees in the same direction as the front wheels on hard cornering whenever lateral acceleration exceeds 0.5*g*.

**Mazda MX-03**
Mazda's MX-03 is not so close to production as the Mid-4, but is full of interesting ideas, particularly in the steering department.

Although a number of Mid-4s have been built for demonstration purposes, performance figures have not yet been published. The official market launch is expected to be early 1988. It was expected that the Mid-4 might be homologated into Group B for rallying, but this Group is now phased out.

Japan's other supercar is not scheduled for production in its present form, but it is full of interesting ideas which may well appear in the showroom before long. Mazda's MX-03 has a triple-rotor engine with two-stage turbocharging, developing 320 bhp at 7,000 rpm. Estimated top speed is 186 mph (299 km/h), with 0 to 62 mph (100 km/h) taking a mere 5 seconds. The four-wheel drive has variable split compared with the Mid-4's fixed proportion of power between front and rear wheels, but unlike the Porsche 959, the Mazda requires manual selection of the torque split. Steering is more complex than on the Nissan, for the rear wheels turn in opposite direction to the front ones for easy manoeuvring at low speeds (seen on Latil 4 × 4 road tractors in the 1930s). As the speed rises the counter steering of the rear wheels diminishes, ceasing at 25 mph (40 km/h). Above that the wheels turn in the same direction as those at the front, helping directional stability. A drawback is

that it is difficult to keep on a straight line while reversing. However, it should not be beyond the bounds of ingenuity to lock the rear-wheel steering as soon as reverse is engaged – provided, of course, that the wheels are already in a straight line.

Whatever the merits or demerits of four-wheel steering, there is little doubt that four-wheel drive will be ever more widely adopted by sports-car makers. Pioneered by Audi on their Quattro and now available on all their models, it is available on Alfa Romeos, BMWs, Fords and Lancias, and even such modest cars as the Fiat Panda and VW Golf, the latter with a sophisticated variable-split system that provides the best balance for all road, and off-road, conditions.

Whether the sports car has a future, then, depends on how you view the concept. It is highly unlikely that the open two-seater of MGB or Spridget type will ever again be made in large numbers, but some models will survive, kit cars will come and go, and ever more sophisticated supercars will be available, even if there are no roads where they can legally be driven anywhere near their limit. Until fossil fuels run out and we are all subjected to electric cars, it seems that sporting motoring will go on.

# INDEX